The Complete Idiot's Reference Card

How to Get Rid of Credit Card Debt

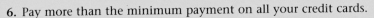

1. Threaten to leave your credit card companies if th~~...~~e. Leave them and find better cards if they don't.
2. Transfer your high balances to your card with th~~...~~
3. Buy large items right after you pay your bill to a~~...~~ two months.
4. Review your bills closely and challenge mistakes.
5. Pay off one card at a time.
6. Pay more than the minimum payment on all your credit cards.

How to Deal with Collection Agencies

Know your rights: Provincial legislation governs the behaviour of credit collection agencies, and it prohibits harassment by creditors: in most cases, they cannot sue you or contact your employer, and they cannot threaten you.

Negotiate: You can often settle your account for pennies on the dollar if you know your rights.

Collection agencies must stop any action against you if you declare bankruptcy.

Common Debt-Reduction Strategies

1. Make more money by working overtime, moonlighting, or starting a small business; just do something to make some extra money until the books balance.
2. Reduce spending by using a budget. A budget need not be a noose around your neck. The right kind of budget does nothing more than help you prioritize your spending. Once you do that, cutting back is easy.
3. Consolidate your debts through a lender into one easy monthly payment.
4. If you can afford the new payments, refinancing your house to take advantage of lower interest rates and draw out some equity may be a good idea.
5. Filing bankruptcy is a last resort, but it can be a good choice in the right circumstances.

alpha
books

How to Radically Reduce Your Tax Bill

You may be able to reduce or eliminate penalties by writing a simple letter of explanation as to why the taxes weren't paid on time.

Canada Customs and Revenue Agency (CCRA), formerly Revenue Canada, enacted fairness provisions in 1991 to allow for the cancellation, reduction or waiver of certain penalties and interest owed.

Usually, exceptions are made due to circumstances beyond someone's control, such as:

➤ natural or human-made disasters, such as flood or fire;

➤ civil disturbance or disruptions in services, such as a postal strike;

➤ serious illness or accident;

➤ serious emotional or mental distress, such as the death of an immediate family member.

How To Reestablish Good Credit

Get a secured credit card. Make sure you pay off the card every month. After a year, you can probably turn it into an unsecured card.

Get an auto loan. If you don't qualify for regular financing, get a dealer-financed auto loan. Look for a dealership that "carries its own papers."

Get a loan from your bank against your bank account. If you open a small savings account at a bank, you can usually get the bank to loan you money against the account and thereby reestablish positive credit.

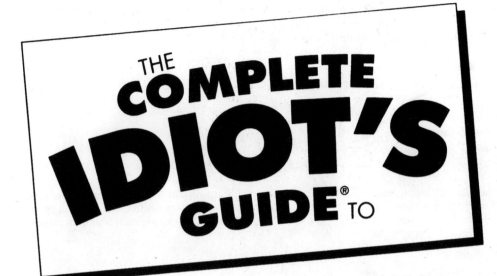

THE

COMPLETE IDIOT'S GUIDE® TO

Beating Debt
for
Canadians

By Janice Biehn, Steven D. Strauss, and Azriela Jaffe

Prentice
Hall
Canada

A Pearson Company
Toronto

alpha
books

Canadian Cataloguing in Publication Data

Biehn, Janice
   The complete idiot's guide to beating debt for Canadians

Includes index.
ISBN 0-13-086726-8

1. Debt. 2. Budgets, Personal—Canada. 2. Finance, Personal—Canada. I. Strauss, Steven D., 1958-   . II. Jaffe,
Azriela. III. Title.

HG179.B53 2000   332.024'02   C00-930173-9

© 2000 Pearson Education Canada Inc.
Toronto, Ontario

Adapted from The Complete Idiot's Guide to Beating Debt © 1999 by Steven Strauss and Azriela Jaffe.

ISBN 0-13-086726-8

Editorial Director, Trade Division: Andrea Crozier
Acquisitions Editor: Paul Woods
Copy Editor: Catharine Haggert
Production Editor: Lori McLellan
Art Direction: Mary Opper
Cover Image: Mike Freeland and Kevin Spear
Interior Design: Scott Cook and Amy Adams of DesignLab
Production Manager: Kathrine Pummell
Page Layout: Gail Ng-A-Kien
Illustrator: Jody P. Schaeffer

1 2 3 4 5 WC 04 03 02 01 00

Printed and bound in Canada.

THE COMPLETE IDIOT'S GUIDE TO and Design are registered trademarks of Macmillan USA, Inc.

This publication contains the opinions and ideas of its author and is designed to provide useful advice in regard
to the subject matter covered. The author and publisher are not engaged in rendering legal, accounting, or
other professional services in this publication. This publication is not intended to provide a basis for action
in particular circumstances without consideration by a competent professional. The author and publisher
expressly disclaim any responsibility for any liability, loss, or risk, personal or otherwise, which is incurred as
a consequence, directly or indirectly, of the use and application of any of the contents of this book.

Visit the Prentice Hall Canada Web site! Send us your comments, browse our catalogues, and more.
www.phcanada.com.

A Pearson Company

Contents at a Glance

Appendices

Contents

Foreword

When you are deep in debt it often seems like there is nowhere to turn. The bills are mounting, the collection agencies are calling, and your peace of mind is plummeting. Soon you are caught in a vicious cycle that results in a truly staggering amount of debt. The truth is, Canadians have never been in deeper debt than they are today. Savings rates have never been lower and many feel like they are only one paycheque away from financial disaster. And the stress from debt problems can affect many areas of life such as work, marriage, sleep, and your overall sense well being.

Well, you are not alone by any means—here are some startling facts:

➤ Household debt reached a whopping 100.4% of disposable income in 1999.

➤ There are over 37,000,000 Visa and MasterCards circulating in Canada today.

➤ Only slightly more than 50% of Canadians pay credit cards in full each month.

➤ In the last decade, there have been no substantial income gains in Canada.

➤ Personal bankruptcies continue to occur at record levels.

As bad as this all seems, there is no evidence that this trend will slow down anytime soon.

But there is help. *The Complete Idiot's Guide® to Beating Debt for Canadians* will help you make, understand and master the various issues involved in getting your financial life back in order. From understanding how collections agencies really work, learning how to budget–and, yes–even invest, this book makes it all straightforward and easy to understand. You will be crawling out from that mountain of debt faster than you might think.

The best thing about this book is the way the authors speak so freely about some of their own financial experiences – from follies to successes – reminding us that we are all human and can learn from our mistakes. As you work your way through this book (and refer back to it again and again!), you will begin to realize that you, too, can triumph over debt and gain important financial skills that will serve you well for the rest of your life.

Laurie Campbell
Program Manager,
Credit Counselling Service

Introduction

It's no wonder that debt is a four-letter word. Financial problems are among the most stressful problems a person can have. Psychologists say that money problems are one of the main causes of divorce.

There are a host of stuffy books out there that will tell you that all you need to do to get out of debt is tighten your belt and budget better. If that's what you're looking for, then put this book down, because we take a different approach.

First, while we certainly offer many budgetary ideas, more importantly, we are determined to help you figure out why you've gotten into debt in the first place, and to offer plenty of practical advice to help you out of debt that goes beyond just putting together a budget. Also, we do not portray debt as an entirely horrible problem. Your authors appreciate the debt that has allowed each of them to start businesses, provide for families, and purchase homes.

Further, this book is fun and easy to read. Although you'll read plenty of fairly technical information, the tone is light, sometimes funny, and always understandable. Finally, although the title for this book may be *The Complete Idiot's Guide® to Beating Debt for Canadians*, we don't treat you like an idiot. We carry no judgments, regardless of how much of a pickle you've gotten into.

What's in It for Me?

Part 1, "Money and Debt," covers the basic problem of why people go into debt and begins to offer some solutions. This section looks at common mistakes that get people deeper into debt than they want to be.

Part 2, "Changing Your Relationship with Money," looks at your beliefs about money and helps you begin to change any negative money attitudes you may have. This section also looks at budgets and helps you formulate some ways to cut back (if you want to) and begin to repay your debts.

Part 3, "When Cutting Back Is Not Enough," offers suggestions that go far beyond what most financial books offer. Find out the best way to get out of credit card debt. Learn how to negotiate with your creditors and reduce your debts. Handle business debt.

Part 4, "A Last Option: Bankruptcy," explores what bankruptcy is, how it works, and shows you when bankruptcy may make sense. Because one of your authors is a bankruptcy attorney, we certainly understand that bankruptcy is sometimes a necessary evil.

Part 5, "Getting Ahead of the Game," helps you see that a life of financial prosperity may not be that far away. Here we show you several methods that you can use to make more money, whether it's for getting out of debt, getting ahead, or retirement.

Throughout this book you'll also encounter many tidbits of information that have been highlighted by friendly icons:

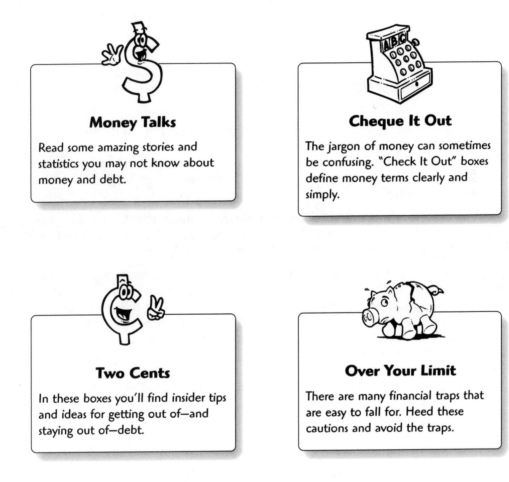

Money Talks

Read some amazing stories and statistics you may not know about money and debt.

Cheque It Out

The jargon of money can sometimes be confusing. "Check It Out" boxes define money terms clearly and simply.

Two Cents

In these boxes you'll find insider tips and ideas for getting out of—and staying out of—debt.

Over Your Limit

There are many financial traps that are easy to fall for. Heed these cautions and avoid the traps.

Dedication

The authors would like to dedicate this book to their great agent, Sheree Bykofsky, who recommended them for the project even though they had some debt of their own.

Acknowledgments

Thanks to my husband, Craig Douglas, who brings new meaning to the job of stay-at-home Dad. Thanks to my daughters who showed remarkable patience when Mommy had to go up to the office to work at the most inopportune times. Thanks to my parents for not always bailing me out of debt in my younger years – they taught me a valuable lesson. —Janice Biehn

Thanks to my co-author Azriela for her help, encouragement, insight, and friendship. Thanks also to Jillian, Sydney, and Mara for their assistance. Special thanks and love to Maria for her patience, love, humor, and support. —Steve Strauss

Thanks, as always, to my husband Stephen, who tolerates and mostly embraces my whole-hearted commitment to being a writer and columnist, and all of the time that this profession requires. Thanks to Nicole Reardon, Co-op student at Millersville University, who spent a summer with me, and learned what it's really like to make a living as an author. Your contribution to my business was much appreciated. Thanks to Deb Haggerty, friend and "Aunt" to our family, who has been generous to our family in times of need. Thanks, Deb. You are family to us and we appreciate knowing that you are there for us. Thanks to Mom and Dad: For being there for me, in good times and in bad. I love you. —Azriela Jaffe

Special Thanks to the Technical Reviewer

The Complete Idiot's Guide to Beating Debt was reviewed by an expert who double-checked the accuracy of what you'll learn here, to help us ensure that this book gives you everything you need to know about beating debt. Special thanks are extended to Warren J. Ladenheim.

Part I

Money and Debt

This part goes over the basics: We define the terms and introduce some simple concepts. But the basics also involve being honest with yourself: How did you get into debt? What do you need to do to get out of debt? Part of the solution lies in examining the problem closely and honestly.

For most people, getting out of debt simply involves looking around. That's why we say, "Take that paper bag off your head when you drive."

Chapter 1

Not All Debt Is Bad Debt

In This Chapter

➤ Why you went into debt

➤ Debt that hurts, debt that helps

➤ Debt you may want to keep

➤ Debt you may want to get rid of

➤ The first rule of holes

➤ Thinking long-term

So you are in debt—who isn't these days? We live in a society that encourages people to go into debt. Credit card commercials encourage us to splurge on that four-star hotel, regardless of whether we can afford it. (That's what your gold card is for, right?) Banks want us to borrow money against our home equity. Credit card companies even line up such an array of "rewards" for using your credit card, such as air miles or points toward a new car, that it's easy to rationalize taking out the plastic.

Yet not everyone is in debt. Many people know how to deal with money. Their debts are manageable, and they have money in the bank. That sounds nice, doesn't it—money in the bank? That is what you deserve. In order to get there, however, you are going to have to change some of your thinking about money and learn a few new methods of dealing with it.

Why Are You in Debt?

People who are not in debt think about and treat money differently than the rest of us. They know a few things about money and debt that escape most of us. Let's call them the "financially literate." If you can begin to relate to money as they do, you will be well on your way to a life that is not only debt-free, but also prosperous. What we hope to do in this book is to show you some of their secrets so you can adopt a few of these ideas and tools to help you get out of debt.

Do not feel too badly if you are not good with a dollar. A lot of people aren't. Money literacy is not always taught in schools, and too often parents are too busy trying to dig themselves out of their own financial hole to help much either. Yet, unfortunately for many of us, we learn more about money from our parents than anywhere else. The good news is that learning how to get out of debt and become more financially literate is not all that complicated.

The first step in the process is to figure out how you created so much debt, because if you don't figure out how and why you got yourself into this pickle, you might get out of debt, but you certainly won't stay out. So the first question to ask yourself is: Why did you go into debt in the first place?

Sometimes going into debt is unavoidable, but often it is not. When money is tight, you have several options; going into debt is just the easiest. Instead of choosing more debt, you might have decided to work overtime and make more money, or possibly you could have tightened your belt and spent less money. Debt was not your only choice.

There are many reasons people go into debt: some are good reasons, and some are bad. It doesn't matter. Did you buy luxuries you could otherwise not afford? Did you lose work time due to an illness or a lay-off, or did a divorce set you back financially? Was debt your way of dealing with some other sudden, unexpected expense? When you look at the reason or reasons why you went into debt, the important thing is to notice whether your spending habits follow a pattern. If you can see a pattern, you need to address that pattern as much as the underlying debt. Part 2, "Changing Your Relationship with Money," will help you break your debt pattern.

Consider Mark and Diane. They both make a good living: he's a psychiatrist, and she's a psychologist. They have two kids to whom they are devoted. They send both to private school, which costs a total of $15 000 a year, and both kids go to summer camp. These expenses add up.

Mark and Diane don't buy luxuries, they don't travel much, and, except for the kids' expenses, they are very frugal. Yet the only way they can pay for everything is by going into debt. They use their line of credit (which is secured by their home) and credit cards to stay afloat. Although they would like to move to a less expensive neighbourhood, they can't because they have no equity in their home, so they are stuck.

Over Your Limit

The average credit card cash advance is $1200. Given normal interest rates for credit cards, if it takes you a year to pay back that advance, it will cost you $1404.

What are they to do? If they are going to get out of debt, something in their lives is going to have to change. The private school is going to have to go, camp may be out, or they are going to have to start making more money. The same is true for you. If you want to get out of debt, you are going to have to identify why you went into debt and change that behaviour or pattern.

Good and Bad Debt

Debt in and of itself is not a bad thing. All of us (the authors) were able to start our own businesses because of debt; Steve began his own law practice, and Azriela began her own entrepreneurial consulting business. As a freelance writer, Janice regularly uses her line of credit—a low-interest form of debt—to pay income tax and cover other emergencies. This prevents her and her husband from having to dip into their retirement savings. So we understand what debt is and why some debt is great debt.

Debt allows you to do things you otherwise normally could not do, such as start a business, go to college or university, or pay for a home. Debt constructs buildings and funds investments and entire corporations—even the government is funded by debt. The trick is to foster debts that help the cause and banish the ones that don't. Not all debts are bad debts.

Good Debt

Debt that helps you, enriches your life, is manageable, and is not a burden can be called good debt. For example, student loans are good debt if they enabled you to get through school and further your life goals. They are bad debt if you dropped out of medical school after one year to become a writer (unless of course, you're following your dream and you haven't a hope in hell of becoming a good doctor). A good debt helps; a bad debt hinders. We want to help you get rid of that bad debt.

Other examples of debt that may be considered good include

➤ **Mortgages.** A mortgage can be a great debt. Not only does it permit you to own your own home, but it also allows you to build home equity. It is an asset. As Chapter 20, "What the Rich Know That You Don't," explains, people who are financially savvy earn interest and equity. People who are not financially savvy pay interest and create money for others.

➤ **Car loans.** A car loan can be a fine debt because you get something long-lasting out of the debt. If you need a nice car for your job (if you are a real estate agent, for example), a car loan may be considered good debt because it helps you in your career. However, a car loan that you cannot afford is a bad debt because it detracts from your life.

➤ **Business loans.** If you can service the loan, and it helps you make more money, the loan is good debt, but if the loan is nothing but a source of problems for you, the debt is bad.

➤ **Credit cards.** Credit cards are fantastic. They are convenient and easy. They can help finance a business or even travel emergencies. The problem with them, as you probably know only too well, is that it is too easy to fall under their siren spell and get in over your head before you know it. That's when they begin to hurt your life more than help it.

Bad Debt Blues

How do you know if your debt is good debt or bad debt? Easy. Bad debts cause stress. You sleep poorly because of them. They cause fights and foster guilt. U.S. Supreme Court Justice Lewis Powell was once asked to define *obscenity*. Hard-pressed to come up with a definition, Powell uttered the famous line, "I know it when I see it." The same could be said for bad debt: You know it when you see it, and it certainly can be obscene.

Bad debt seems impossible to pay back. You create bad debt when you charge things you don't need or when you borrow for things that you consume quickly, such as clothes,

Money Talks

Tight for money? Here are some simple ways to save a little extra: Don't use ABMs at other banks and avoid user fees; cancel your movie channels on cable and save about $20 per month; put all of your change at the end of the day in a jar and save about $50 a month; hold a garage sale and make about $200; cancel your cell phone (unless it is solely used for business) and save at least $50 a month.

meals, or vacations. The things quickly disappear, but the debt has a nasty habit of sticking around, seemingly forever. Bad debts can become very bad debts because of interest and penalties. For example, if you buy a CD player for $200 and don't pay it off by the end of the year, and your credit card company charges a usurious 18 percent APR (18 percent per year), you owe $220 by the end of the year. If you do this with five items, you owe $1100, and that's a lot of money.

You can create bad debt when you agree to pay these crazy interest rates that some creditors charge, because the debt seems to grow exponentially. Credit cards are the prime culprit, but they are by no means the only one. High interest can also come with personal loans, business loans, or unpaid income taxes.

You probably purchased this book because you have a lot of these bad debts, debts you are having a difficult time handling and that cause you anxiety. They are the debts you avoid thinking about, the phone calls you don't answer, and the bills stuck in a pile. Avoidance dances with guilt only to be tapped on the shoulder by your new suitor, fear.

You know what the bad debt dance looks like; anyone reading this book does: New bills are coming in before you've cleared out those from last month. You're surprised to find that the phone bill is still unpaid. Somehow the dentist was never sent his cheque. You know what past-due notices look like. Your Visa and MasterCard bills include late payment penalties. There is more month left at the end of your money, and payday seems far away. Worst of all, these things don't surprise you anymore.

Avoidance is a common coping mechanism to deal with a budget that doesn't balance. The problem is, it can create even more problems than you already have:

Your property could be repossessed. The electronics store can come take its TV back. The finance company can come take your car.

You could get sued. If that happens, your wages could be garnished, or your bank account could be levied upon. Imagine your surprise when you go to transfer that

$1200 out of your chequing account to pay your mortgage and you find that it has been seized by one of your creditors.

A lien can be placed on your real estate. Failure to pay a bill now means that a creditor can get a judgment against you and force you to pay it later when you sell your house, only then you will pay it with steep interest.

Loss of services. You could lose your insurance or your utility services if you avoid paying those bills.

Over Your Limit

When someone sues you and wins, it is called getting a judgment. A judgment can be used to empty your bank account, garnish your wages, or put a secured lien on your house.

Yet, as much as you have been avoiding the problem, the truth is that your debts are neither crushing nor hopeless. They are simply a problem—one for which there is a solution. But no one ever eliminated a problem until he or she recognized and admitted that there was a problem. You began to do that the moment you bought this book. As you read it, you will need to begin to formulate a debt-reduction plan that will work for you. As you do, you need to determine which debts are necessary and which are not.

Debts You Want to Keep

Steve, one of the authors of this book, is a bankruptcy attorney. One day, an old acquaintance named Bill came into his office and said that he needed some help getting out of debt, but he also wanted to avoid bankruptcy if at all possible. They talked, came up with a plan of action, and Bill went on his way. About four years later, Steve ran into Bill again and asked how things were; Bill relayed the following story.

Bill had $30 000 in credit card debt and was behind two months on his mortgage when he left Steve's office. That day, Bill finally decided that something had to change. He wanted to pay everyone back, put some money in savings, and keep his house. His mortgage was his largest, and favourite, debt because he loved his house.

Bill's first order of business was to prioritize his debts. Wanting to save his house, Bill called his lender and found out that it had a program that would enable him to roll his mortgage *arrears* onto the end of his loan. He was therefore able to keep his most important debt and focus his energies on getting rid of the debts he didn't want anymore.

Bill put together a credit card repayment plan by consolidating his debts into one monthly payment at his bank (these are also available at trust companies or credit unions). He started living a bit more frugally, making some extra money by moonlighting, and paying more on his credit cards than the minimum. He was diligent, but not always perfect. Although it took him several years, he finally did get out of debt. He also kept his house and even created a little nest egg. Bill did it, and you can too.

Debts to Get Rid Of

If you want to prosper financially, there are plenty of debts that you will want to wipe out. The most obvious are those where you are paying high interest and penalties, things such as credit cards, lines of credit, taxes, or any other debt that is much higher than inflation. In Chapter 9, "Call Your Creditor and Say 'Hi' (The Plan)," you will see how to formulate a plan that will enable you to get out from under these burdensome debts. But as you contemplate this plan, you also need to prioritize certain debts and pay them on time:

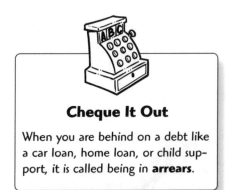

Cheque It Out

When you are behind on a debt like a car loan, home loan, or child support, it is called being in **arrears**.

➤ **Rent or mortgage.** Make paying your rent or mortgage a top priority. Payments on a home equity line of credit or second mortgage are also essential because you can lose your house if you don't pay.

➤ **Car payments.** Make the payments. If you don't, the car will be repossessed.

➤ **Utility bills.** These services are important, and the bills usually have heavy late-payment penalties.

➤ **Child support or alimony.** Not paying these debts can land you in jail.

➤ **Taxes.** Taxes should not be put off, but if you can't pay, you still need to file. We talk more about this later on in the book, but if Revenue Canada is about to take your salary, bank account, house, or other property, you should set up a repayment plan immediately.

The First Rule of Holes: Stop Digging!

The goal of this book is to help you get out of debt within the context of making your life work. You will not be asked to make radical, unreasonable changes in your life because doing so rarely works. Instead, important, sometimes gradual, small but significant changes can make a big difference.

If you are going to start getting out of debt, you have to stop going into debt. One way to start is to begin to wean yourself from the credit card teat if you think that is part of your problem. You don't have to cut up all your credit cards; that would be impractical and unreasonable. Start slowly, but build up to it and get strong. You can do it. The only way to stop going into debt is to stop going into debt. You might as well start now because the sooner you start, the sooner you will get out of debt. The longer you wait, the longer it will take.

In subsequent chapters, we will show you how to easily trim your budget (well, almost easily) so that you need not incur more debt to stay afloat. But begin now. Down the road you will see that this is one of the most important steps you can take in getting out of

Two Cents

If you were able to put $2000 a year away in an RRSP beginning in your twenties, you would have over half a million dollars by the time you are 65.

debt. You will thank yourself for this gift. Remember the first rule of holes: Stop digging!

Long-Term Goals

Now is the time to begin to think about your long-range financial vision. What is it you hope to accomplish by getting out of debt? Changing some habits? Paying off your MasterCard? Probably what you really want is a less stressful life, one that's free from money worries. But you can have even more. Getting out of debt is one thing, but prosperity is another thing altogether.

You have read this once already, and you will read it again in this book: If you don't begin to do some things differently, to change the way you think and treat money, you might get out of debt, but you won't stay out of debt. If you do make some simple changes to your thinking and your behaviour, not only will you get out of debt, but you also will get ahead. You will get what you deserve: a life of abundance.

The Least You Need to Know

➤ Going into debt for essentials makes financial sense; doing so for nonessentials does not.

➤ Not all debt is bad debt.

➤ You may want to keep debts that enhance your life and get rid of the rest.

➤ Stop adding to your debt right now.

➤ Cultivate a long-term plan of action.

Chapter 2

Early Warning Signs of Trouble

In This Chapter

➤ Money signs

➤ Banking signals

➤ Evading the inevitable

➤ Emotional problems

How serious are your debt problems? The spectrum of possibilities ranges from negligible to severe. The fact that you bought this book indicates that debt is something you are concerned about. As you read this chapter and review the most common signs of debt problems, consider that the more signs that apply to you, the more serious your situation is.

Where Have All the Dollars Gone?

The first sign that debt is becoming more of an issue in your life than it should be is the incredible shrinking bank balance. Although you make enough to pay your regular bills, more and more of your monthly income goes toward servicing your rising debt. It gets to a point where money is tight, and you feel like you are choking because there is never enough money. Unfortunately, this situation creates a negative domino effect upon the rest of your financial life.

But I Still Have Room on My Card

The first to fall is the credit card domino. Your lack of funds causes you to begin to take cash advances to pay your minimum balances or basic living expenses. You know that your gold card still has about $5000 left on it, so you begin to use it to live on. Or, even worse, you begin to accept all of those credit card offers that come in the mail, and before you know it, you have 10 open credit cards.

Two Cents

"He who restrains his appetite avoids debt."

—Chinese proverb

You take out $100 here and charge $500 there. "No big deal," you think. After all, you are used to paying off your cards, or at least paying enough that the debt has not, so far, seemed burdensome. You begin to rationalize. You tell yourself that you're just in a temporary cash crunch, that this is why credit cards were invented. Feeling better, you take out another $500.

The Balance Transfer Shuffle

"Not to worry," you tell your partner or yourself. You have a plan. These stupid credit cards can't outfox you. You will just transfer your balances from the card with the high balance or the high interest rate to a different card. You are smarter than the credit card companies.

Not only do you transfer balances, but you start to use those convenient cheques the credit card companies are always sending you. You begin to pay one card with another card. In the meantime, not wanting to upset your precarious financial balance, you

Money Talks

When you use your credit cards to withdraw cash, extra fees kick in. Cash advances carry an upfront fee of up to four percent of the amount advanced. There is a higher interest charge for cash advances than regular card charges, and many issuers also require you to pay down the balances for purchases before you pay down the higher-interest cash advance balance. Finally, cash advances carry no grace period; interest charges begin to mount as soon as the ABM spits out the money.

Money Talks

Debt got you down? Consider these rules penned by Thomas Jefferson: 1. Never put off till tomorrow what you can do today. 2. Never trouble another for what you can do yourself. 3. Never spend your money before you have it. 4. Never buy what you do not want because it is cheap; it will never be dear to you. 5. Pride costs us more than hunger, thirst, and cold. 6. Never repent of having eaten too little. 7. Nothing is troublesome that we do willingly. 8. Don't let the evils which have never happened cost you pain. 9. Always take things by their smooth handle. 10. When angry, count to 10 before you speak; if very angry, count to 100.

begin to use your cards more to pay for everyday things.

The bills grow. Whereas you used to be able to pay more than the minimum, now the minimum is more than you can pay. In an effort to conserve your rapidly dwindling cash reserves, you decide you have no choice but to save money—by using your credit cards more!

Relief is in sight. Using your cards more and not spending your precious cash to pay off these credit card balances gives you a (false) sense of security. Your money situation is not that bad. For a few months, things seem back to normal. Anyway, those tiny classified ads you are going to start running all over the country are going to make you rich, and then you will pay off all of your cards, and this situation will be something to laugh about in five years.

Two Cents

When looking at credit card offers, check how long the introductory rate lasts, the annual percentage rate after that teaser rate expires, whether the teaser rate applies only to transferred balances, any annual fee, late fees, over-the-limit fees, and balance transfer fees.

Then the card with the low interest rate jacks up your rate to 18.9 percent. You have a $10 000 balance on that card! It's OK. Stay cool. You still have two more cards with room on them. All the while, you are getting deeper and deeper in debt.

What do you do? Eureka, you have a solution! You can apply for more cards, get some more low "teaser" rates, and transfer some more balances. So you do, and so it goes. Sound familiar?

Dog Logic

Soon, the mailman becomes your enemy; all he brings is bad news. Maybe you're not smarter than the credit card companies after all. Every bill you get from them now is shocking. You can't afford to pay them. So you start to only pay some of the bills on time.

Paying some of the cards late frees up some cash, but now you are incurring late fees and extra finance charges because of your ever-increasing poor bill-paying habits. The problem is, you are so far in over your head that all of your bills begin to look like messages from the enemy. Soon, you start to create a pile of unopened bills.

In order to make it through until payday (if only that little ad had generated some phone calls!), you start to pay your other bills late. Late fees pile up on late fees. You begin to get threatening letters from your creditors. Soon, you get letters from collection agencies.

Finally, you become a juggler in a three-ring circus of your own making. The cable is about to get turned off. "I'll run down and pay it today!" "Yes, I know, I understand I am behind; I'll drop a cheque in the mail tomorrow." "Maybe," you think to yourself, "they won't get it until next week, and it won't hit my bank until next Friday." That's the ticket!

The small brushfire that began back home is beginning to burn out of control.

Don't Bet on It

Compounding the personal debt problem in this country is the new access to recreational gambling. While Canadians have been lining up to gamble $2 a week for years at lottery booths, and crowding Bingo Halls by the bus load, government-funded casinos in the 1990s have turned gambling into a multi-billion-dollar industry, says Statistics Canada in the 1998 report "The Gambling Industry: Raising the Stakes." Though they are not the epitome of glamour that James Bond would have you believe, casinos in Canada do legitimize gambling as a harmless recreational activity, akin to a night on the town or at the theatre.

According to the 1996 Family Expenditure Survey, eight out of every ten households in Canada gambled some money on at least one gaming activity, spending an average of $423. The higher the family income, the more money that was risked and lost. The poor, however, spend proportionately more of their income attempting to cash in on the big prizes that are offered in lottery wins, Bingo prizes, and casino pay-outs. If you look at the money as an entertainment cost, it is easy to rationalize. But for the two to five percent of families for whom recreational gambling becomes "problem gambling," the dollar values soar well beyond what is affordable says Roberta Boughton, an addiction therapist at the Centre for Addiction and Mental Health in Toronto. "The problem becomes the solution," says Boughton, referring to the circular pattern that develops of gambling to try to pay off other gambling debts. "Most gambling addictions begin with one big win at some point. But soon the addict begins circling the drain, chasing losses in desperate attempts to recoup lost money." Gambling is an invisible problem, often shrouded in secrecy by the problem gambler. The family often doesn't even know about the extent of it until considerable financial damage brings it to a crisis.

If you or your spouse has a gambling addiction, you can seek help from a gambling therapist. If you think your spouse has a bad gambling habit, take steps to ensure your security by keeping finances separate, particularly credit cards, bank accounts, and retirement savings. You could be on the hook for your spouse's debt if your name is on all of his or her assets.

Bye-Bye Savings

The next indication that things are getting out of hand financially relates to your bank accounts. You might have entered this period proud of the fact that you had some money in the bank. Maybe you were saving for a rainy day or maybe for a special trip that you wanted to take.

Sadly, by this point, your savings are probably long gone. Despite the penalties, your RRSPs have probably been raided, too. Equally bad, your previous valiant efforts to do the right thing and consistently save some money have probably gone by the wayside as well. With money as tight as it is, you don't see how you can afford to begin to save some money again. Your pride is hurt, and your ego is wounded. You might begin to feel depressed over the sad state of your financial affairs. That rainy day has come.

Money Talks

Record bank profits in the past few years have left Canadians rather cynical about banking. With fees charged for everything from opening to closing a bank account, it's no wonder electronic banking has taken off. It seems the less contact we have with the bank, the better. The Canadian Bankers Association estimates that over 85 percent of banking transactions are now done electronically, through ABM, direct payment cards, or Internet banking. In 1998 Canadian banks recorded $825.4 million in cash withdrawals, $204.2 million in deposits, $59.2 million in bill payments, and $65.7 million in account transfers.

Cheque It Out

Often, even if a cheque you write to a creditor does not clear the bank the first time, that creditor may try to deposit it again before deciding that the cheque is no good. These creditors are **putting the cheque through twice**.

What's My Balance?

More and more Canadians are paying bills electronically rather than writing cheques, but if you're in debt, chances are you're in the latter category. (After all, electronic banking doesn't let you bounce a cheque. Either you have the money, or you don't.) You have probably figured out how to just skate by.

It could be that you go to pay the phone bill at the last possible moment on Friday afternoon, knowing that the cheque won't get to your bank until probably Tuesday of the next week (but hopefully Wednesday!). That will work, because you get paid next Wednesday.

Maybe you do what Tom does. When things get really bad, he pays the bills on time, but "accidentally" puts the cheque for the phone company in the Visa envelope and vice versa. By the time the mix-up is fixed, two weeks have gone by, and he's gotten paid again. He fixes the problem and makes it through another month.

Or, like Jessica, you just stop balancing your chequebook altogether. What's the point? After all, when you go to the ABM, you check your balance! Jessica can't bear to figure out how much she owes to whom and refuses to keep track of her ABM withdrawals, so she just continues to write cheques and take out money, keeping a rough balance in her head and hoping that it will be all right. This is the next signpost on a debt-end road: evading, avoiding, and ignoring the truth of the situation.

How to reduce your ABM charges:

1. Don't use an ABM machine belonging to an institution where you don't bank.

2. Consider using a credit union. Its ABM fees are usually lower.

3. If you use an ABM regularly, withdraw larger amounts of money to reduce the number of times you are charged a fee.

4. Avoid ABMs that surcharge.

End of the Line

Creditors are now starting to close your accounts. Credit card companies, once your good friends, want nothing to do with you. Your accounts have been assigned to collection agencies. Sadly, they do want to talk to you.

You stop answering the phone. You get caller ID. Finally, you change your phone number, get an unlisted number, and give it out only to your friends.

At this point, you have a chronic debt problem. You know it, too, but you would rather ignore the problem or explain it away:

➤ **You are concerned only about today.** Although your debt problems are now constant, and every month is as bad as the month before, your only concern is this month. Getting the rent paid, paying back Dad, and keeping the heat on are your concerns. The fact that you have the tax bill or insurance payment due next month is of no concern to you today. You will solve that crisis when you get to it.

➤ **You have lost track of how much you owe.** You don't even bother to look at the balances on the statements you get; you can't pay them anyway. If you do have any credit cards left, you don't care what the interest rate is; all you know about your cards is how much room you have on any one of them with which to charge.

Two Cents

"When I look back on all these worries, I remember the story of the old man who said on his deathbed that he had had a lot of trouble in his life, most of which had never happened."

—Winston Churchill

➤ **You have become the king or queen of rationalizations.** You refuse to take a good hard look at your financial affairs and instead have reasons for why things are the way they are. "The divorce killed me." "I'm too busy with my novel to worry about something as mundane as my bills." "I'm no good with numbers." "I'll deal with it after the first of the year."

➤ **You are in a state of constant worry, but do nothing.** You may be frozen with fear. The problem looms so large that you don't know where to start, so you start nowhere.

Your Money or Your Life

What began as an isolated skirmish in the outback of money country has now spilled over to the rest of your life. It could be affecting your health, your job, your relationships, and even your life.

Marriage and Money

Money troubles are the leading cause of divorce in this country, and now you know why. Your debt issues are now beginning to affect your relationship. Your mate is angry with you, scared about the well-being of the family, and concerned that your problems will affect his or her financial life as well. Here are some signs that you're in drastic debt:

➤ Your mate is afraid to apply for credit with you for fear that your problems will spill over.

➤ The constant phone calls from creditors cause pain and anger in your mate.

➤ The constant worry about money takes its toll on your sex life.

➤ Your mate is worried that the boss will find out.

Finally, you resolve to do something and face your money demons. Congratulations, buying this book is an important first step.

Two Cents

Before they walk down the aisle, couples should have a money session to avoid surprises down the road. From student loans to car payments to credit card bills, it's best to come clean on every "I owe" before saying "I do."

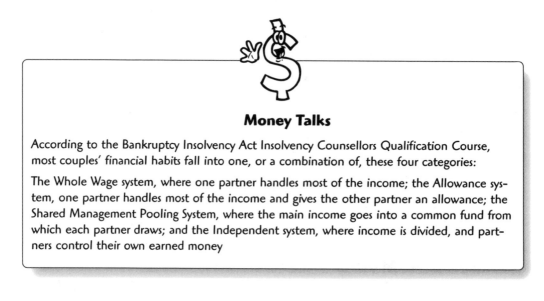

Money Talks

According to the Bankruptcy Insolvency Act Insolvency Counsellors Qualification Course, most couples' financial habits fall into one, or a combination of, these four categories:

The Whole Wage system, where one partner handles most of the income; the Allowance system, one partner handles most of the income and gives the other partner an allowance; the Shared Management Pooling System, where the main income goes into a common fund from which each partner draws; and the Independent system, where income is divided, and partners control their own earned money

Test Yourself

As we said at the beginning of this chapter, debt issues can range from mild to severe. Take the following quiz to see how serious your debt situation is:

Are your debts making your home life unhappy?

Do your debts make you careless with the welfare of your family?

Are your debts a source of constant friction with your mate?

Are your debts affecting how people view you?

Do your debts affect how you view yourself?

Do your debt problems distract you from your work?

Do you fear that your employer, family, or friends will learn the extent of your total indebtedness?

Have you ever lost a friend because of your money habits?

Have you ever lied in order to obtain credit?

Do you expect a negative response when you apply for credit?

Have you ever borrowed money without considering how you will pay it back?

Have you ever borrowed money without considering the interest rate?

When faced with a difficult financial situation, is your first thought to go deeper into debt?

Have you ever lied to your creditors regarding payment of a bill?

Does the pressure of your debts cause you difficulty in sleeping, or cause you to overeat, undereat, smoke, or otherwise affect your health negatively?

Has the pressure of your debts ever caused you to drink more than you should?

Do you think about your money problems a lot during the day?

Do you justify your debts by telling yourself that you are superior to the "other" people, and when you get your "break," you'll be out of debt overnight?

Have you ever developed a strict regimen for paying off your debts, only to break it under pressure?

Have you seriously considered bankruptcy?

Scoring:

1–5 yes answers: Your debt issues are not bad and are easily resolvable.

5–10 yes answers: Your debt issues are more serious, but not out of control.

10 or more yes answers: Your debt problems are very serious and deserve your immediate attention. You must begin to take corrective action now.

You see that you need to take action to resolve your debt situation, which is good news. Consider these ideas:

➤ Continuing to run from the problem will only get you in deeper trouble.

➤ Respond to your creditors and show them that you have an interest in working things out. (We'll show you how in Chapter 12, "Talking to the Lion: Dealing with Creditors.")

Two Cents

"Our lives improve only when we take chances—and the first and most difficult risk we can take is to be honest with ourselves."

—Walter Anderson

➤ Acknowledge to yourself that you have made some irresponsible decisions.

➤ Get professional counseling if it is warranted.

➤ Share your problems with a close friend or your spouse.

➤ Know that there is a way out and that this process and a debt-free destination are probably a better experience than the stress in your life today.

Today is a turning point in your life. There is plenty you can do to turn this situation around, and it may not be nearly as difficult as you think. The remainder of this book helps guide your way.

The Least You Need to Know

➤ The first signpost on the road to indebtedness is a lack of money and an increase in money worries.

➤ When you begin to have problems with your bank accounts, things are getting more serious.

➤ Evading and avoiding the problem make the matter worse.

➤ When your home life is affected by money troubles, it is time to take action.

Chapter 3

Take That Paper Bag Off Your Head When You Drive

In This Chapter

➤ Paying bills late

➤ Falling for the credit card trap

➤ Not saving

➤ Believing in scarcity

➤ Working for others

➤ Overspending

There are many ways to fall into debt. One person may overspend while another blindly ignores the mounting bill pile, believing that the problem will somehow magically improve. The reason for your indebtedness could be poor planning, a spending addiction, or a combination of bad habits. Whatever the reason, it is important to identify what you are doing wrong so that you can begin to make some changes. (Of course, there are many reasons for going into debt that have nothing to do with anything you may be doing "wrong," such as a medical crisis that leads to a loss of earning power, or starting a business. These types of situations are dealt with in other chapters.)

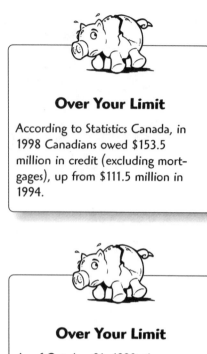

The Cheque Is in the Mail

One reason why people end up in debt is that they were never taught basic financial skills, such as paying bills on time. Failing to pay your bills in a timely manner only compounds your debt problems because late payments can hurt you in so many ways. This problem should be easily fixed.

The first way comes from the costs incurred for the "privilege" of paying late. Say that you have a $139 credit card payment due on the 15th. If you end up paying that bill on the 20th, you will probably pay at least another $25 in late charges.

In and of itself, a lone $25 late fee is no big deal. Usually, however, we are not talking about a single late fee; paying late can be a bad habit. If you multiply this late fee times, say, six bills—a couple of credit cards, your mortgage, a car payment—you could be easily losing at least $150 a month. That is a big waste of money.

What's worse is that the late payment habit can cause you to fall even deeper into a vicious cycle of debt. Money is tight, in part because of late fees, and then you pay late because money is tight. If paying late has become a habit, it could cost you upwards of $1000 over the course of a year.

Paying your bills late hurts you in other, more insidious, ways as well. A history of late payments will ruin your credit rating, making getting other credit more expensive and thereby costing you even more money. (Note, however, that it takes 30 days from the date the bill was due for the negative remark to hit your credit report.) A bad credit rating can really kill you financially.

Suppose you went to get a $20 000 car loan with good credit. At 6 percent over five years, you would pay roughly $6000 in interest for that loan. If persistent late payments have hurt your credit rating, you might pay 15 percent for that same loan. Interest on that loan would cost you up to $15 000.

The good news is that it is not that difficult to get off the late payment train. A month or two of budgeting can get you back on a normal payment schedule and save you a lot of money in the long run (and in the short run).

Congratulations, You've Been Approved

Credit cards can be a boon or a bust, depending upon how they are used and treated. The responsible use of credit cards makes living a lot easier for many people. They fund business startups and treats for your spouse. We have no problem whatsoever with the reasonable and responsible use of credit cards.

The problem is that being unreasonable and irresponsible with credit cards is just so darn easy. Convenient and fun to use, credit cards can too easily become more of a curse than a blessing. With interests ranging from 8.99 percent to 18.9 percent, credit card debt is easy to create but difficult to erase.

You must be especially wary of what we call in this book "the credit card trap." This trap is very easy to fall into and very difficult to get out of. You fall into the trap when

➤ You run up a card with, say, an 18 percent interest that you know you can't pay off.

➤ You use credit cards to buy easily consumable things, because you will be paying exorbitant interest for items that quickly disappear.

➤ You use credit cards for luxuries that you could not otherwise afford.

➤ You pay only the minimum payment due.

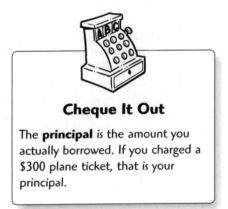

Cheque It Out

The **principal** is the amount you actually borrowed. If you charged a $300 plane ticket, that *is* your principal.

Once you have fallen for the trap, you have a card on which you owe a lot of money, on which you pay only the minimum payment, and on which the principal never seems to decrease.

Like so many of us, Nancy fell for the credit card trap. After graduating college, she moved to New York and got a job waitressing while she looked for acting jobs. She used her credit card overdraft protection to balance her chequebook every month. After a year, she was about $10 000 in debt.

She decided that she had to get rid of these debts before they got more out of hand. Although she used a method that we hadn't thought of before hearing her story, it worked for her, and that's the important thing.

Nancy took every extra cent that she made and started to pay off the card with the smallest balance, while paying the minimum on her other three credit cards (since the minimum amount due was a relatively small amount), until that card was paid off. She then did the same thing with the next smallest card, but instead of making only minimum payments on the other two cards, she made double the minimum payment, which she could afford to do because one card was paid off already. She then repeated

Two Cents

If you tell your credit card company that you will cancel your card unless you get a lower rate, you just might get a lower rate.

this strategy with each of the last two cards.

It took her a little over a year, but at the end, Nancy was completely out of the credit card debt that had been overwhelming her. Also, and equally importantly, because none of the payments had been late or behind, her good credit remained good.

Of equal consequence, Nancy did not cut each card up as she paid it off or cancel the accounts as people are often advised to do. Instead, once each account was paid in full, she wrote a letter canceling it, saying that she was in the market for a card with a substantially lower interest rate. She was amazed when she started getting offers for cards with much lower interest rates from the very same credit card companies that had been charging her such horrendous rates.

Nancy then began teaching herself how to properly use credit cards. Instead of grabbing each offered card, she carefully read everything about each and selected two that offered the best overall terms, not just the lowest rates. She treated each one like an American Express card: It had to be paid off in full each month, unless she used it for an unexpected emergency. No matter what, her rule was, revolving balances had to be paid off within three months. So you see, there is a way out of the credit card trap and out of any debt if you make a few simple adjustments to your money habits.

Two Cents

In 1997, Statistics Canada noted that of the taxfilers aged 25 to 64 who put money away, the average amount was more than $6000, approximately 11.8 percent of their average income.

Savings? Who Needs Savings?

Many people have no savings at all. Although we all know that we are supposed to have some money saved, between bills and kids, it just seems too hard most of the time. It's kind of like losing weight. We know it would be good for us, but it's awfully hard to do.

Yet the great thing about having a little money in the bank is that you can use it for things that you would have otherwise have gone into debt for. Instead of charging that $400 trip to the beach, going further into debt, and paying more in interest, if you can save $400 you will be in much better financial shape. And it doesn't have to be that hard.

If you would like to begin to save, try these easy-to-implement ideas:

Realize that small steps can yield big results. Put 10 percent of your spending money away at first, even if it's just 10 percent of your pocket change. Over time, small amounts add up, and you probably won't even miss 10 percent of your pocket money.

Eat more cheaply. Eliminate a trip to a fast-food restaurant, make a cheap dinner one night a week, or bring your lunch to work. Save the savings.

Use 10 percent less. Stretch your shampoo, laundry soap, and dishwashing detergent. Just stretching by 10 percent will enable you to meet your weekly savings goal.

Change brands. Prices fluctuate, and without brand loyalty, you can get the best prices.

Applied consistently, these ideas and others you come up with can yield enough savings to make a difference.

I Believe in Santa Claus

Another way to get in debt and ensure that you will stay in debt is to pretend that the problem will somehow magically disappear. You will win the lottery or make so much money next year that you need not worry about your mounting debts today. Wishful thinking can happen to anyone, for any reason; it happens to all of us for different reasons at one time or another.

Money Talks

If you put all your spare change in a jar, rustle up coins from the laundry room and in the crevices of furniture and your car, you would probably be surprised to see how much money you have that you don't even know about.

Over Your Limit

At the height of his career, Art Schlichter made over $1 million a year, but he is now in prison for forgery.

The problem with this thinking is that it allows you to avoid responsibility for your financial problems. You need not take any corrective action because there will be a magical solution.

Dangerous wishful thinking happened to Mitzi Schlichter, former wife of pro-football quarterback Art Schlichter. When she married Art, she knew that Art liked to gamble, but she didn't think he had a problem. She had her first inkling otherwise when, on the flight home from their honeymoon in 1989, Art told his bride that he had $10 000 in new gambling debts.

It took nine years of broken promises, debt, and heartache for her to realize that they had a serious problem with money and gambling. She divorced Art and now works at a treatment centre for gambling addicts. Her ex-husband, once a number one draft pick and a starter for the Indianapolis Colts, is in prison for forgery.

You may win the lottery, but most likely not. Getting out of debt takes work, being straight with your creditors, and being honest with yourself.

Believing in Scarcity

Your beliefs have as much to do with your current economic situation as almost anything else. When you are in debt, it is easy to see the world as one of lack. But the fact is, there is a lot of money in this world.

The story is told of a famous movie actor (who shall remain nameless) who enjoyed making millions and then blowing it all, every single penny. This actor is said to have done this time and again. He apparently liked the challenge of having to create a new fortune over and over again.

It takes a lot of courage—or stupidity—to do this, and there is no guarantee in life, certainly not in the movie business where some new actor is always coming along as the latest flavour of the month. After blowing his fortune for the third or fourth time, there was no guarantee whatsoever that this actor would ever make millions of dollars again acting in movies. But he did it again anyway.

Besides chutzpah, what this actor had was a belief in abundance. He believed in it so much that he put his money where his mouth is. If he believed in scarcity and were afraid that he would never work again, he never would have done what he did. He credits his bedrock belief in abundance for his ability to keep working and making money.

No, you are not a Hollywood actor, but the moral of the story still applies. As the saying goes, "As a man thinketh, so is he." In the next few chapters, we will look at how to change some limiting beliefs you may have about money.

Working for Others

Another reason you may be in debt, probably a big reason, is that you don't make enough money. If you are tight for cash, the usual solution is to borrow by getting a credit card advance or asking your brother for help. But the fact is, when the books don't balance every month, you have three options; it just seems like going into debt is the only one.

Instead of incurring more debt, you could cut back and spend less, or you could make more money. Either of these options would work. The important idea to realize right now is that you don't have to quit your job to make more money. There are plenty of ways to increase your income every month that have nothing to do with your job. As you will see in the last section of this book, an entrepreneurial mindset can go a long way toward getting you out of debt.

Money Talks

The Lillian Vernon company sells household items, has revenues over $200 million a year, and is listed on the American Stock Exchange. Lillian Vernon started the company in 1951 from her small apartment while pregnant to make some extra money to help out the family finances.

Time for a Plan

Most of us have negative connotations when we hear the word budget, likening it to a financial diet. But budget does not have to be a bad word. Honest!

(We ask you to suspend your negative beliefs about budgets for a little while and see whether creating one might help you far more than hurt you. If, at the end of the next few chapters about budgeting, you are not convinced that a budget can help save the day, by all means revert back to your former budgetary beliefs. Just give us the benefit of the doubt for a little while. Thank you.)

A budget is a money plan. You can use it to organize and control your financial resources, set and realize goals, and decide in advance how your money will work for you. A budget allows you to know how much money you have to spend every month and where you are spending it. As such, a budget is the one of the most important steps you can take toward maximizing the power of your money.

Over Your Limit

In 1996, 79 361 Canadians went bankrupt—a record number that prompted the Office of Consumer Affairs of Industry Canada to contract Carleton University and COMPAS Inc. to conduct an empirical study to gain a better understanding of the people who file for bankruptcy protection.

An architect would never start work on a new house without a blueprint. An auto manufacturer would never begin construction of a new car without a detailed set of design specifications. Yet many of us spend money without a plan to guide us. At the very least, a budget should allow you to find extra spending money in your paycheque every month.

Compare a budget to driving a car. In an automobile, you get plenty of feedback on how you're doing. When you drive, you use mirrors, speed limits, and the instrument panel to get information about your driving, and you know that a small mistake can cost lives. If you go too fast, you get a ticket. There is plenty of feedback from both within and without the car to tell you whether you are doing a good job.

Think about what would happen if you took some of that feedback away. Suppose you didn't have a gas gauge, or an oil pressure monitor, or a rearview mirror, or a speedometer? What if you had no windshield? Driving would be beyond dangerous. You need feedback to know where you are going. Managing your finances without a budget is like driving a car with a blindfold on.

The Overspender

Compulsive overspending is a sure way to get deep in debt. Maybe you are the overspender, or maybe your spouse is (maybe you both overspend). An overspender is someone who loves to spend money to bring pleasure. Budgeting, saving, and investing are not part of the plan. The spending is such a problem that it gets in the way of paying normal bills.

Over Your Limit

With the Internet adding to cable television, at-home shopping will top $100 billion in sales in the next few years.

Overspenders may use the spending of money for many different, and not altogether healthy, reasons:

➤ As a substitute for love

➤ As a way to avoid problems at work

➤ To avoid intimacy

➤ To relieve guilt

➤ To feel important

➤ To gain power

➤ To gain confidence

A compulsive overspender spends money whether he needs to or not. He celebrates an important event by blowing a wad of cash or running up a credit card. He does not stop to think whether he can afford something, if he wants it, for whatever reason, he gets it.

One of your authors, Janice, used to spend this way. When travelling through Europe as a university student, she bought expensive souvenirs with her Citibank Visa card that she shared with her mother, which thus had a high spending limit. "It's only money," and "You only live once" were her common rationalizations for wool rugs from Greece and leather jackets from Italy. It took her two years to pay off the credit card through part-time jobs, and she hasn't let credit card debt rack up since.

Compulsive overspending can ruin a relationship. The other partner may become so angry at the precarious financial situation the overspender has put the couple in that she pulls away. Or she might become an enabler, helping the overspender by making up the difference and then resenting it.

There are several things a spouse can do to help the overspender or that an overspender can do to help himself:

Money Talks

According to Statistics Canada's General Social Survey in 1998, 43 percent of the population surveyed reported spending an average of 1.9 hours a day shopping for goods and services; 19 percent of the population reported spending an average of 1.6 hours per day eating meals in restaurants.

➤ **Realize that overspending is usually a symptom of a deeper problem that is not being addressed.** Counselling might be in order to help the overspender figure out what the real problem is and begin to deal with it.

➤ **Be honest.** An overspender may deny that there is a problem, thinking that he is just a misunderstood, fun-loving guy. The spouse must tell the truth. The overspender must admit the truth.

➤ **Come up with a financial plan of action.** You, or you and your spouse, need to set some financial goals and decide how you will begin to achieve them. (Read the rest of the book!)

➤ **The spouse cannot rescue the overspender.** She can help, she can love him, but rescuing him just makes the problem worse. She may even have to separate herself financially by opening up a separate chequing account and getting credit cards in her own name. For example, Carol finally had to divorce her husband to avoid getting sued by his creditors, although she continued to love and live with him.

➤ **Try a role reversal. Go to a department store and switch roles.** The frugal wife should become the overspending husband, and the husband should be the one that constantly says no. Watch how your mate behaves and notice how it feels to act differently. You might be embarrassed to see yourself through your mate's eyes.

For Mark and Jean, this last simple exercise helped them see things just a bit differently. Mark was the overspender, and Jean was the practical one. He just loved to binge shop, and she loved to hoard things. She was in charge of their finances and paid all the bills. Needless to say, they constantly fought about money.

After their relationship took a turn for the worse because of money, they sought counselling. After a few sessions, they realized that Mark's overspending was rooted in his poor childhood; spending money helped him feel powerful. Jean also learned

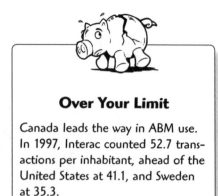

Over Your Limit

Canada leads the way in ABM use. In 1997, Interac counted 52.7 transactions per inhabitant, ahead of the United States at 41.1, and Sweden at 35.3.

something; she learned that making money and not spending any was a way to make her husband feel guilty and gain some power in their relationship.

That was when they went on their excursion to the department store. That trip helped her see why Mark liked doing what he had been doing; it was fun to spend money. For his part, Mark didn't like what he saw when Jean acted like him. She looked out of control and irresponsible. Though it took time, both began to change and become a bit more like the other.

If you are an overspender, or know one intimately, there are solutions. If the problem seems out of control, you should also read Chapter 15, "Credit Counselling," to see whether that group might be a solution for you.

The Least You Need to Know

➤ Paying bills late hurts you in many ways.

➤ Beware the credit card trap.

➤ It is not that hard to start saving if you start small.

➤ Your beliefs affect your material world.

➤ Be open to the possibility of budgeting.

➤ Overspending is usually a symptom of a bigger problem.

Part 2
Changing Your Relationship with Money

Here we introduce the solutions to the problem. Not everyone is in debt. What do they do that you do not do? What did their parents teach them when they were growing up? These are some basic, simple ideas that everyone should know, but that many people do not know.

People do not avoid debt effortlessly, but it just requires a little work every month. We lay the process all out step-by-step, and explain what we're doing at every point along the way. We'll teach you what to do and why to do it.

Chapter 4

A Frank Talk with Mr. Loonie

In This Chapter

➤ Your family and money

➤ Your money history

➤ Uncovering hidden beliefs

➤ Money talk

Getting out of debt will take more than making more money or sticking to a budget. Money is an emotionally charged subject, and what you think and how you feel about money has as much to do with your level of prosperity as anything else, if not more.

If your debt problems were not caused by a sudden emergency, but instead because of a pattern, then we think that it is important that you discover your negative money beliefs so you can change them. Because unless you change your beliefs about money, change these patterns, and begin to relate to it like wealthy people do, you may get out of debt, but you won't stay out of debt. The first step in that process is to understand that you learn more about money from your family than from anywhere else.

Your Money History

Like any relationship, your relationship with money can take many forms. It can be good or bad. It can be dysfunctional, or it can be healthy. Most people with chronic debt problems have some sort of an unhealthy relationship with money.

The key word is chronic. Many people who have a healthy relationship with money consciously choose to go into debt because it enables them to do things they otherwise could not, and these people have a plan for how they will service the debt. Debt becomes a symptom of an unhealthy relationship with money when debt is created unconsciously or when it is unmanageable. The fact that you bought this book probably, though not necessarily, indicates that you are probably no longer creating debt unconsciously.

Do as I Say, Not as I Do

As we grow up, we learn about money from our parents. Unfortunately, for many people, plenty of these lessons were negative. One reason is that our parents learned about money from our grandparents, many of whom lived through the Depression. As a result, a lot of people learned that money was a scarce item, and owning it was something to be afraid of or embarrassed about.

Sam learned this lesson in childhood. Sam's father was a successful entrepreneur who made a very good living. But he had always told Sam that he was "not made of money." Despite the fact that Sam's dad made plenty of money, money was still a constant point of argument and worry in the house.

When Sam's first daughter was four, he found himself one day telling her that she could not have a new toy because he "was not made out of money." Realizing that he was merely mimicking a family belief about the scarcity of money, Sam decided to buy her the toy, more for his own good than hers.

That experience was the first step in a long process of rethinking his money values and fixing his relationship with money. From that day forward, Sam would say to himself, "I am made out of money." Of course, he wasn't made out of money, but by using this statement to change the family belief that he had unwittingly learned and unconsciously accepted, he began to unleash himself from some of his family's suffocating beliefs about money.

Linda had almost the opposite experience. She was

Over Your Limit

A recent survey in the American women's magazine, *Redbook*, found that 44.3 percent of wives and 31 percent of husbands made a purchase and fibbed about either its price or its very existence to their mates.

raised in a family that constantly tried to "keep up with the Joneses." Overspending was less important than appearances. As a result, the message she received from her parents was that budgets were bad and overspending was good. As an adult, she realized that she had some work to do.

Two Cents

"When I was young I thought money was the most important thing in life; now that I am old, I know it is."

—Oscar Wilde

What Were You Taught About Money?

Some of us adopt our family's attitudes regarding money without even realizing it; others knowingly and consciously rebel against their parents' money beliefs and actions. Either way, your parents are still molding your behaviour. What you should strive for is to relate to money in a manner that reflects your values today and the values you want to pass along to your children. You begin this journey by noticing what you learned from your parents about money:

➤ **What were their actions regarding money?** Was it a source of constant worry? Did they avoid talking about it? Did they always argue about it? Did they blame each other or you and your siblings for money problems? Did they act as if they never had enough, or maybe as if they had more than they really had? What did this teach you?

➤ **Do you remember any traumatic incidents that may have affected your beliefs about money?** Maybe your parents had to close a business or were ashamed of having to file for bankruptcy. Maybe you didn't have enough money to go to the prom or felt ashamed of how you had to dress for school. How did this make you feel about money?

➤ **What did you know about your family's financial situation?** Was it ever discussed? If it was a secret, why do you think that was so? Was money a source of pride or embarrassment? What did you learn from this?

➤ **What was the main message you were taught about money?** You may have learned that the husband earns the money and the wife spends it. If your family was struggling financially, you may have learned that your family at least had love and been told that rich families do not.

When you were a child, you were likely told not to ask or talk about money. Now think about that for a second. What is the subliminal message being sent when a topic is taboo? If your family avoided talking about money, did that send you a signal that money is not only a forbidden subject, but also a bad thing?

Money Talks

As a general rule, families with healthy attitudes about money are not afraid to discuss financial matters with their children. Kids are brought up knowing how much Mom and Dad make, where the money is invested, and how much the monthly mortgage payments are.

Over Your Limit

Youth broadcaster YTV commissioned a survey of the growing nine- to fourteen-year-old market, known as 'tweens, and discovered that nine out of ten kids have influence over the purchase of their own clothes and shoes. With gifts, babysitting, snow shovelling, paper routes, and allowance, these kids made up almost $1.4 billion worth of spending power in 1998.

We do not mean to suggest that all the things you heard about money were dysfunctional, but we would not be surprised if that were mostly true. What you need to do is look at what you were taught about money and see how that may be affecting your life today. The good news is that you can change this pattern with your own children and teach them to have a positive relationship with money so that they don't continue the debt cycle you've gotten yourself into.

Money Stories

How your family earned, spent, saved, wasted, thought about, and perhaps even fought about money has had a powerful role in shaping your financial attitudes and behaviours today. For example, it dawned on Laurie why she had grown up to be a compulsive overspender when she finally started to think about her family's money history. Her father was quite strict and always very tight with both a dollar and his emotions. Her mother, though, had been very loving and was rather extravagant with Laurie. Don't tell Laurie that money can't buy you love; she learned differently. Laurie grew up equating money with love.

As an adult, Laurie realized that she had learned that spending money (even when she didn't have any) had become a way to feel loved. That simple realization began her process of financial solvency.

Not all families' money attitudes are bad. Born and raised in Boston, Michael learned what he considered to be "powerful lessons" about frugality, ingrained by three centuries of New England conservation, typified, he says, by the clean-your-plate admonishment that "children are starving in China."

He tells the story of walking down the street one day with a friend, when he watched "incredulously" as a man in front of him casually tossed the four pennies he'd just received as change onto the sidewalk. "With barely a moment's hesitation, I scooped up the discarded pennies. My friend was clearly embarrassed. She couldn't believe that I would literally and figuratively 'stoop that low'." Michael did not care. He had been raised to believe that with four pennies here and a dime there, you would soon have some real money. It was a belief he appreciated.

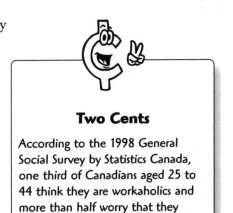

Two Cents

According to the 1998 General Social Survey by Statistics Canada, one third of Canadians aged 25 to 44 think they are workaholics and more than half worry that they don't have enough time to spend with their families and friends.

Money Makes the World Go 'Round

Answer the following questions honestly. You might want to write your answers on a piece of paper. It is not necessary, but it could help. As you do, notice which questions tend to make you uncomfortable. Those are the important ones.

➤ If your family had a motto about money growing up, what would it be?

➤ Did you get an allowance growing up? Did you have to work for it or was it given to you? What did that teach you about money? Is that what you do (or plan to do) with your own children? Why or why not?

➤ Was money ever discussed in your family? If not, what do you think were some of the unsaid beliefs your parents had about money?

➤ Were you taught the value of a dollar growing up? Did you have a savings account?

➤ Did you have to work as a teen? What happened to the money you earned?

➤ When did you first go into debt to get something that you wanted? How did you feel going into debt? Was this the beginning of a pattern?

➤ When was the first time you remember losing money? What did that teach you? Was it helpful in some way, or did you learn to be afraid of money?

➤ Did money influence your choice of careers? Was that a good idea?

➤ How do you feel about money now? Is it your friend or your enemy? Do you love it or resent it? Do you pay too much attention to it or not enough?

Simply becoming aware of some beliefs and patterns helped Mara. Growing up, whenever she asked for a special treat, Mara was always told by her father not to be "greedy." She heard this again and again until it was finally ingrained. Making matters more difficult was the fact that Mara adored her father.

As an adult, Mara always deprived herself. To be kind to herself meant, on some level, to

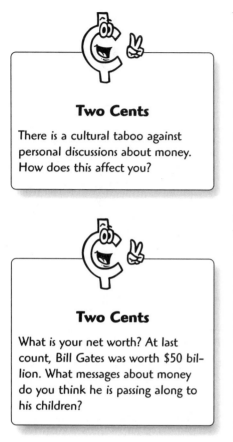

Two Cents

There is a cultural taboo against personal discussions about money. How does this affect you?

Two Cents

What is your net worth? At last count, Bill Gates was worth $50 billion. What messages about money do you think he is passing along to his children?

be a greedy, disobedient daughter. Her finances reflected this. She was always broke and always ended up in low-paying jobs. When she finally took stock of her money history, one of the first things she realized was that she would have to rethink her beliefs about "greed" and accept the fact that wanting something did not mean she was a bad person or daughter.

So, what were you taught about money? All of these lessons created your personal money belief system. This belief system is firmly established in most children by the age of 14. After that, because there is a cultural taboo against personal discussions about money, you probably accepted your money beliefs without question.

Your money belief system forms the basis of your relationship with money. It tells you whether to spend or save, whether to invest in stocks or to buy a new car, and even how to price your services. Your money belief system decides whether you will be a borrower, a lender, a saver, or a spender—even whether you will be rich or poor.

Do you doubt this? How can you ever expect to get rich if you believe that money is the root of all evil? Your actions, based upon that belief, would repel money away from you. You may assume others around you have the same beliefs and values about money, but guess again. It is safe to say that Bill Gates has different beliefs about money than you do. (Or than we do!)

Money Beliefs

Let's begin with the supposition that your beliefs create much of your life. If you believe that it is important to be a good person, you will behave accordingly. If you believe in sacrificing your own needs for the good of your children, you will make life choices based upon that belief. People who believe that they can drive after a few drinks make different choices than those who don't.

The funny thing about a belief is that it may or may not be true. How does anyone know whether money figuratively grows on trees? Is money the root of all evil? No one knows for sure. The great thing about a belief is that it can be changed, as you will see in the next chapter.

We all have money beliefs, and although you may not know it, many of yours may be quite negative. Just look at some of the most common sayings and beliefs about money:

Money Talks

A pastor made the following announcement before the offering: "I would like to remind you that what you are about to give is tax deductible, cannot be taken with you, and is considered by the Bible to be the root of all evil." (By the way, the actual biblical expression is "The love of money is the root of all evil.")

➤ Money is the root of all evil.

➤ Money doesn't grow on trees.

➤ Money isn't everything.

➤ Money can't buy you happiness.

➤ Money can buy you happiness.

There are plenty of money slogans reflective of negative societal beliefs about money: blood money, drug money, dirty money, funny money, and so on. Is it possible that you may have unknowingly adopted some of these negative beliefs about money? Yes, it's possible. Actually, it is more than possible; it's probable.

How do we know? Look at the facts: you are deeply in debt. Being in debt is a symptom of unhealthy beliefs and attitudes about money. Becoming more aware of your money beliefs is your next step toward resolving your indebtedness.

Over Your Limit

In her book *Money Demons*, Dr. Susan Forward says, "Conscious beliefs represent only a fraction of our personal belief system. Like the tip of an iceberg, the stuff that sinks ships is hidden beneath the surface, in our unconscious."

Other Sources of Money Beliefs

You can receive money messages from many sources, not just your family:

➤ What did your religion tell you about money? Many religions foster a belief that money and spirituality are mutually exclusive. Were you given the message that to be successful financially meant you had to be a bad person?

➤ What did you learn about money from your friends? Was it cool to be struggling for money? Maybe it was cool to be driving a BMW. Did you unintentionally pick a money mode so that you would be like (or different from) one of your peers?

➤ What did you learn about money from society? Jeff grew up wanting to be an artist and became enamoured with the "struggling artist" lifestyle. Although he was ready to finally make some money by the time he turned 40, he had a difficult time believing that he was not "selling out" by wanting to draw a cake and eat one, too.

You should begin to notice a theme in your life with regard to money; a theme that had its genesis in your childhood.

Two Cents

Henry Ford, one of the richest men to have ever lived, once said, "Everything I did, I did to prove the power of faith."

A Heart-to-Heart Talk with Money

You have a lot of strong feelings about money and your relationship to it that you probably have never before expressed. As you begin to become aware of these feelings, (and in order to become more aware of your hidden beliefs about money), it might help to sit down and have a heart-to-heart talk with money.

We're serious here. Money has controlled a lot of your life, and if money could listen, you'd probably have plenty to say. So we want you to say it. It will help crystallize things for you and further elucidate what you have been taught about money and what you believe to be true.

Get over the silliness of this exercise, take out a twenty-dollar bill, go to a quiet place where no one can see you (hopefully!), and give money a piece of your mind. Tell money

➤ What I want from you is:

➤ My biggest mistake when it comes to you is:

Money Talks

Debbie Fields always believed that she could turn her great chocolate chip cookie recipe into a business, although no one else did. She started small, renting the corner of her local grocery store, and gave away a lot of cookies. In 1994, her belief paid off. She was paid $100 million for Mrs. Fields, Inc.

➤ What needs to change about our relationship is:

➤ The reason I haven't changed it is:

➤ What gets me angry with you is:

➤ A secret I have about you is:

➤ My biggest fear about you is:

Go for it, have some fun, get it out, and don't stop here. You surely have plenty to say to Mr. Money. Tell him what you think. As you do, look for some beliefs you have that you may not have noticed before.

Conversations, by definition, are a two-way street. What do you think money might have to say to you if it had the chance? Consider the following:

➤ If money had one piece of advice for you, what would it be?

➤ If money had a secret to tell you, what would it be?

➤ What would money say about how you treat it?

➤ If money could sum up the main thing that needs to change about your relationship with it, what would it be?

➤ What would need to change for you to become best friends with money?

We are asking you to do a bit of soul searching in this chapter. Some of these things may be uncomfortable, but remember, that is where the gold is. Stick with it. Choosing some positive new beliefs about money and getting out of debt and ahead of the game is far more important than any bad feelings that may bubble up.

Two Cents

"Money is congealed energy, and releasing it releases life's possibilities."

—Joseph Campbell

The Least You Need to Know

➤ We learn more about money from our families than from anywhere else.

➤ Many of the messages we get about money are negative.

➤ You probably have some negative beliefs about money that you may not be aware of.

➤ Becoming aware of your money beliefs is the first step toward changing them.

I AFFIRM...

Chapter 5

Money Affirmations

In This Chapter

➤ Changing your belief system

➤ Visualizing and change

➤ Feeling and change

➤ Thinking and change

We've said it before, and we'll say it again: If you do not change the way you think about money, you might get out of debt, but you won't stay out of debt. In this chapter, we provide you with a variety of techniques and tools you can pick and choose from to change some of your money beliefs.

Fake It 'Til You Make It

One way to change a belief is surprisingly simple. You just change your thinking. If you have been conditioned to believe that money is hard to come by, catch yourself when you think that and consciously choose a different thought.

Jim used this technique. He was a struggling comic in Toronto, and his family was quite poor. At one point his dad was fired, and Jim's family ended up living in a van. Jim had every reason to believe that money was a scarce item.

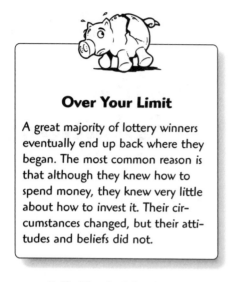

Over Your Limit

A great majority of lottery winners eventually end up back where they began. The most common reason is that although they knew how to spend money, they knew very little about how to invest it. Their circumstances changed, but their attitudes and beliefs did not.

Eventually Jim moved to Los Angeles to try to make a go of his career. Despite a failed sitcom and flagging hopes, one day Jim wrote himself a cheque for $10 million. In the little note section on the cheque, he wrote, "acting services rendered." He dated the cheque for 10 years in the future.

Every night, Jim would drive up to the hills above Los Angeles, take out the cheque, look at it, and believe it to be true. He tried to make his entire being believe that he was worth and had $10 million. Jim says that he would not leave and go back home for the night until he truly believed that the cheque was real.

Ten years later, the day before the cheque was set to be "cashed," Jim inked a deal to be the first actor in Hollywood history to be paid $20 million for one picture. That picture was *Ace Ventura: When Nature Calls*. That's right, Jim is Jim Carrey, and now you know the rest of the story.

Jim did several things right, things that you can do, too, if you want to change a limiting belief you have about money. First, he made a conscious decision to change the way he thought about money. At the time he boldly wrote his cheque, he had no evidence that it would ever be real. He was an unknown, broke actor. Yet he made himself believe it was real. He changed the way he thought about himself and money.

Second, it was not just his thoughts Jim worked on. Mr. Rubberface says that it was a whole-body experience. He felt the emotions of having that much money, of believing that he was worth that much money. He says he made himself physically feel the experience and joy of being rich. He was so committed that he would not go home until he felt the feeling.

Jim also used repetition to his advantage. Think about it. Whenever you have had to learn something new in your life, wasn't repetition a key component of the process?

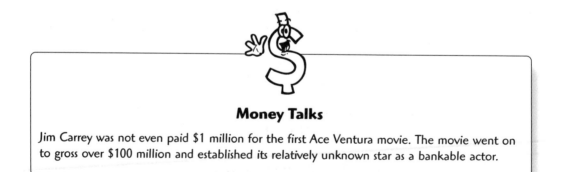

Money Talks

Jim Carrey was not even paid $1 million for the first Ace Ventura movie. The movie went on to gross over $100 million and established its relatively unknown star as a bankable actor.

How else did you learn your ABCs, geometry theorems, or how to sink a three-pointer, if not by repetition? Alrighty then; if Jim can do it, so can you.

Creative Visualization

Another thing that Jim Carrey did right was to use a physical object to change his belief. Holding an actual cheque made visualizing the cheque when he wasn't on his mountain a lot easier.

Creative visualization is the technique of using your imagination to change a belief or otherwise achieve a goal. With creative visualization, you create an idea or mental picture in your mind and regularly focus on it, thereby setting in motion the event.

You use visualization every day of your life. Whenever you create something, you create it first as an idea in your head. A thought always precedes creation. "I think I'll make dinner" precedes the meal. "I want to write a book about getting out of debt" precedes the book. Creative visualization is using this simple concept toward purposeful ends.

The Process

Here is how the technique works: First, think of something you want or would like to change. Let's say that you want to create a new belief regarding abundance. Go to a quiet room and get in a comfortable position, either sitting or lying down. Relax your body completely. Breathe deeply and slowly.

When you are deeply relaxed, begin to imagine the belief you want to adopt: "I have more than enough money for anything I want. I am able to pay for whatever I want in cash!" Imagine what it feels like to truly believe that. What would you own? How would you feel? What could you give to those you love? How would that make you feel? Imagine yourself in the experience of abundance. What are people saying? What does it look like? How does it feel to be finally out of debt? Create a complete and thorough picture.

Do this for a few minutes. Have fun with the experience and make it enjoyable—

Two Cents

"Repetition is the mother of skill."

—Anthony Robbins

Two Cents

A wise woman once said that worry is nothing but "negative visualization."

Cheque It Out

Positive statements made to yourself are called **affirmations**.

Money Talks

Visualization has become commonplace in the field of self-improvement. Athletes use it all the time, imagining a knockout or a personal best. It is said that Mark McGwire used visualization as he chased 70 home runs.

having complete abundance should be enjoyable! Now, make some very positive affirmative statements to yourself. "I am so fortunate to finally have abundance in my life." "I love this new car!" If doubts arise, just let them flow on through. Don't fight them or resist them.

End your visualization with a statement, such as "This, or something better, is now mine in satisfying and harmonious ways, for the highest good of all concerned." This statement reaffirms that visualization works only when it is best for all concerned.

This exercise can take anywhere from five minutes to half an hour. Each time you do it, it may be different. Try to do your visualization as often as you can, usually two or three times a day.

Don't get hung up on the term visualization. It is not necessary to "see" an image. Some people do see a very clear image in their heads; others do not. The important thing is to feel the experience, to believe it is so.

Set a goal. Decide on something that you would like to have, work toward, or create. It can be a physical thing, a new belief, or even a relationship. Start with things that are achievable fairly easily in the near future until you get the hang of this technique and believe that it works.

Create a clear vision, idea, or picture. Create it in your head as if it already exists. "I love my new car!" Get a picture of the car you want. Write yourself a cheque for $20 million. Make your desire clear and specific.

Be positive. Think about your goal in a positive, energetic way. Make strong positive statements to yourself about it: that it exists, that it has come to you, that you appreciate it—that sort of thing. See yourself with it, feeling it and accepting your blessing. Don't be too serious.

Rinse and repeat. Bring your mental image to your mind often, both in quiet times reserved for this exercise and in the middle of your busy day. This repetition helps integrate the image into your life. Repeat this exercise until you have achieved your desired goal, or your desire for the goal disappears (which sometimes happens in life).

Money Affirmations

There are many things that you can say to yourself as you visualize the change you want in your life. Some good money affirmations that you may want to adopt are the following:

➤ I have abundance in all things; my needs are met easily and effortlessly.

➤ I now give and receive money easily.

➤ The more I have, the more I have to give.

➤ Every day, in every way, I am becoming richer and richer.

➤ I now have a perfect, satisfying, well-paying job.

➤ I now have enough money to do whatever I want.

➤ The world is abundant and easily shares its bounty with me.

➤ Abundance is my natural state of being.

➤ Every day I am becoming more financially prosperous.

➤ The more I have, the more I give, and the more I give, the happier I am.

➤ I am finally out of debt.

Two Cents

Use a notebook to serve as your money changes workbook. In it, write down exercises in this chapter that inspire you and record your thoughts and feelings. Write down some affirmations or old and new beliefs that you are working on.

As you say these things to yourself, your old beliefs will bubble up and tell you that you are a liar. The thing to do then is to acknowledge your past, accept these feelings, let the feeling fade away, and go on creating a new belief. Soon you will have a new belief and new feelings.

New Beliefs

Besides visualization and affirmation, emotion and experience can also change beliefs and money values. A bad experience changed one of Robert's money values in an instant.

Robert always used to pay his rent late. His landlord kept warning him to stop, his wife kept telling him to stop, but Robert ignored the warnings. After nine months, Robert had gotten very comfortable with this arrangement, until he came home one day and found an eviction notice tacked to his front door. The shame and embarrassment he felt having to see his wife's tears and tell his kids that they all had to move deeply affected Robert. After moving to a new place, Robert never paid his rent late again.

People want to avoid repeating negative experiences. Being mugged makes you more cautious. Getting hit by a car jaywalking probably means you will never jaywalk again.

After losing World War II, Japan amended its constitution and disavowed war, searching for greatness through peace, which it achieved.

For our purposes in this book, the good thing about a negative experience is that it can change a belief in a hurry. But you don't have to wait to be a victim of a bad experience. You can create a negative experience in your mind and emotions and thereby create a shift in attitudes and beliefs in a hurry. We are not talking about creating an actual negative event, just feeling the experience of one, like a sense memory. If you link actual emotional pain to your negative money beliefs, you can change these beliefs.

The reason this technique works is that researchers have discovered what you inherently know: a highly emotional experience, usually a negative one, can have a lasting impact on what you think and feel. The following exercise uses this fact for your benefit instead of your detriment.

Go to a quiet place and answer the following questions. As you do, allow yourself to feel bad—really, really bad. Linking the pain to your outmoded money belief will create the desired change:

➤ What can't you do because you do not live in abundance? How has a lack of money damaged you? What would you have done with more money? Have you not traveled somewhere? Is there something you want to own that you cannot? How does that make you feel?

➤ How has your limited thinking about money negatively affected those you love? What were you not able to do for your family because of your money belief system? How many times have you told family members that they can get something they want or do something they desire "later"? How much pain has that caused them?

➤ Do you know someone who has needed your financial help, but you were unable to help him? Does someone you know need some medical help that you cannot afford to pay for? How does this make you feel?

➤ Would you like to be able to buy your parents a home, or send your sister on that vacation she always dreamed of? Is there a certain school you would like to send your children to? How does it make you feel not to be able to do these things?

Make yourself feel the pain. If your brain associates negative feelings with a lack of money, it will want to change your money beliefs.

To create a true change in a money belief with this system, you need to associate positive feelings with abundance as well as associating negative feelings with lack. Let's look at the abundance side of the coin. As you answer these questions, allow yourself to feel great:

➤ How would you feel and what could you do if you had financial abundance? What would you do if money were no object? What would you buy? Where would you go?

➤ Who could you help if you had an abundance of money? How would that make you feel? What would be said about you if you gave away as much as you wanted to?

➤ What experiences could you have if you were financially free? What could you learn? What could you do? Is there a dream you have that you have never been able to ful-fill? How would you feel about yourself if you conquered your money demons?

➤ How would it feel to pay off all of your debts?

➤ How free would you be without money wor-ries? Feel that freedom. Would you feel more secure? Would you have peace of mind? How would your mate feel if you created financial abundance for the two of you?

Two Cents

"Affluence is the experience in which our needs are easily met and our desires spontaneously fulfilled. Affluence is reality. When we are grounded in the nature of reality and we also know that the same reality is our own nature, then we realize that we can create anything."

—Deepak Chopra

Try doing this exercise every day for a week and see whether you begin to feel differently about money. After doing this exercise, many people begin to create such negative feelings about their lack of money that they automatically adopt new, more positive beliefs about money. Others vow to take all necessary actions to get out of debt and get ahead.

A pattern emerges. Jim Carrey's trick, creative visualization, and the preceding exercise all require that you feel the feelings of abundance. Creating a physical change in your body causes an emotional change in your head.

Think and Grow Rich

Do you doubt that thoughts are things, that as you think so too you create? "As a man thinks, so is he" is one way of saying this. Even the Bible says (paraphrased), "As you sow, so shall you reap."

Probably the most well-known book about creating wealth also happens to be one of the best, if not the best. *Think and Grow Rich* was written by Napoleon Hill in 1960 at the behest of Andrew Carnegie. Carnegie, who amassed his fortune in steel, is one of the richest people to have ever lived; the book contains his secret for creating wealth. *Think and Grow Rich* is one of the best-selling books of all time. It is now in its twentieth printing.

According to Carnegie, there are six steps by which a desire for wealth (or any change for that matter) can be transmuted into actual wealth:

1. Decide the exact amount of money you want. Be definite and state a specific amount.

Money Talks

Among the people who unwittingly used Carnegie's secret in their own endeavours are Henry Ford, Charles Schwab, Theodore Roosevelt, Wilbur Wright, John D. Rockefeller, Thomas Edison, Woodrow Wilson, and Alexander Graham Bell.

2. Decide what you intend to give for that money. You cannot get something for nothing.

3. State a definite date by which you are committed to having the money.

4. Create a specific plan for carrying out your desire and immediately put this plan into action.

5. Write out a clear, concise statement of this plan. For example, "I will have $100 000 by January 1 of next year, and I intend to give _____ through my plan of action to get it."

6. Read your statement aloud, twice a day. Once upon waking up and once right before bed. As you read, see and feel yourself in possession of the money.

If these steps seem surprisingly similar to the other exercises in this chapter, you are correct. If you think these six steps could be used to create any change in your life, you are correct again.

What is interesting about Napoleon Hill/Andrew Carnegie's recipe is that it requires action on your part. This aspect is important to realize. Changing your beliefs is only one part of the plan. In addition, you need to take action. In part 5 of this book, we give you several different things you can do to make more money.

The confluence of positive beliefs and new actions creates different results. If you always do what you've always done, you'll always get what you've always gotten.

What you are doing with all of these exercises is messing with your own head. To the extent you have limited or negative beliefs about money, the more you begin to introduce some new ideas into your brain, the more you will begin to believe in, and thereby create, a more affluent life.

The Least You Need to Know

➤ Changing your belief system often depends on linking new feelings to new beliefs.

➤ Visualizing a new way works for many people.

➤ Forcing yourself to confront the negative effects of a lack of money can quickly cause a change in beliefs.

➤ Putting your plan to paper and rereading it daily has worked for some of the wealthiest people who have ever lived.

Chapter 6

Money Is a Family Matter

In This Chapter

➤ Marriage and money

➤ Children and money

➤ Teens and money

As we have seen, your parents were instrumental in the creation of your money belief system and debt problems. Your own family is an opportunity to put an end to this cycle and implement some new beliefs, although it may not be easy. Not only will you need to accommodate your mate's money beliefs and money style, but you will also have to teach your children some things about money that may seem foreign to you.

For Richer, for Poorer

When figuring out how to resolve your debt problems, you and your spouse must be on the same page. Getting to this point is a two-step process. First, you need to figure out what your different money styles are. Then, you need to merge those two styles to create a unified front and plan of action.

Money Talks

A recent survey found that 34 percent of women and 35 percent of men admitted to having a hidden stash of cash their spouses don't know about. Women reported socking away around $500; for men the amount was $1000 to $5000.

Who Are You?

That John Gray's book *Men Are from Mars, Women Are from Venus* is one of the best-selling books of all time is strong evidence that the sexes have inherent differences. This is as true for money issues as it is for anything else.

Compounding gender differences are other problems that make money peace a difficult thing to achieve at home. Even today, men usually make more money than their wives do and thus tend to wield the financial power in the relationship. In 1990, the Canadian Advisory Council on the Status of Women reported that women earned roughly 61% of what men earned. And according to a new StatsCan labour market report on trends in the 1990s, while women continued to earn less than men, real weekly earnings among women rose 12 percent between 1989 and 1996. Income growth for women has outpaced those of both low- and high-income earning men.

Further, all people have different money styles based upon beliefs and backgrounds. The most common styles are

➤ **The spender.** This person spends money regardless of financial circumstances. Going into debt is no problem for the spender.

➤ **The cheapskate.** This tightwad is so afraid of losing money or going into debt that he deprives both himself and those around him of the joys that money can bring.

➤ **The worrier.** This person worries so much about money that he has a difficult time enjoying it, even when he has it.

➤ **The free spirit.** The free spirit is the opposite of the worrier. Bounced cheques, late charges, and too many bills? No problem, dude!

➤ **The dreamer.** "Don't you know that our lottery win will save the day?"

➤ **The planner.** The healthiest of all the styles, the planner plots out his financial future while trying to still enjoy the present.

Over Your Limit

In her book, *You Just Don't Understand: Women and Men in Conversation*, Deborah Tannen says, "Women speak and hear a language of connection and intimacy, while men speak and hear a language of status and independence, [therefore] communication between men and women can be like cross-cultural communication, subject to a clash of conversational styles."

Two Cents

Most first-generation millionaires create wealth by combining money styles. Not only do they take risks and invest wisely, but they also live below their means and clip coupons.

The labels are not what matters; the important thing to realize is that partners have different money styles that must be accommodated. Maybe you and your mate are the same type, and maybe you're not. A union of different types can cause a lot of money problems. On the other hand, different styles can also give you a balance you would otherwise not normally have.

David was a classic spender; his wife Ellen was a worrier. Whenever they would get some extra money, his first thought was to go shopping. She wanted to save every penny. She wanted every bill paid on time (even if it meant doing without), and he thought the bills could always wait a while.

David and Ellen fought constantly about money. After several years, they finally had a talk that made a difference. They sat down, admitted and discussed their respective money styles, figured what their joint core values were with regard to money, and created a plan of action that met those values. A bit of each of them went into the plan. He could spend some money (but not as much as he wanted), and she could save some (ditto). They merged their styles for the good of the whole.

David and Ellen's styles, like those of many couples, were practically polar opposites. Merging styles, values, and attitudes is no easy task. Yet it is a necessary one.

Janice, one of the authors of this book, and her husband Craig are another case in point. She a spender by nature (as we've already established) and Craig is a saver who enjoys the research behind a purchase more than the purchase itself. The couple came to a middle ground after a few years of marriage. Janice does not buy expensive clothes or other items on impulse, and Craig agrees to spend some of the couple's hard-earned money on big-ticket items. Though they use their one credit card liberally, (so much so that after four years they were able to buy a surround sound stereo system through the credit card's award catalogue) they never carry a monthly balance.

When Worlds Collide

Although each of the money styles has its strengths and weaknesses, you and your spouse need to combine the best of both. Combining the styles will help you teach your children some consistent values about money and enable you to put together a debt-reduction plan that you both agree with.

You absolutely need to compromise and come up with an agreeable joint plan that will accommodate both partners' money needs. If you do not agree at the outset about how you are going to go about solving your money crisis, your chance of succeeding is quite poor. Solving this issue is critical to your financial health and may even save you from divorce. The number one reason for divorce is financial difficulties.

There are three key elements to this process:

Communication. Sit down with your partner and make an honest assessment of where you are financially and how both of your styles and family histories have contributed to the current state of affairs. Honestly admit what you have been doing right and what you have been doing wrong. Acknowledge both your own and your partner's money strengths and weaknesses. Tell your spouse what you admire about his or her money style.

Get out whatever old grudges and resentments you have about money. Because this discussion will hopefully be the foundation of a new financial future, you had best get the past out of the way. Finally, tell your partner what the optimum result of your financial problem would look like to you. Lay it all on the table.

Over Your Limit

A serious debt problem can either be a symptom of trouble in the marriage or the cause of the conflict. Few things cause as much marital friction as money. Sometimes, it takes counseling to resolve these issues.

Two Cents

If you and your partner do not usually butt heads over spending versus saving, it is unlikely that your problem is a difference in beliefs or styles. Instead, a good talk about priorities is probably in order.

Compromise. Next, you must find some mutually agreeable middle ground. This is the negotiation phase of the discussion. Set some joint goals and agree in a general way on issues such as debt reduction, savings, investments, and bill-paying habits. Realize what you have been doing wrong and agree to what you will do differently in the future.

You need to set both short-term and long-term money and debt-reduction goals. Do you want to begin to invest a little bit of money in some mutual funds? Do you want to pay off two credit cards completely within a year? Where do you want to be financially in five years?

Often money matters are so emotionally charged that it is difficult to have a rational discussion. If you are in that place, it may make sense to see a counselor to work through these issues.

Plan of action. The remainder of this book will help you with this part. You need to create a plan based upon your goals. The plan should specifically state what you both want to accomplish financially and when you plan to have each item completed. Your plan may look something like the following plan.

Sample Action Plan

Goal	Completion date
1. Transfer all credit cards to card with lowest interest rate	1 month
2. Save $1000	6 months
3. Send kids to summer camp	9 months
4. Pay off orthodontist bill	1 year
5. Buy a new car	1 year
6. Buy a rental property	3 years

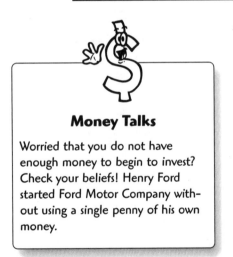

Money Talks

Worried that you do not have enough money to begin to invest? Check your beliefs! Henry Ford started Ford Motor Company without using a single penny of his own money.

A plan of action that is based upon a frank and honest discussion and mutual values and goals and that includes something for everybody is a plan that has a great chance of success.

Kids Are People, Too

The rich are different than the rest of us. Not only do they think about money differently than most people, but also, for the most part, they teach their children different values about money. Rich people tend to teach their kids about saving and investing; the poor and middle class usually teach their children about spending and borrowing.

Your children are your opportunity to break the familial money cycle of which you are an unwitting participant. Teaching your children to have a healthy relationship with money today means that you won't have to lend them this book tomorrow.

Teaching your kids the right way to deal with money has the added bonus of reinforcing what you are now learning. Showing them how to deal intelligently with money helps you do the same. Concentrate on three main areas when it comes to young kids and

Money Talks

Dear Ann Landers: My husband and I have two sons. The oldest one calls me and complains incessantly about his finances and borrows money often, yet he and his wife dine out often and see several movies or plays every week. Our younger son has moved back home, still runs through money as fast as he earns it, and borrows from us whenever he needs cash. Where is it written that children have a right to expect such things from their parents? Had It in Kentucky.

Dear Kentucky: You are making this possible by your actions. It's time you stopped being enablers.

money: earning, saving, and spending. Teaching teenagers about money is a separate matter taken up at the end of this chapter.

Whistle While You Work

How do you teach your kids good money values? Remember what you were taught and do the exact opposite! We're just joking. Children need to learn that money is good and that it can be their friend if they treat it with respect.

For instance, it is helpful to show children that one of the reasons you go to work every day is to make money, which is good. They need to see the connection between work, the money it generates, and what that money can be used for.

Lily never saw this connection growing up. Her single mother struggled for every dollar. Lily recalls one particular day when she was about nine years old and her mom was complaining about a lack of money. "Mom," Lily said, "just go to the bank." "What?" her mother replied. "Just go to the bank, and they hand you money." Lily and her mother had a good laugh about this comment years later.

Probably the best way to teach children the value of money and work is to allow them to earn some money at home. We advocate paying children for jobs they would not normally do. This way, they learn that "fun" money comes from extra work. Children also need to learn that work is not just about making money, but that money sure is a great benefit of a job well done.

Jerry Seinfeld once said this about money and work: "I never consider the money. That's the most financially sound approach you can take in business. When you don't consider

Two Cents

A recent survey found that 74 percent of parents give allowances, and 66 percent tie them to chores. Of the parents who give allowances, 54 percent require their kids to save a portion. In her book *Kids are Worth It!*, parenting expert Barbara Coloroso advocates keeping chores and allowance distinctly separate, arguing that kids should learn they have to do chores because they are members of the family, not with the incentive of money. Allowance should be given solely to give children the experience of learning to save and manage money.

the money, then you can make the right choice. And the right choice always leads to money."

Consider the following ideas when you hire your children:

➤ Tell them what you want done, but let them figure out how to accomplish the task. This should foster independence, a desire to do a good job, and a better appreciation of the financial rewards of their work.

➤ Pay by the job.

➤ Evaluate their performance. Praise a job well done and consider a small "bonus" for exceptional work.

You Teach Best What You Most Need to Learn

After your kids have earned some money, the next trick is to teach them the value of saving some of it. The problem is that saving money for its own sake, or for a rainy day, or to invest is just too amorphous a concept for most young kids to understand. Instead, find something they want to buy that is too "expensive." Then show them that by saving their money, they could get it. Imagine the difference in what they will learn if you teach them to save and spend versus if you taught them to charge and spend! The idea, at least initially, is to just get them into the habit of saving. You have that habit, don't you?

For instance, your six-year-old daughter may want a special Barbie that costs $20. Put her to work and show her that if she saves some of her earnings, then she could buy that Barbie in three weeks. Saving money will then equal Barbie. Now that's a powerful connection for any six-year-old girl!

Imagine the difference if she has to work and save to get that special Barbie versus if dad pulls out the credit card and charges it to see the smile on his precious daughter's face. Sometimes, love means having to say no.

Although a piggy bank for savings is a nice idea, a savings account is better. A piggy bank is just too easy to dip into. A trip to the bank, though, is a special event. The feeling of importance and mastery your child will feel when she goes to deposit some money in her own account will surely pay dividends in more ways than one.

No Lessons Required

Spending, the final frontier. "Teach them how to spend," you say. "Now you're talking, spending is the easy part." We agree. Teaching someone to become an intelligent consumer, one who respects his hard-earned and long-saved dollar, is easy compared to breaking a lifetime of bad habits.

Two Cents

Experts agree that there are certain things you can do to teach your children to be financially literate. Among the things most often cited are: Start early, encourage saving, give allowances, pay for chores, teach them about shopping, buy them a good money book for kids, show them how to invest in the future by buying a stock, make finances fun, and remember to have family discussions about money.

Teach your kids the things about shopping that you had to learn the hard way. Always keep the receipt. Find out what the store's return policy is. Read the label. Compare prices. Look for sales. The most expensive item is not always the best. Name brands cost more. The picture on the box always looks better. Television commercials are not always 100 percent truthful. Read the fine print. There is nothing wrong with buying at a consignment or second-hand store.

Teen Time

It is never too late to begin to teach your children the right way to deal with money. It should help them to avoid some of the mistakes you have made and will also help reinforce your new ways.

Teens have special money issues that younger kids don't share. They need to be financially prepared to go out into the world. They need to be taught such simple things as how to write a cheque and how to balance a chequebook. You may even take a further step to show them about Internet banking and the importance of tracking automatic debit card spending. They also need to be made aware of just how easy it is to go into debt but how difficult it is to get out of debt.

Credit card companies target high school graduates with incentives and card applications. Make sure your teenagers know about the credit card trap and how to avoid it. Teenagers should be made aware of the following:

➤ They will be solicited with an introductory interest rate, but it will jump, and many credit card interest rates are well above 15 percent.

Over Your Limit

There are 400 million VISA cards and MasterCards in circulation worldwide.

➤ Charging up a storm is easy, but maxing out the card and paying the minimum payment ensures that the card will never be paid off.

➤ Late fees and penalties make a credit card balance difficult to reduce.

➤ Credit cards should be used for their convenience, not when you don't have the money, or foresee having the money, at the end of the month.

➤ The smart way to use a credit card is to pay it off every month.

Teaching teens to be respectful of money and fearful of debt is one of the best parting gifts you can give them before they leave home.

The Least You Need to Know

➤ Everyone has a money style.

➤ Spouses need to learn to blend money styles and create a plan of action to get out of debt.

➤ Children are your chance to teach (and learn) correct money values.

➤ Teens need to be made aware of the dangers of going into debt.

Chapter 7

The "B" Word

In This Chapter

➤ Budget *is* not a bad word

➤ Keep a record

➤ Make a plan

➤ Create a budget

➤ A sample budget

➤ Budgets and your computer

Most of us view budgets as a necessary evil at best and something to be avoided at worst. The traditional view is that a budget is a restrictive plan forcing you to deprive yourself of what you want.

The truth can be far different, if you want it to be. A budget should be a guide, not a constraint. A reasonable, good budget is a tool that allows you to do what you want. That's why you went into debt, right, to get what you want? And guess what? If you spend more than you wanted to one month, you don't go to jail. Your budget is your tool; it can be as friendly as you want it to be.

Over Your Limit

Seen on a bumper sticker: "How can I be overdrawn? I still have cheques left."

Two Cents

If you plan ahead and begin to budget accordingly, it is easier to save for a vacation, because you will be able to get the best rates by booking far in advance.

Budget Is Not a Four-Letter Word

Most people who go deeply into debt have no idea how much they spend on groceries, entertainment, clothes, or restaurants every month. As we said in an earlier chapter, not knowing the state of your finances (except for the fact that you are in debt) is like driving with a bag over your head. A budget allows you take the bag off and get a good look at where you are going financially. If you don't like what you see, make some changes.

Maybe budget is the wrong word to use. A plan is more of what we are talking about here. You need to come up with a plan that lets you see what comes in, what goes out, and what you want to go out.

For example, maybe on the first of the month after reading this chapter, you decide that you would like to spend $200 a month on entertainment (it is your budget after all). The first part of the plan would be to find out what you normally spend on entertainment. So for the whole month, you would spend money as you usually would, keeping close track of your entertainment expenses.

At the end of the month, you would add up those expenses and see what you spent. If the total were $300, that would be valuable information to have, would it not? You could then decide that you want to spend $300 a month the next month and cut back somewhere else, or you might decide to watch your entertainment spending more closely. Maybe you had no idea that you were spending $300 a month on entertainment. Either way, the budget, the plan, is working for you, not against you. It takes the blindfold off, see? (We will explain how to make this plan in a tad more detail later.)

So the first of many benefits of budgeting is that you know what is going on. Planning (we will use the terms planning and budgeting interchangeably) is a tool that shows you how your funds are allocated, what your priorities are, and how far along you are toward reaching your goals.

Creating a budget has several other benefits:

You are in control. A budget enables you to take charge of your finances. It helps you get a grip on your spending so that you can make sure your money is used properly. It will help you have enough for essentials, and actually allow you to create enough extra left over for "nonessentials." With a budget, you decide what is going to happen to your hard-earned money and when. You can control your money, instead of having your money control you. Now that would probably be a welcome change.

You are more organized. A basic budget divides funds into categories of expenditures and savings. Beyond that, however, budgets can record all your monetary transactions. They can also provide the foundation for a simple filing system to organize bills, receipts, and financial statements.

You are more communicative. If you are married, have a family, or share money with anyone, having a budget that you create together can resolve personal differences about money handling. Your budget is a communication tool to discuss priorities for where your money can best be spent.

You don't lose opportunities. Knowing the exact state of your personal monetary affairs and being in control allows you to take advantage of opportunities that you might otherwise miss. Have you ever wondered if you could afford something? With a budget, you will never have to wonder again. You will know.

You will be more efficient. A budget means that all of your finances are automatically organized for creditor communications, for tax time, and for any query that may come up about how and when you spent money. Being armed with such information saves time digging through old records.

Most importantly, you will have extra money. Hidden fees and lost interest paid to creditors can be eliminated. Unnecessary expenditures, once identified, can be expunged. Savings, no matter how small, can be accumulated and made to work for you. A budget will almost certainly produce extra money for you to do with as you wish.

Even if you don't use the budget you draw up, just the homework involved in creating it can be instructive because you may find that you are spending more than you want to on various items.

There are three steps to creating a budget. The first step is to keep track of where your money goes in a normal month before you create your budget. After reviewing where your money is spent, the second step is to decide where you would rather see it applied. The last step is to create a budget and track your spending.

Keep a Good Record

Getting out of debt requires that you know how much you spend every month and where you

Two Cents

More money-saving ideas: Select a cheaper long-distance carrier; avoid impulse purchases; turn off unnecessary lights, heat, or air conditioning; get rid of premium cable channels; shop at consignment stores. Eat out less, car pool.... The list is endless, isn't it?

Two Cents

Keeping your receipt from the ABM will help you keep track of where the money goes because you will know where and when you took out money.

spend it. Vicky was shocked when she began to keep track of her spending habits. She had no idea how much she was spending on lunches at work and on music. She didn't know where her money went every month until she kept track. Do you? If you don't, do you see how knowing this could be immensely helpful? That is the purpose of keeping a good record.

Spend a month writing down, every day, exactly what you do with your money. How much do you spend on food, cabs, gas, and magazines? Create categories, carry a little notebook with the categories listed, and keep a daily log of every expenditure. If you are not keen on the notebook method, many personal finance computer programs enable you to do the same thing. Either way, every day, you need to record every expenditure for at least one month. Yes, this process sounds like a pain in the rear, but what you discover will be worth the effort, and it's not as hard as it sounds.

List every little thing, to the penny: lunch, movies, books, dry cleaning, haircuts—everything. On days that you pay large bills (your car payment, for example) enter those in one of your categories too. Having 20 to 30 categories is not uncommon. Every time you spend money, record it in a category or add a category.

This is not as much work as it sounds. You only need to create this list once, in the beginning. It will be the basis for any budget you create later on. Your categories, the more specific the better, should include:

➤ Rent/mortgage

➤ Housing-related expenses (repairs, decor, furniture)

➤ Utilities

➤ Groceries

➤ Insurance (Car, home, life, disability)

➤ Clothes

➤ Fast food/Restaurants

➤ Entertainment (be specific)

➤ Transportation

➤ Child care (including school tuition)

➤ Sundries (magazines, newspapers, personal health care products)

➤ Prescription medication

➤ Miscellaneous (gifts, charitable donations)

If you are a student, you'll want to include tuition, text books, supplies etc.

You may be wondering how we'd think you'd have money for gifts or charitable donations, but you may be spending money on these when in fact you should be reducing these expenditures substantially until you are in a better situation to give more. Carefully consider how much money you spend on a friend's birthday gift. Remember, it's the thought that counts.

At the end of the month, tally the results. Make sure that you also include all cancelled cheques, labeled ABM receipts, and itemized credit-card statements so that all of your expenditures are accounted for. The picture should be illuminating. Maybe you never knew that you spent $30 a month on late video charges. Maybe those computer games added up. Whatever the case, this record will help you see where the problems lie.

Your Plan

Once you see where things are, you can decide where you want them to be, put yourself back in control of your finances, and begin to make more intelligent decisions. You can decide that less needs to be spent on vitamins, for example, or that more should be spent on clothes for the kids. Instead of blindly spending whatever cash you have in your pocket on whatever need you may have on any given day, you start your month by planning ahead.

Madeline decided that she could easily spend a lot less on fast food every month. Next to the $300 she had in that category's recorded total, she added a category called "budgeted" and listed $150. On the first day of the next month, she went to the market and loaded up on her favourite items and made sure to keep some with her each day as the month progressed. That first month, she spent less than the $150 projected, and for the first time in a long time, she ended the month without a money crisis.

This type of plan is flexible, can be changed, and does not control you; you control it. The whole idea of the record and plan is to enlighten you and enable you to make intelligent decisions. A budget is simply your plan for how you can best utilize your money. It's restrictive only to the extent that you want it to be.

Two Cents

Different stages of life require different budgets. A university student will have fewer categories of expenses and different priorities than a single parent of four will.

Creating a Budget

After you monitor your spending, the process of putting together a budget is quite easy. The simplest budget of all would consist of just adding one more column to the record you made and listing how much you plan to spend on each item the next month. You would then need to continue to track your expenses to see whether they meet your goals. Voila! You created the dreaded budget.

However, because a budget is a planning tool, it is wiser to create a more elaborate one. For example, you may have had no prescription expenses the month that you tracked your spending habits. That does not mean, however, that you do not want to budget some money every month for that purpose. What you should do, then, is to create a budget that covers everything that you plan to put money toward in any given month.

Although adding more detail into your budget plan will be time-consuming initially, doing so will give you more information and make your plan more useful in the long term. It will also enable you to put aside money every month for specific reasons and make paying bills quicker and easier because there will be no fights over priorities; you prioritize your discretionary spending up front. Your budget will be broken down into three sections: income, fixed spending, and discretionary spending.

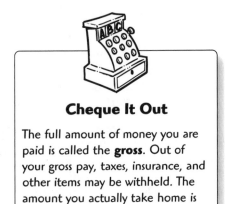

Cheque It Out

The full amount of money you are paid is called the **gross**. Out of your gross pay, taxes, insurance, and other items may be withheld. The amount you actually take home is called your net.

Income

Whether you use a computer program to help you with your budget or do it by hand in a notebook, the first category will be your income. Before you can decide how best to spend your money, you must know exactly how much comes in every month.

Income will include your net pay, money from freelancing, tips, alimony, child support, trust funds, interest, dividends—everything. All revenue streams must be included. If your income varies every month, then the best thing to do is to use an average month calculated from income generated over the past year. Let's say that last year you took home about $30 000. Some months you made $2000, and some months you made $3000. Average it out. $30 000 over a year is an average of $2500 a month.

Fixed Expenses

Fixed expenses are expenses that stay the same every month, month after month. You have no discretion when it comes to fixed expenses. This part of your budget will include:

➤ Mortgage or rent payments: Yes, your rent or mortgage may go up or down, but budgets change as your life changes. Whatever your housing costs currently are, put them here.

➤ Utility bills: These bills include gas, electric, phone, heating, water, garbage, cable TV.

➤ Car payments.

➤ Taxes: If you make ongoing payments to Revenue Canada for past taxes, or if you are self-employed, you need to budget some money every month (or quarter) for this expense.

> ➤ Loan repayment: Student loans or other personal loans are included in this category.

> ➤ Child support or alimony payments.

> ➤ Insurance premiums.

> ➤ Any other fixed expense or regular monthly payment.

Discretionary Expenses

Your budget will make a difference in the area of discretionary expenses. What are your priorities? Upon reviewing your record, you will probably decide that you need to spend more in some areas and less in others. That's the whole idea. By reallocating these expenses, you will be able to re-focus your finances. You can decide to spend less on food and more on saving or whatever works for you.

This is not how most people view a budget. Instead of something that is always telling you "no," we see a budget as something that says "yes" to your most important values. This kind of budget tells you to spend more, not less, on those things most important to you. If spending money on your children is important, then you can create a budget that reflects that desire.

This part of the budget will include

> ➤ Food: Include all food and household goods spending at grocery stores, bulk-food stores, farmer's markets, and so on.

> ➤ Eating out: Dinners, work lunches, breakfast meetings, and so on.

> ➤ Home-related expenses: Furniture, electronics, home improvements, the gardener or handyman expenses, and maintenance belong in this category.

> ➤ Clothes.

> ➤ Entertainment: These expenses would include concerts, clubs, movies, video rentals, and so on.

> ➤ Work: Any work-related expenses not covered in the clothing or food categories would go here.

> ➤ Accounting and legal: Even if you don't have ongoing expenses here, you might want to budget for that yearly trip to the accountant at tax time.

> ➤ Automobile: Gas and upkeep.

> ➤ Health and medical: Here you account for health items such as vitamins and your gym bill, as well as any potential expenses not

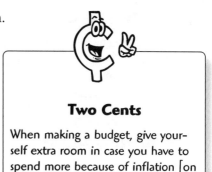

Two Cents

When making a budget, give yourself extra room in case you have to spend more because of inflation [on gasoline, for example] or an unexpected emergency.

covered by your benefit plan, which in some cases includes certain prescriptions, eyeglasses etc.

➤ Travel: Toll road expenses, airline travel, and so on.

➤ Taxes: Ideally, you will have enough money taken out of your taxes by your employer that you won't owe any at the end of the year. But if you normally owe taxes, account for it here. If you are self-employed, you probably don't need to be reminded to budget for taxes.

➤ Books and magazines: We can't forget to buy books!

➤ Vacation: If you spend $500 every summer taking the kids camping, you save a little for it every month.

➤ Children: Monthly child care expenses, baby-sitting, piano lessons, school expenses, and everything else.

➤ Saving: You said you were going to start saving, right?

➤ Debt repayment: As you will see in Chapter 9, "Call Your Creditor and Say "Hi" (The Plan)," it is very important to budget some money, whatever you can comfortably live with, toward repaying your debts.

➤ Fun: If this isn't in your budget, what's the point?

➤ Miscellaneous.

Although the goal here is to have your spending stay within the limits you've set, a concurrent goal should be to discover if some of your figures are unrealistic. If so, adjust them. There is no point in making a budget that you can't live with. You will probably have to change it two or three times before you come up with a useful, workable budget.

Optimally, your goal should be to reduce your spending to about 90 percent of your income. Why? That way, you will be saving 10 percent of your income and hopefully earmarking it toward investments (discussed in the last section of this book) and your other long-term financial objectives. If you reduce your spending and invest the savings, not only will you get out of debt, but you also can get rich.

Two Cents

Discuss budget items with everyone in the house. When it affects others, budgeting is a family affair.

A Sample Budget

Let's look at Chris and Amy's budget. Their problem was that, although both made a good living, they were running in the red every month and borrowing from their credit cards to make up the difference. Chris brought home $1500 a month, and Amy took home $2200 a month. They had two kids.

They bought a computer program to help them create a budget. Every day for a month, they each dutifully kept track of their normal spending habits, and every night for a month, they spent about 10 minutes entering it into their computer. They agreed up front not to fight over how the other one was spending money. At the end of the month, they had made $3700 but had spent $4000. Let's look at how they solved the problem.

Their fixed expenses included a mortgage payment of $1100. Car payments were $600 a month, and utilities were $200 a month. Their fixed expenses totaled $1900 per month.

Their discretionary spending broke down this way:

➤ Food: Chris and Amy spent an average of $800 a month at the market, although their record disclosed that they spent quite a bit at the convenient and expensive small market down the street. By shopping at a less expensive grocery store and making a run for bulk items once a month, they figured they could save about $100.

➤ Eating out: The family ate out or ordered in three times a week. They decided to cut back to once a week (if that), intending to save another $200 a month.

➤ Entertainment: Chris and Amy had a standing Saturday night date for movies and dinner. Between this and the baby sitter, they spent $60 a week. They decided to cut out the dinner portion of their date sometimes and stay home once a month, saving another $100.

➤ Children: Both kids participated in activities such as music lessons, kung fu, and soccer at a cost of $200 a month. Each child had to cut out one activity. This saved another $100.

➤ Saving: They had no savings when they started but decided to allot $100 a month to start with.

➤ Debt repayment: They also began to pay $100 extra toward paying down their credit cards.

Once they saw where their money was going, Chris and Amy were able to cut $500 out of their budget and put their money where they thought it would be better served without radically changing their lifestyle. They wanted to avoid borrowing from their credit cards, begin to pay them off, and start to save some money. These things were more important than another date or the convenience of shopping down the street. A budget does nothing more than assist you in prioritizing your finances.

Over Your Limit

Have patience. Take your time when setting up a budget. It does not have to be done in one sitting. Also realize that it may take a few months to begin to see real results from your budget.

Mary had a different problem. A stay-at-home mom, Mary found it difficult to get through to the end of the month because her husband was paid only once a month on the first. By the 25th, she was always out of money and had no credit cards to borrow from.

Mary decided to be fairly strict with herself and her family after reviewing her record. Now, on payday, she pays all the bills for fixed expenses and utilities, and then subtracts from her balance the amounts for automatic withdrawals, such as the mortgage payment and student loans. She transfers money into the savings account for long-term savings and for unscheduled expenses like car repairs and emergency funds.

Then she takes the remaining amount and divides it by four to use as a weekly allowance for groceries, gas, and incidentals. She withdraws that amount in cash from the bank on Monday and pays only cash for purchases. At the beginning of the next week, she takes her allowance again. Mary's method of budgeting demonstrates that a budget can be as flexible and creative as you want it to be.

Budgets and Your Computer

As we said, you can create a budget by hand or with the help of a computer. If you have a computer, you can take advantage of some of the great budget programs that are available.

Both Quicken and Microsoft Money (to name just two programs) make it easy to draw up a budget and monitor compliance. Quicken, for example, comes with a set of categories that handle most of the basics. You can edit the list to create categories that make better sense for your particular household. If you're away from home, you can even track expenses at the Quicken Web site and then download the transactions to your computer later. Also with Quicken (we use this program as an example because it is the market leader), you can produce monthly spending reports in categories you select.

The drawback to electronic budgeting is that entering and categorizing all of your income and outflow can be quite a tedious chore. You can reduce the tedium to some degree by judicious selection of categories. If you are only worried about tracking your spending for recreation and leisure, then you could create categories that cover those types of expenses and let everything else accumulate under "miscellaneous revenue" or "miscellaneous expense."

The problem with that approach is that you forego the opportunity to spot problems in other spending areas

Two Cents

One drawback of monitoring your spending by computer is that it encourages overzealous attention to detail. Once you determine which categories of spending can and should be cut (or expanded), concentrate on those categories and worry less about other aspects of your spending.

that you may not even be aware of. A better solution is to track expenses using electronic banking. That way, you can download your payments and deposits directly from the bank, rather than having to enter them by hand.

The Least You Need to Know

➤ Budgets are a tool to help you.

➤ Creating a record of your expenditures will help you see where you spend your money.

➤ Creating a budget will allow you to prioritize your finances.

➤ Computer programs make budgeting fairly easy.

Chapter 8

How and Where to Cut Back

In This Chapter

➤ Attitudes

➤ Food

➤ Kids

➤ Work

➤ Travel

➤ Pleasure

➤ Love

You need to live below your means if you are going to get out of debt. That is a fact. It's like losing weight. Unless you consume less and do things differently, nothing will change. Permanently ridding yourself of debt, like permanently ridding yourself of extra weight, requires a change in habits.

In this chapter, you will find many good ideas that will enable you to trim your budget without too much sacrifice, ideas that you can adopt for the long term. Pick and choose the ones that work for you and implement them into your overall debt reduction plan.

A Good Attitude

Most likely, you are going into this cost-cutting process with a sour attitude. Money is tight, cutting back is not fun, and admitting you made mistakes is not easy. Yet, as with anything else in life, if you attempt to get out of debt with a negative attitude or while carrying around bad feelings, the chances of success are diminished.

In many ways, getting out of debt and living below your means can be enjoyable instead of miserable. Cutting back will require that you change some habits, but if you keep in mind that your old habits are probably what got you into trouble in the first place, replacing them with new ones can be a fun adventure.

Two Cents

Getting out of debt is a precursor to getting rich (if that is your desire). Many of the skills that you use to get out of the money pit are the same ones you need to get ahead in life. So do not be too sad. Cutting costs is good training.

It's all a matter of having the right attitude. Spencer's grandmother had an apropos saying in this regard. Always a witty and active woman, Gram was eventually forced by age and ill health to live in a senior community. One day, Spencer went to see her. He asked how she was doing. She was silent for a second, looked at Spencer with a twinkle in her eye, and said: "I'm in good shape ... for the shape I'm in!" That is the type of attitude we are suggesting.

We know it is not easy; if cutting back were in your blood, then this book would not be in your hand. However, we cannot emphasize enough that you have to do some things differently if you are to get out of debt. Starting with a positive attitude makes the process easier.

Food for Less

Let's see how a positive attitude can affect the bottom line. Aside from mortgage or rent payments, food costs for a family are probably the largest item in the family budget; depending upon the size of your family, food costs can be bigger than car payments.

Money Talks

A survey conducted by American International College discovered that 80 percent of those surveyed said that they would pay an additional 20 percent on a $200 purchase like a gas grill if they didn't have to assemble it themselves.

It is not difficult to reduce the cost of food. Bulk and discount stores are easy to find. What is difficult is getting out of the habit of paying for convenience. Although it may be much easier to buy tonight's dinner at the corner store down the street, planning ahead and buying at a less expensive supermarket can save you a lot of money every month.

A key concept to reducing your food bill could be called "shop and stock." Buy food when it is cheaper and stock it away until you need it. You can dramatically reduce your food costs by doing so and still eat what you like. Shop for food at a less convenient and less expensive market. Buy in bulk. Buy on sale.

We especially recommend buying on sale. When you shop, look for items that you regularly use that are on sale, even if you don't need them. Freeze them or put them in the back of your cupboard. Shop and stock. If you get really good at this, you need never pay full price for anything again, because everything in the market eventually goes on sale. If a favourite item goes on sale, buy it, even if you don't need it at that moment (feels like old times, no?). Although it might seem odd to buy things you don't immediately need, the savings are realized in the future when you do not have to buy that chicken that was on sale two weeks previously.

Susan started shopping this way and saved an average of $40 a week feeding her family of five. She then earmarked that extra $160 a month to pay down her credit cards and paid off one of them within a year. Who knew that creamed corn on sale could do battle with the mighty MasterCard and win?

There are plenty more ways to save on food costs:

➤ **Buy markdowns.** Day-old bread and pastries are usually half-price.

➤ **Use coupons.** Coupons can save you a lot of money, but they can also be a hassle. If you find coupons for a thing you use consistently, they can save you lots of money.

➤ **Buy in bulk.** As a general rule, the more you buy of an item, the less each indi-vid-ual portion costs. Bulk purchases of rice, beans, flour, chicken, cheese, and vegetables can all be divvied up into smaller portions and frozen or stored in plastic containers. If you think that you don't have enough room or people to buy in bulk, buddy up with a friend or relative and shop together. Just be sure to avoid thinking that you really need 48 granola bars!

➤ **Buy generic.** Mark was a struggling director forced to live on almost nothing because of his choice of professions. He learned to buy some generic foods and sundries to save money. Now, although he directs television shows and makes a bundle, he still buys generic because he sees no difference in quality.

If you eliminate the need for convenience, you can still eat the same foods you always have at a fraction of the cost.

Over Your Limit

Prepared frozen meals and snacks are among the most expensive items you can buy at the market. According to the Roper organization, sales of prepackaged frozen meals increased by 35 percent in the 1990s. You will save a lot of money by avoiding these frozen foods.

Is It Possible to Save Money If You Have Kids?

Yes, you can have the joy of raising children without going broke. No, it will not be easy, especially given their proclivity for saying, "I want one of those!" Larry's father often told Larry, "My name is not get me, buy me."

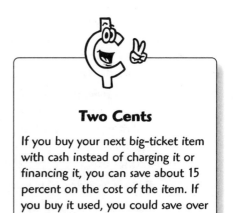

Two Cents

If you buy your next big-ticket item with cash instead of charging it or financing it, you can save about 15 percent on the cost of the item. If you buy it used, you could save over 50 percent.

We discussed kids and money in detail in Chapter 6, "Money Is a Family Matter," but a few things need to be reiterated here. Although we live in a very materialistic society, it is incumbent upon all of us to teach our children well. They will feel the tug of peer pressure, the "need" to have $130 Air Jordans. If you can teach them money literacy early, you will have gone a long way toward saving them years of financial and emotional grief.

Kids learn best by example. If they see you buying new shoes every month, they will want new shoes. If you get the newest computer every six months, they will want the new Nintendo. If they see you being smart with a dollar, they just might learn that, too.

There are scores of ways to have fun with your kids, teach them positive values, and still save money. What is your favourite Halloween costume of all time? It is probably safe to say that it was not some prefab, store-bought costume, but rather a homemade, creative masterpiece. Keep that in mind as you strive to give your kids the best without teaching them the worst.

Art projects are a fine example. Children love to make art, to express themselves with pictures when words may be hard to find. Crayons are great for the little ones, and most newspapers sell (or even give away) newspaper end-rolls (just the paper, not the print) for a song just to get rid of it. Add some scissors, glitter, string, markers, beads, and buttons, and you have an afternoon of relative peace and quiet. Maria has a special "gallery" (a wall) where she hangs the best pieces of the week. Why not keep all the packaging you throw away every week? Anything can be a part of a work of art. Large boxes are especially prized as the makings of a great clubhouse or creative "box-car."

Other great, inexpensive activities include

➤ **Cooking and baking.** By incorporating children into your kitchen activities, you kill two birds with one stone. They play (for free), and you get some work done.

➤ **Music.** Teaching children to love music is a reward unto itself. Whether they are listening to Mozart on CD, playing the flute, or drumming that wooden spoon, music can be a compelling, wonderful, affordable activity.

➤ **Reading.** If children learn early enough, they can't stop. That you can check out endless books for free from the library makes reading that much better. Books can also be purchased cheaply at yard sales, book fairs, and church bazaars. Have children write their own books. Read to your children every day.

➤ **Computer.** If you have a home computer, the possibilities are endless. CDs make learning fun and can often be found in the bargain bin at the computer store for a few dollars. The Internet is a vast resource of fun and learning. AOL Canada, for instance, has an entire area for kids only. Install an inexpensive blocking program, and let them go explore the world.

➤ **Sports.** Sports can usually be played for the cost of a football, basketball, or Frisbee.

➤ **Games.** They need not be expensive. Puppets can be made out of lunch bags. Use old clothes for dress-up. Puzzles are pretty cheap. (Old puzzles that are missing pieces make great craft fodder.)

➤ **Money.** Help them start a business. The kids can solicit neighbours for a summer pet-sitting or pet-washing service. They can wash cars or sell lemonade. In the winter they can shovel snow. They can baby-sit.

It Takes Money to Make Money

Work-related expenses can devour a budget. Utilize these ideas and save a bundle:

Bring lunch. Let's say that you and your spouse could each save a conservative $5 per day by brown-bagging it three days a week. At the end of a year, you would have saved over $1500.

Buy clothes on sale or even used. A new silk tie may cost $40. On sale, it is $30. Used, it is $5. The same holds true for a suit or dress. Of course, you must look sharp

Over Your Limit

According to the Fall 1998 Canadian Radio Listening Habits and Lifestyles findings by the BBM bureau of measurement, families with household incomes between $50 000 to $80 000 make up 30 percent of the fast-food clientele, the largest percentage distribution. The middle class know how to eat cheaply, but they could save even more money by eating at home more often.

to get ahead at work; no one is saying that you should dress like Cosmo Kramer. We are saying that you can dress your best for less.

Save on dry cleaning. People can spend over $1000 a year on dry cleaning. If you shop around a bit, it is probable that you can find a convenient dry cleaner that will do the same work for one third less. Having that jacket cleaned every other time instead of every time you wear it can also save money. Better yet, check the tags before you buy to avoid purchasing items that are "dry clean only."

Use mass transit. Remember, convenience costs. If saving money is going to become a priority, then something will have to give, probably convenience. Driving to work may be quicker, but gas and parking are expensive, and a bus is a lot cheaper. (You may even be able to save on your car insurance premiums if you commit to commuting via public transit.)

Save on coffee breaks. Snacks from home can replace that daily $3 bagel and juice, although giving up your latte may just be too much to ask.

Two Cents

Each of these savings alone may be miniscule, but when you add them together, they can make a big dent in your expenditures. When you use that money to pay off credit card debt and corresponding high interest rates, you are really beginning to change your situation.

We are not telling you that you must become a miserly saint. As Maude said in the movie *Harold and Maude*, "You can't be good all of the time; it spoils the fun!" Pick and choose what works for you.

Traveling on a Budget

Traveling, too, need not be outrageously expensive. If you are willing to spend a little more time getting to your destination, you can save a lot more money.

The Only Way to Fly

Plane flights now can be quite inexpensive. No-frills charter carriers like Canada 3000 and Royal are cheaper, and ticket brokers sell discounted airline flights.

If you are really adventurous, you can become an air courier. Large companies ship packages every day around the world, and they require someone to accompany the package. That person is you, the air courier. As a courier, you can fly to Europe, Asia, South America, almost anywhere, and do so at a heavy discount (The catch? You have to travel light). Whereas a flight from New York to Oslo might cost $2000 roundtrip, on a courier flight it might be $395. Sometimes, in a pinch, it can be free. Pick up a book on air courier

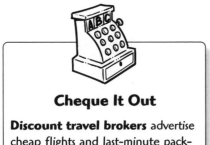

Cheque It Out

Discount travel brokers advertise cheap flights and last-minute package deals in the weekend section of major newspapers.

travel, and you are off. The other downside is that you usually don't get to choose how long you can stay abroad, and bringing the kids along is impossible.

Other ways to save on airfare include:

➤ Travel during off-peak times of year.

➤ Travel over a weekend. The cost of a major air carrier's flight from Toronto to Vancouver, for example, that left on a Monday was three times as high as one that left on a Saturday.

➤ Fly standby.

➤ Give up your seat on an overbooked flight and get a free voucher. Tim books a flight every year for December 23 from Denver to New York (making sure the ticket is exchangeable) without ever planning to go. He goes to the plane that day, happily gives up his overbooked seat, gets a free flight anywhere in the country for being so reasonable, and uses his exchangeable ticket on a flight he will use later in the year.

➤ If and when necessary, don't forget to use compassion fares. Airlines offer discounted bereavement fares if you can show proof of death and explain your relationship to the deceased.

Traveling Cheaply

Once you get to your destination, you can save even more money. Go to the local Chamber of Commerce and get a tourist kit; inside will be discounts and lots of great offers. Traveling by bus or subway saves money, and if you will be there for awhile, consider getting a bus pass.

Lodging can be very expensive or very cheap. If you are going to travel overseas, you can exchange homes with a family in the country you are going to. You can rent an apartment instead of staying in a hotel, which will allow you to prepare some of your own meals and avoid eating out every single night. You can stay in a discount motel instead of a hotel. You can stay in a college dorm instead of a motel. You can camp.

Be sure to use any discounts available to you. Seniors are offered discounts on car rentals, airline tickets, lodging, admissions, mass transit, and restaurants. Other groups that are often offered similar discounts are members of the military, students, auto club members, and union members.

Young, Broke, and in Love

David and Leslie took one of their most memorable trips ever when they were young and had no choice but to be creative. They took a train from Los Angeles to Tijuana and hopped a plane to Mexico City, because flying within the country was much cheaper than flying internationally.

Once in Mexico, they grabbed an overnight train to the pyramids (saving on a hotel room). They then took a 24-hour bus ride to Cancun (saving another night of hotel expenses). In Cancun, they stayed at the youth hostel for $4 a night. They hitched south (which is not safe nowadays) and found a room on the beach for $10 a night. There they got engaged with a $25 silver ring David had bought earlier in the trip. They just celebrated their 15th anniversary, and although they don't travel like that anymore, they miss it a lot.

Pleasure on the Cheap

Eating out need not be so expensive either. Your newspaper is full of coupons for inexpensive meals for adults and families alike. If you eat out often, dining clubs offer two-for-one deals, and discount coupon books sold by civic organizations pay for themselves in meals many times over, if they are used. Other ways to eat cheaply include:

➤ Utilize "early bird specials."

➤ Eat á la carte instead of ordering a full meal.

➤ Share your food.

➤ Don't order a drink.

➤ Go out for lunch instead of dinner.

➤ Just go out for dessert.

Two Cents

Movie theatres don't make their real money at the box office; the concession stand is what you need to be wary of. If you are so inclined, bring your own candy and soft drink in a bag, and you will save $10. Malcolm pops his own popcorn before going to the movies and sneaks it in, in his backpack. (We told you this could be fun.)

Movies are usually half price for a matinees. If you are patient, that new Mel Gibson movie will turn up at the discount theatres in a few weeks. If these ideas don't appeal to you, stay home and make it a Blockbuster night.

We are so used to spending money for entertainment that it comes as a shock to realize just how much there is to do for almost nothing:

➤ Go on a bike ride.

➤ Go to a museum.

➤ Take a drive in the country.

➤ Garden.

➤ Attend a free lecture at a university.

➤ Go to the library.

➤ Play a free sport—tennis, baseball, basketball.

➤ Make art.

➤ Go to a street fair.

➤ Go camping.

Money Can't Buy You Love

Going on a date can also be inexpensive if you use your imagination. (When Tom was a child, he thought his mom was telling him to use his "magic nation.") A picnic in the park or at the beach is quite romantic and a bargain to boot. A walk around the city, stopping for coffee, and browsing in galleries are equally fanciful and similarly inexpensive.

The possibilities for fun, economical dates are endless, if you use your own "magic nation." Use these ideas to get you started:

➤ Find a dark cafe and spend the night chatting and drinking.

➤ Test drive a dream car.

➤ Explore a new neighbourhood.

➤ Take a walk in the woods.

➤ Fly a kite.

How about this idea: Act as though you and your spouse were going on a getaway for the weekend. Find someone to take the kids, pack your favourite clothes, plan a special Saturday afternoon and Sunday brunch, and stay home. Do it all and have a blast, just do it from home. Dress up, light the candles, feed each other food, trade massages, and go wild. You may end up doing things you have never done, seeing parts of your city you have never been to, and saving a small fortune in the process.

The Least You Need to Know

➤ Having the right attitude is essential.

➤ When it comes to food, you pay for convenience.

➤ Kids can be as happy playing as they can be spending.

➤ Traveling on the cheap can be a great adventure.

➤ Romance need not be expensive.

Chapter 9

Call Your Creditor and Say "Hi" (The Plan)

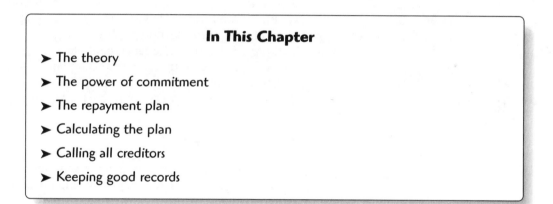

In This Chapter

➤ The theory

➤ The power of commitment

➤ The repayment plan

➤ Calculating the plan

➤ Calling all creditors

➤ Keeping good records

In the last chapter, you began to take a look at your monthly budget and possibly make some changes. Even if you didn't, it remains a fact that the only way you are going to get rid of those debts that hinder you and stress you out, short of bankruptcy, is to earmark some money every month to repay them.

The best way to do this is to formulate a repayment plan. Before you even say that you can't, that it's impossible, that there is no room at the inn, let us say that we will not ask you to make impossible sacrifices in order to get out of debt. This book and this plan are about getting out of debt within the context of making your life work.

Cheque It Out

When a creditor finally decides that it can no longer collect the debt from you, it will **charge off** the debt. This does not mean you don't owe the money anymore. It just means that your creditor probably sold the debt to a collection agency at a steep discount and will get a tax break for the loss.

Two Cents

"Whether you think you can, or that you can't, you are usually right."

—Henry Ford

Get Out of Debt, Now

Your creditors are probably not too happy with you right now. Although some people start on the path toward financial solvency still current on all of their bills, most people do not. Their utilities may be close to being turned off, and their credit cards are so maxed out that they can no longer even use the cards to pick a lock.

Late payments like these create even more debt, which in turn may cause more fear and avoidance. Avoidance can then cause more late payments, creating even more debt. Debt begets more debt. Maybe you'll go on a binge-shopping spree to feel better. In this hellish cycle, debts grow and grow and grow. You can put an end to this cycle by putting together a practical repayment plan.

Of course, we realize that some debt is unmanageable and that such debt is bigger than a repayment plan. If that is the case, bankruptcy is probably a better option. We understand that and even endorse that option. After all, one of the authors of this book is a bankruptcy attorney. The repayment plan being presented here is for those of you who plan to get out of debt without declaring bankruptcy. Bankruptcy is discussed in Part 4, "A Last Option—Bankruptcy."

Commitment

To make this repayment plan work, give it your full commitment. Commit totally to repaying everything and everyone to whom you owe money. Of course, it will take time and won't be simple, but that is no excuse for not starting.

A 31-year-old man once asked his wise father whether he should go back and finish his university degree. The man was worried that it would take three years and that he would be 34 years old when he finally finished school. His father looked at his son and asked him, "How old will you be in three years if you don't go?" How old will you be in three years if you don't commit to repaying your debts? You'll be three years older and several more dollars in the hole.

Making a commitment to pay everyone back is very significant. If you do it, you will feel better about yourself. It will give you the confidence to call up your creditors and work out a repayment plan. Fear will begin to evaporate and will be replaced by strength. A commitment to keep your word, have integrity, and live up to your responsibilities fosters self-esteem. It is good for the soul.

Commitment is a very powerful thing. Buckminster Fuller (1895–1983) is best known for inventing the geodesic dome, but he was also a prolific author, mathematician, cartographer, speaker, scientist, and inventor. At one point, he had the longest entry ever in the history of Who's Who.

What many people don't know about Bucky is that he was a complete failure for much of his life. He was kicked out of Harvard twice (once for blowing his entire semester's allowance on an evening with showgirls), had several businesses fail, and was grieving for a daughter he lost to a childhood illness. An unhappy, unknown failure at 30, Buckminster Fuller decided to kill himself.

As he walked to Lake Michigan in the dead of winter, intent on throwing himself in, Fuller realized that his mistake had been selfishness; if he fully committed himself to helping the greatest number of people he could, he could be a success. He vowed on his deceased daughter's memory to do just that. It was only after making this commitment that he turned his life around and became a lovable genius some dubbed "the da Vinci of the twentieth century."

W.H. Murray wrote the following in *The Scottish Himalayan Expedition*:

> Until one is committed, there is hesitancy, the chance to draw back, always ineffectiveness. Concerning all acts of initiative and creation, there is one elementary truth the ignorance of which kills countless ideas and splendid plans: that the moment one definitely commits oneself, then providence moves too. All sorts of things occur to help one that would never otherwise have occurred. A whole stream of events issues from the decision, raising in one's favour all manner of unforeseen incidents, meetings and material assistance which no man could have dreamed would have come his way. Whatever you can do or dream you can, begin it. Boldness has genius, power, and magic in it. Begin it now.

You don't need to change the world; you just need to make a commitment to yourself and for yourself that you are going to repay all your debts.

The Plan

Again, this plan to pay off your debt will not be at the expense of the rest of your life—in fact, it cannot be done that way. If you set up a plan that involves renouncing all you enjoy, you will not stick to the plan. Because you will not have been spending any money, when you do break your budget plan you may well binge, putting yourself worse in debt than before you started. You will continue to eat, live, entertain, go to school, have lunch out, and so on. You will just be adding one more category to your expenses: debt repayment.

Your payments may not be that much at the beginning; whatever you can afford is what

Money Talks

A 1996 poll conducted by the Angus Reid Group sponsored by Ernst & Young found that three-quarters of Canadians reported having a bank credit card, and one-half said they had a department store credit card (58% of these respondents were women). Two-fifths of Canadians have a personal line of credit.

Forty percent of Canadians with at least one credit card said they carried outstanding balances; those from the Atlantic provinces were more likely to fall into this category, with Quebec residents being the least likely. This tendency to carry debt from month to month decreased with age.

you should pay. This is going to be a plan that works, one you can live with. Although it might be a modest beginning, creating such a plan is a significant moment in your financial life.

Calculating the Plan

Get out a sheet of paper and write down every single creditor you owe money to on the left-hand side. Next to each name, list how much you owe them. Let's use Ryan as an example. Here are his outstanding debts:

Calculating Your Debt (Example)

Creditor	Amount Owed
CIBC Visa	$5000
Royal Bank MasterCard	$1000
Aerogold Visa	$2000
The Bay	$1000
Mom	$2500
Total:	$11 500

You then need to figure out what percentage each debt is of the entire amount. It's not that hard to do. First, add up your total debt. In Ryan's case, it is $11 500. To figure out each creditor's share of the whole debt, divide each creditor's amount by the entire debt. For example, the CIBC Visa bill ($5000) divided by the entire amount ($11 500) equals 0.43, or 43 percent. That bill is 43 percent of Ryan's total indebtedness.

The next thing to do is to add that figure onto your list, next to each creditor's name and the amount owed. In Ryan's case, the list would look like this:

Calculating Your Debt Percentages (Example)

Creditor	Amount Owed	Percentage
CIBC Visa	$5000	43%
Royal Bank MasterCard	$1000	9%
Aerogold Card	$2000	17%
The Bay	$1000	9%
Mom	$2500	22%
Total:	$11 500	100%

This list tells you how much each creditor is going to get each and every month, depending upon how much you can afford to pay. How much can you afford to pay? If you have a budget, you know. If not, you still intuitively know how much you can afford to repay every month—$25, $50, $200, whatever works.

Let's go back to Ryan and see how this process works. His budget will allow him to dedicate only $100 each month toward these bills. (We are not saying not to pay your bills if you can afford to pay them. This tool is for those bills that you have fallen behind on and/or feel overwhelmed by.) Each creditor will get its percentage of that $100:

Debt Payment Calculations (Example)

Creditor	Amount Owed	Percentage	Repayment
CIBC Visa	$5000	43%	$43
Royal Bank MasterCard	$1000	9%	$9
Aerogold Card	$2000	17%	$17
The Bay	$1000	9%	$9
Mom	$2500	22%	$22
Total:			$100

Over Your Limit

If budgeting has failed for you in the past, it may be because you failed to plug the cash leaks. Although keeping track of rent and car payments is easy enough, your ABM card may be the dreaded culprit. It's easy to take out $20 or $40, forget to account for it, and wonder where $200 went at the end of the month.

To figure out how much each creditor gets, multiply its percentage by the amount you can afford to pay (we promise there will be no more math after this!). Because Ryan can afford $100 a month and his mom gets 22 percent, he needs to multiply her percentage, 0.22, by $100: 0.22 x $100 = $22. If Ryan could afford $200 a month, The Bay would get 9 percent multiplied by $200: $18.

Ryan, like you, would then need to pay these amounts each and every month to his creditors. As it stands, Ryan will devote $100 to getting out of debt, with each creditor getting a percentage according to how much Ryan owes them.

This is where your commitment comes in. You must set aside that amount, whatever it is, every month and earmark it toward these debts. Each creditor will have to share whatever it is you can afford. The only way to get out of debt is to get out of debt. It is not easy. That is why you must be committed.

For various reasons, your plan may not exactly reflect how much you owe each creditor. One debt may have such high interest that it must be paid more, or another creditor may be bothering so much that you just want to get rid of it as fast as possible. These adjustments are fine; the important thing is to create a plan that works, that you can live with, and that you are committed to.

For example, you may decide that the best course of action is to get rid of the credit card with the highest interest rate first and then worry about the others. We have no problem with that—in fact, it's smart. The important thing is to create a plan that you believe in and that works. Pick a plan, any plan. Once you do, the important thing is that you will be getting out of debt instead of going into debt.

Remember Me?

At this point, you may be thinking that The Bay won't take $9 a month. Maybe not, but maybe it will. Actually, some of your creditors might be very happy to hear your voice. Especially if you have been avoiding them and reneging on your responsibility to pay what you owe them. A phone call with a repayment plan, even a small repayment plan, can be seen as better than nothing.

Explain to each creditor on your list what you are doing. Tell the creditors

➤ You are sorry for allowing this debt to get out of hand. If you express regret, you may find that the creditor will be far more willing to work with you.

➤ You have every intention of paying them back in full.

➤ Paying them back will, however, take some time. You owe a lot of people money, not just them.

➤ You have a plan of action to pay everyone back, and in it you will be treating each creditor equally. The creditor to whom you owe the most money will be paid the most. It is a fair plan.

➤ You understand that they want more money each month than you are proposing, but at this time, you are doing you best. In time, as the debts shrink, you hope to be able to pay more.

➤ You would like their cooperation. If they could stop adding interest, they would get paid sooner, and your job would be easier.

Two Cents

Creditors are people, too, and those customer service representatives have more authority than they let on. Customer relations experts say that customers who treat the person on the phone with respect have a far greater chance of getting what they want.

Sam had ignored his Canadian Tire bill for five months and owed them $1100 when he finally created a plan that called for him to pay them $75 a month. Once he got up the nerve to call customer service, Sam explained his situation, apologized, and proposed his plan.

Creditors don't have to agree to anything, certainly not a cessation or reduction of interest. But if you are honest with them and if they see that you are endeavouring to do the right thing, they just might agree. After all, the last thing they want to see is a default.

If they tell you they will not accept $9 a month, that they will sue, or will write off the debt and sell it to a collection agency, listen politely, and send them the money anyway. The odds are that they will cash the cheque, however unhappily.

Over Your Limit

Studies have shown that creditors are less likely to sue over debts under $1000 and more likely to sue for debts over $5000.

Credit card companies might not be so generous. They are usually very difficult to deal with and do not often negotiate. Yet, as with other creditors, an honest attempt on your part to settle your bill can go a long way. Do your best to get them to lower interest and finance charges, pay what you can afford to pay, and begin to make some headway. (Make sure to read Chapter 11, "Taming the Credit Card Goliath," and Chapter 12, "Talking to the Lion: Dealing with Creditors.")

There are downsides to this sort of plan. By consistently paying less than you owe there is a possibility that your creditors may report you as paying late every month. Or they may cancel your credit altogether. If this is of concern to you, you may want to pay those creditors whose credit you still want more and the others less, at least until they are paid off.

Keeping Good Records

As you go about restructuring your debt and paying off your bills, you need to keep good records. Good records will help you stay organized and ensure that you know what you are talking about when you deal with a creditor.

Buy a three-ring notebook that you can devote to your debt reduction plan. One section will be the list of creditors and your proposed repayment percentages that you created. Another section will keep track of communications between you and each creditor. The final section will tally your balances and amounts paid.

Keeping Track of Creditors

Designate a separate sheet of paper in your notebook for each creditor with its name and phone number at the top. Especially early in your debt reduction plan, you may be talking with your creditors a lot. As you do, you want to be able to keep track of what is said and agreed to, as shown in the following example:

Tracking Creditors (Example)

The Bay, 879-7972

Date	Content of discussion
9/27	Spoke with Darla in accounts receivable. Offered to pay $9 a month. She says she doubts it, but will speak with her supervisor.
10/13	Called Darla again, left message to call back.
10/15	Darla called, says her supervisor agreed, but wasn't happy. I told her I would send my first payment on the first of next month.

Have a separate sheet for each of your creditors. If a dispute ever arises, this information will give you plenty of ammunition. Even if a dispute does not arise, memories are short, and it helps to have the name of your contact person and what was last said. Although you can try and get these agreements in writing, many creditors refuse to do that. It never hurts to ask though.

Keep a Tally of Your Payments

The final part of your notebook is a running tally of what you have paid, when you paid it, and what you still owe. Again, each creditor should have its own subsection. You may even want to put your monthly bills in their proper place in the notebook. You can even put each cheque as it clears your account in this section.

You can monitor payments and outstanding debt in various ways:

➤ You can do it by hand by subtracting your payment each month from your previous month's balance.

➤ You can use a spreadsheet. Spreadsheets are part of many computer systems; Microsoft Works, which is found on many PCs or Macs, has one built in.

➤ You can buy a computer program, such as Quicken, to help you. These programs have some cool charts and graphs that will let you see your debt shrinking in 3-D.

Two Cents

Customer service representatives type the content of every conversation they have with a customer into their computer. This way, the next representative who deals with that customer knows what was said in the last conversation. If you ever make a deal over the phone, make sure the representative inputs it into the computer.

If you adopt this program and see it through, you should begin to see some dramatic results in a short period of time. Just as debt seems to have an almost mystical way of growing in the blink of an eye, so too does it have a way of shrinking when you begin to take action. As time goes by, and as your debts reduce, you will be able to devote even more money toward your debt-reduction plan, making it shrink all the faster. Before you know it, you will be out of debt.

The Least You Need to Know

➤ You must make a commitment to repay every one of your debts.

➤ You need to create a repayment plan that you can live with.

➤ Each creditor should get its percentage of your debt repaid every month.

➤ Your creditors may be more willing to work with you than you realize.

➤ Keeping good records is essential.

Part 3

When Cutting Back Is Not Enough

This chapter is for special situations. We look at several types of debt; dealing with each can require special knowledge. From income tax to student loans to credit card debt, there are pitfalls that trap thousands of Canadians every year. These are common problems, and they have solutions.

If one of these chapters applies to you, please read it carefully. We've packed a lot of information into a few pages.

Chapter 10

Refinancing Your Home

In This Chapter

➤ Knowing when to refinance

➤ A risky proposition

➤ Types of refinancing

➤ Counting the cost

➤ Helpful hints

Sometimes, no matter how much fat you trim from your budget, you still don't have enough money to get out of debt. At that point, other measures are needed. We hope you see that there are many different ways to get out of debt and that the best method of all is a combination of different ideas that work for you.

For instance, your plan may include some new money values, a tighter budget, and some negotiated settlements with creditors (see Chapter 12, "Talking to the Lion: Dealing With Creditors"). Or it could be that changing some bad habits and working things out with the Canada Customs and Revenue Agency, or the CCRA (formerly Revenue Canada) suits your situation. Another tool to add to your debt-reduction arsenal is refinancing your mortgage. A fine option, it must be used cautiously.

Refinancing your mortgage has two different meanings. On the one hand, it is synonymous with "renegotiating" your mortgage for a lower interest rate, and will definitely save you money. On the other hand, it refers to actually changing the term and amortization rate of your mortgage to come up with a smaller monthly payment that you will make for a longer period of time. The latter situation is done at a lender's discretion. A bank, for example, does not want to see you default on your mortgage. It is not cost-effective for a bank to foreclose on you. If you approach your lender proactively, it is more likely to agree on a refinanced mortgage plan that will help your debt crisis. However, if you get yourself into a situation where you have begun to miss mortgage payments, the lender may not be as likely to cooperate.

When Refinancing to Save Money Makes Sense

There are basically four situations in which refinancing seems attractive:

1. **The current mortgage rate is much lower than what you negotiated when you bought your house.** Back in the early to mid-nineties, many Canadians bought homes with interest rates floating at 9.5 percent. Then in 1994 they dropped to the lowest rate in years — as low as 6.25 percent. Renegotiating the mortgage made sense for a lot of people, who saved hundreds of dollars a month on mortgage payments.

2. **The variable interest rate is about to go up, and you want to lock-in at the lower rate.** Perhaps you weren't sure which way interest rates were heading when you bought, but now are certain they will go back up.

3. **You have been "riding" the low variable interest rate and your nerves can't take it anymore.** Many people play the variable interest rate game and do manage to save quite a bit of money. But unless you're willing to keep a close eye on rates, it's worth it to lock in and give your stress levels a chance to rest.

4. **You need cash.** The fourth situation in which refinancing seems attractive is when

Cheque It Out

Know your lingo: A **variable mortgage rate** is a loan that goes up and down in conjunction with interest rates in general. A **fixed rate loan** is a loan that has a set interest rate for the duration of the loan, no matter what interest rates in general are doing. A **balloon payment loan** is a loan with a large lump-sum payment due at the end of the loan.

you need some extra cash and you want to refinance the house in order to pull out some money. This proposition is inherently dangerous, and we do not recommend it. However, if you have plenty of equity in the house and are in a severe debt crisis, refinancing may be an advisable approach to solving your problem. Read on.

The first three situations make sense because you will likely be saving money, but the last option is inherently dangerous. Let's look at each situation a bit more closely and show you why you may want to refinance.

Does Refinancing Make Sense for Me?

If you have an open mortgage (which means you haven't locked in for a set period of time, and are taking advantage of variable interest rates); either or a mortgage insured by the Canada Mortgage and Housing Corporation, which automatically becomes open after three years; or a long-term mortgage in which you are at least five years into the loan, you can refinance your mortgage with little or no penalty. Otherwise, refinancing can be an expensive proposition that may not save you much money in the long run. Crunch the numbers carefully.

"The lowest rates we've seen in years!"

There are three main factors to look at when determining the costs and benefits of refinancing:

1. **What will be the difference between the present rate and the new rate?** An old rule was that if you could lower your interest rate by two percent, refinancing was worth it. Anything less than that would have been eaten up in costs and fees. Today, there are many more loan options, so the old rules do not apply. If you can lower your interest rate, you are well on your way to making a good decision.

2. **What are the total costs associated with the refinance transaction?** The costs of refinancing have decreased greatly in the past several years. With no-point loan options, for example, borrowers can save thousands of dollars upfront. Your mortgage lender or broker should give you a specific breakdown of all closing costs so that you will be able to calculate your savings exactly.

3. **How comfortable are you with possible payment changes over the life of your mortgage loan?** If you are not saving money, there is no point in refinancing.

Risky Business

Refinanced home loans can take many forms: a refinanced first mortgage, a second mortgage, and even a third mortgage. Refinancing to lower your interest rate or to get a loan that you are more comfortable with makes sense to us. Refinancing to pull equity out of your house (so-called equity loans) should be considered with caution.

Over Your Limit

Don't get greedy. Once you decide to refinance your house, you may be tempted to wait for rates to get their "lowest." Rates go up and down every day, and waiting a day too long to refinance a loan has burned many a homeowner. Are you going to hit the bottom? Probably not. Are you going to save money? Yes. If you want to gamble, go to Las Vegas. It's a heck of a lot more fun.

It is understandable why you would want to use your home equity to help you get out of debt. Home equity has replaced the savings account for many Canadians. Instead of dipping into their savings when times get tough, they take out a home equity loan.

To understand why this option looks better than it is, you must first understand the difference between secured and unsecured debts. A secured debt is one that is tied to some sort of collateral. For example, a bank would be happy to loan you the $25 000 you need to buy a new car, as long as it holds title to the car. If you do not pay the bank back, it will repossess the car. The car, which is the collateral, secures the loan.

With an unsecured debt, there is no collateral protecting the creditor. A credit card is an example of an unsecured loan. When you get a new Visa card, the card issuer does not ask you to pledge any property as collateral to secure the debt you will incur using the card. You simply promise to pay back the debt. That debt is unsecured. The majority of debts people have, such as credit cards and department store bills, are unsecured debts.

A home equity loan, or a second mortgage, can be very risky because you are trading unsecured debt for secured debt. When you stop paying an unsecured debt, all a creditor can do is write demand letters, make a lot of phone calls, and possibly sue you. Although this activity may prove to be annoying, it certainly is not devastating.

But failure to pay back a secured debt can be devastating. When you stop paying a secured debt, not only do you get the same letters and threats, but, far worse, you also lose the collateral that secures the debt. If you fail to stay current with that second mortgage you took out last year to pay off your credit cards, your lender can foreclose and sell your home out from underneath you. That is far worse than getting sued by a credit card company.

This is exactly what happened to Sandy. She was having a difficult time repaying the $40 000 she owed on her eight different credit cards. Sandy decided to take out a second mortgage on her house at 8 percent interest, which was substantially less than the interest rate on her credit cards, and pay off all of her debts.

Money Talks

Ted Turner owns the most real estate in America. He owns 1.3 million acres in New Mexico, Montana, Nebraska, Florida, Georgia, and South Carolina. Among his holdings are 1.15 million acres in New Mexico, amounting to 1.5 percent of the state. Included in his holdings in New Mexico, according to Forbes magazine, is the 578 000-acre Vermejo Park Ranch, purchased for $80 million; the oil rights to the land sold for an estimated $81 million over several years (and he keeps the land).

Unfortunately, two years later, she lost her job, was unable to continue to pay both mortgages, and lost her home in a foreclosure sale. Had Sandy not swapped her credit card debt for a second mortgage on her house, she would not have lost her home.

Had she not taken out the second mortgage to pay off her debts, Sandy probably would have had about $50 000 in credit card debt when she lost her job. At that point, she could have stopped paying the credit cards and earmarked any money she did make to pay her existing mortgage. Although she undoubtedly would have received many nasty phone calls from her credit card companies, an unsecured creditor cannot foreclose on a house like a secured lender can. Sandy would have kept her home.

If you are refinancing to pull money out of your house, you'd better be very careful. You need to be pretty darn sure that you will be able to pay the new secured debt. On the other hand, if you are refinancing in order to reduce your interest rate and thereby make your monthly budget work better, go right ahead; we're with you.

Types of Loans

With more and more families investing money into their homes, tapping into that home equity is becoming more popular. If you're house rich and cash poor, as the saying goes, then using some of the money you have built up into your home's equity over the years may be a viable way to pay for certain things, such as home renovations or as emergency cash. One of the writers, Janice, and her husband, have even used their line of credit to maximize RRSP contributions. Unlike interest on mortgages, interest on funds borrowed to invest in non-registered investment, is tax-deductible.

A home equity loan or line of credit is basically like a second mortgage. If you paid the standard 25% downpayment on your home when you bought it, your mortgage was originally 75% of the property's value.

Over Your Limit

Many equity lenders say that they can loan you up to 125 percent of the equity in your house, that it is easy to apply, and that you can be approved in a matter of days. Why are they so anxious to loan you money? Because they know they cannot lose. You will repay the loan either voluntarily or involuntarily through the sale of your home.

How much can you get now? Lenders usually allow you to borrow between 66 percent and 75 percent of the home's resale or market value, provided the outstanding mortgage is less than 75 percent of the value of the property. To figure it out, here's the math:

   A. current home value $200 000

   B. 75% of home value $150 000

   C. mortgage outstanding $125 000

   D. amount available to borrow(different between B and C) – $25 000

You can have the money accessible in a sort of bank account; however, there is usually nothing preventing you from simply withdrawing the entire amount at once, which means you have a very affordable pre-approved loan at your fingertips. You will have to meet the lender's conditions before you get the money, of course. These conditions are in place to make sure you are able to handle the excess debt and monthly payments. There are also administration fees, similar to those charged for setting up a mortgage. If you can arrange the line of credit when you arrange the mortgage, you'll save on these costs. In fact, most lenders are happy to offer a line of credit to home buyers, because they know there are often loads of unexpected bills and emergencies that crop up.

What About Interest?

Interest rates for home equity lines of credit is usually a fixed amount over the prime rate, typically, half a percentage point higher. You will have to pay monthly minimum interest payments, as well as some payment toward principal. Because a line of credit is a demand loan, your lender can also turn the tables and demand repayment in full whenever it sees fit—usually if the monthly payments are not being made, for example.

When Not to Use Your Home Equity

Be careful of using a home equity line of credit to pay off unsecured debts, such as from a credit card. Remember, never trade unsecured debt for secured debt, unless you are absolutely sure your debt situation will be resolved in the short-term. Though you may be able to pay off a high interest rate credit card, you are adding extra debt to your mortgage. If you have trouble making those payments down the road (maybe because you end up racking up more credit card debt), then you are really in a pinch.

Equity Lines of Credit

The typical home equity credit line is different than an equity loan. An *equity loan* is a lump-sum loan secured by the house. An *equity line of credit* is a revolving line of credit. A borrower is approved for a specific amount of credit, which will become the maximum amount that can be borrowed under the plan. Lenders usually require the line to be at least $5000, but total credit lines can range up to $500 000.

Once the home equity line is in place, a borrower can borrow up to the credit limit at any time. Many plans require a minimum draw against the line of between $250 and $500. The borrower is usually required to repay at least the minimum interest due each month for the first 10 years. The interest rate on home equity lines is variable, is usually based on the prime rate, and is capped at a maximum that ranges from 15 to 20 percent.

Money Talks

Lenders look at a borrower's credit bureau rating when determining whether to give the loan. The lower the score is, the better the credit risk. Components of a low credit rating include good credit, the ability to handle debt, and adequate, documented monthly cash flow.

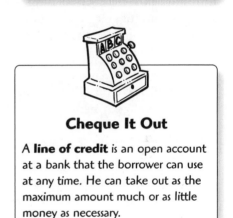

Cheque It Out

A **line of credit** is an open account at a bank that the borrower can use at any time. He can take out as the maximum amount much or as little money as necessary.

Qualifying for a New Loan

How does a mortgage lender decide to approve or deny an application? Basically, there are three fundamental areas that a mortgage underwriter looks at when making his decisions. Those areas are commonly referred to as the three Cs of refinancing underwriting. They are credit, character, and collateral.

➤ **Credit.** The first C, credit, refers to qualifying for the mortgage payment based on your monthly income. There are two ways the lender will calculate this: the

Money Talks

Canada's chartered banks (Bank of Montreal, The Bank of Nova Scotia, CIBC, Canadian Western Bank, Citizens Bank of Canada, First Nations Bank of Canada, Laurentian Bank of Canada, Manulife Bank of Canada, National Bank of Canada, Royal Bank of Canada, Toronto Dominion Bank) lead the way in holding mortgages with 61%. Credit unions and caisse populaires hold 14%, finance companies hold 7%, while trust & mortgage loan companies are tied with life insurance companies, each holding 5% of the country's mortgages.

gross-debt service ratio, which stipulates that your housing costs, including heat, utilities etc., must not exceed 30 percent to 32 percent of your total monthly family income; or, the total debt service ratio, which stipulates your housing costs plus debts must not exceed 37 percent to 42 percent of your total monthly family income.

➤ **Character.** This area has to do with how faithful applicants are in making their credit payments on time. It is the most crucial indicator, because if someone has paid credit cards, car payments, and a previous mortgage on time, he will be more likely to pay his new mortgage on time as well.

➤ **Collateral.** Collateral refers to the home being refinanced. An appraisal may be done to ensure that the house is worth the amount being loaned. An independent appraiser uses recent sales of comparable homes in the area to determine whether your price is similar.

How Much Will This Cost?

The total loan size (independent of the value of the property) also determines the interest rate for many lenders. A $7500 home equity loan may carry a rate of 9.75 percent, but a $100 000 loan may be charged only 8.5 percent. Some programs also carry introductory teaser rates for the first three or six months, often at 6 percent or less.

The last factor affecting rates is based on whether the borrower or the lender will pay closing costs. Some lenders give borrowers the option of a lower rate if they pay closing costs, which include appraisal, attorney, recording, and other fees that, usually, are under $2000.

Other lenders tie closing costs to the total loan amount. If the lender knows the

Money Talks

Banks are prohibited from practising "tied selling," where it is deemed that the bank is coercing the client to use another bank product in order to obtain a loan or mortgage. The bank is allowed to offer services at competitive or discounted prices ("relationship pricing") in order to entice a would-be borrower, and it is also allowed to insist that some products or services be used as a way to manage credit risk.

Over Your Limit

Don't say you were not warned. One leading lender even has this caveat on its Web page: "Simply because lenders are lending furiously to anyone who will borrow, consumers should be extremely wary of not getting in over their heads with home equity debt. Home equity loans of any type should never be used for day-to-day expenses."

borrower will take out $25 000, for example, then the lender will not mind paying the closing costs because it will make back the costs with interest payments within a few months.

You should pay the closing costs if doing so will mean a lower rate of interest. Throughout this book, we have emphasized the need for long-term thinking. People primarily go into debt as a result of short-term thinking. Refinancing a home loan is a perfect example of this.

A debtor thinks short-term, "I need the money, so paying closing costs is a bad idea." A saver thinks long-term, "I want a lower interest rate more than I need an extra $1000 right now, so paying closing costs is not so painful." The saver knows that paying 7 percent instead of 8 percent on a $40 000 loan over 30 years, even if it means paying $1000 in closing costs, would save him a lot of money over the life of the loan. Debtors never prosper.

Cheque It Out

A **lender** is the financial institution that makes the loan to you. You can deal directly with a lender or you can deal with a **broker**. For a fee, a broker will shop you around to different lenders, trying to find you the best deal.

Over Your Limit

Brokers may not issue a rate lock-in agreement themselves; they may only transmit a lender's lock-in offer to an applicant.

Winning at Refinancing

When looking to refinance your house, you need to know about a few things that can help you in this process. The first thing is to determine whether you would prefer to deal with a lender or a broker.

Lender or Broker?

One of the advantages of applying for a loan with a lender, such as a bank, trust company, credit union, or caisse populaire in Quebec, is that you will deal directly with the entity (person or company) that will make the decision on whether to approve your loan application. This direct contact offers less opportunity for miscommunication to occur during the application process. Brokers, in contrast, are unable to make credit decisions or issue mortgage commitments.

Nevertheless, you may find that a broker can provide you with more choices of loan products than any direct lender. If you have bad credit, brokers may be better because they can shop difficult applications to a variety of direct lenders.

Although there are no fixed rules to determine whether you should choose a direct lender or broker, you should know, when submitting your application, which type of mortgage organization you've selected.

Lock It In

It is also important to find out whether you are getting a *lock-in agreement*. A lock-in agreement is a lender's agreement to make a loan at a particular rate, with or without certain points, provided that the loan is closed by a specified date.

This is known as pre-approved, and it typically lasts for 60-90 days. That means you have two to three months to close the deal from the time the mortgage is offered at a given rate. Most lenders will give you the lowest rate available on the day of the sale. You can usually get a lower interest rate if you don't "lock-in." However, if mortgage rates suddenly spike, which they have been known to do, you could end up being stuck with a higher rate than you would have had if you had locked in from the beginning.

Keep in mind that lenders do not need to comply with the terms of the agreement if the

Money Talks

Beware of fraudulent loan brokers. They lurk in the classified sections of newspapers and are responsible for the bilking of hundreds of dollars from unsuspecting, desperate Canadians. How? By asking for an "up-front fee" which they say is an administrative charge, a processing fee, a charge for insurance on the loan, a file preparation fee, a sign-up fee, or a retainer. If any loan broker asks you for money before he gives you the loan, chances are he is not legitimate. For information on where to report a fraudulent loan broker, contact your provincial office of consumer affairs, or visit the federal government's Industry Canada Web site at http://strategis.ic.gc.ca, and look under Consumer Connection.

information they request is not provided promptly. If, after a deal is made, an applicant fails to comply with all of the conditions contained in a loan commitment, or if any information given in the application proves to be significantly inaccurate, the mortgage will be invalid.

Be sure to meet all of your obligations. Be sure that your application contains detailed and accurate information. Lenders may find errors while processing your application and inaccuracies will needlessly delay the process. Provide all the additional information requested by a lender and retain documentation. If you are unclear about what a lender needs, request a clarification. Do not make assumptions.

Final Thoughts

When applying for a new mortgage, you can help your loan officer by supplying as much information as possible at the time of application. Information such as tax returns for the last two years, a recent paycheque stub, and your last two monthly bank account statements will help move your mortgage application through the processing system smoothly and quickly.

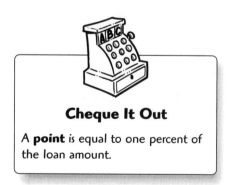

Cheque It Out

A **point** is equal to one percent of the loan amount.

From the beginning of the process, be honest about any credit problems you have had in the past. Doing so gives the loan officer the opportunity to confront any negative credit history head-on. Most credit problems can be easily explained.

The Least You Need to Know

➤ Refinancing makes the most sense when it means you will lower your monthly mortgage payments.

➤ Exchanging unsecured debt for secured debt must be done judiciously.

➤ Many types of loans are available today.

➤ Be a saver, not a debtor. Think long-term.

Chapter 11

Taming the Credit Card Goliath

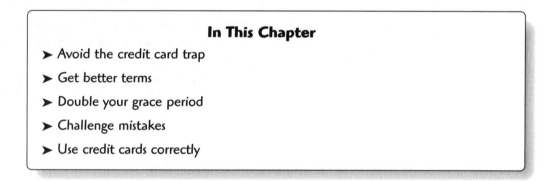

In This Chapter

➤ Avoid the credit card trap

➤ Get better terms

➤ Double your grace period

➤ Challenge mistakes

➤ Use credit cards correctly

Credit card debt is probably the most common debt issue that people face today. It's a terrible cycle. The cards are easy to use, but before you know it, the interest rate makes them difficult to pay off. In this chapter, we will show you some tactics that you can use to drastically reduce both your overall credit card indebtedness and your interest rates.

Credit Quicksand

Throughout this book we have consistently warned you against falling for the credit card trap—charging, taking cash advances, getting stuck with a huge bill, paying a big interest payment every month, and thereby ensuring that the balance is never paid off. It's a trap because you are caught in a predicament that is difficult to get out of.

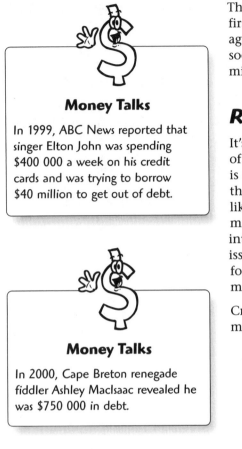

Money Talks

In 1999, ABC News reported that singer Elton John was spending $400 000 a week on his credit cards and was trying to borrow $40 million to get out of debt.

Money Talks

In 2000, Cape Breton renegade fiddler Ashley MacIsaac revealed he was $750 000 in debt.

There are two ways to fall for the credit card trap. The first is to not understand or care about what you agreed to when you took out the card and thus get socked with needless fees. The second is to fall for the minimum payment ploy.

Read the Fine Print

It's amazing how many people don't know the terms of their credit card agreements. All they know is that it is difficult to pay off the cards. Because one way to pay them off is to make more money, here's an idea: Do like the credit card companies do. Issue a credit card, make unrealistic promises that you can break, charge interest rates that would make a loan shark blanch, issue fees for the slightest infraction, sit back, and wait for the dough to roll in. That situation is in fact what many people have agreed to.

Credit card companies have a lot of ways to make money. The smart consumer will be wary of them:

➤ **Exorbitant interest rates.** The Bank of Canada lends money to banks at around 5 percent interest. Banks loan money for mortgages at around 6 percent and to commercial customers at around 8 percent. The average credit card interest rate is 17 percent.

➤ **Diminishing grace periods.** The grace period is the time you have to pay the

Over Your Limit

If you applied for a credit card in your name alone, the responsibility to pay for charges on that card is yours. Even if you had another card issued to a spouse later on, if that person's name is not on the application contract, that debt is yours alone. Conversely, if you co-signed for someone but never used the card, you are equally responsible for the debt on that card.

money back without paying interest. It is usually between 10 and 30 days, although some cards have eliminated it altogether.

➤ **Cash advance thievery.** To get a cash advance on a credit card, you usually pay a transaction fee of around 3 percent per advance, and there is no grace period. Interest is charged from the moment the money lands in your hands.

➤ **Disingenuous offers.** Credit card issuers will offer a card "as low as 8.9 percent" and then send you one at 15.9 percent. Or they send you the card at the advertised rate, but don't clearly mention that the rate will triple in three months.

➤ **Fees, fees, and more fees.** Late fees of $42 on a card with a $50 balance seem to be legal only in the world of credit cards.

You fall into their trap if you fail to see or just don't care about what they are doing to you. All of these tricks can be avoided if you are educated and know what you are doing. After you read this book, you will be!

The Worst Trap of All

The amount of interest you pay each month is based upon the interest rate you have agreed to pay and your remaining balance. Most card issuers have a minimum payment, which is 2 percent of the balance or $15, whichever is greater (if only $15 were greater!).

Many people get their bill, look at the minimum amount due, and pay that amount. *This is the absolutely biggest mistake you can make with credit cards.* Minimum payments can stretch your payments on, ad nauseam, and guarantee that you will pay for what you bought many times over.

Say that you have a card with a $7000 balance and an interest rate of 17 percent. How long do you think it will take you to pay off that balance paying a minimum payment of 2 percent? Three years? Five years?

Let's do some simple math. A monthly interest payment of 17 percent (your interest rate) on $7000 is $104. Adding that to your balance means that you will have a new balance in month two of $7,104. Your minimum payment is 2 percent of that amount, which is $142. So if you just paid the minimum, your balance the next month would start at $6962. Thus, by paying the minimum payment of $142, you knocked a whopping $38 off of your original balance.

Over Your Limit

According to the Canadian Bankers Association, as of October 31, 1998, there were 35.3 million consumer credit cards in circulation in Canada, and $23.9 million in outstanding balances.

If you followed this minimum payment course of action, it would take (get ready for this) over 40 years to pay off the entire card! Don't worry; it gets worse. You would also end up paying almost $14 000 on your $7000 balance. And you wonder why you are in debt?

There Has to Be a Better Way

As you can see, the cost of paying the minimum payment on your credit cards is high indeed. To reduce your credit card debt, then, you must begin to pay more than the minimum amount on your cards.

The results of doing so can be impressive. In the preceding $7000 example, the 2 percent minimum payment amount goes down every month as the principle decreases. However, if you keep paying the original minimum payment of $142 instead of the new, lower minimum, you will decrease the time it takes to reduce your credit card debt from 40 years to just about 5 years.

The key then to the first way to reduce credit card debt is to pay more than the minimum payment due, as much more as you can afford. Use the information in the chapters on budgeting to help you figure out how much you can pay. If you could increase the payment from $142 to $242, that $7000 debt would be repaid in just less than three years. (Unless you fall for the seduction of getting more cards once your balance starts to decrease!) Another way to accomplish the same goal is to make 13 payments a year instead of 12.

If you are able to cut back on some other expenses and pay more on your credit card debt, you can get out of debt before you know it. Although paying more than the minimum is just one way to free yourself from the credit card trap, it is probably the most important.

The Balance Transfer Dance

One of the easiest, and best, methods of lowering both your monthly credit card payments as well as your overall credit card indebtedness is to transfer the balance on your cards with a high interest rate to a card or cards with a much lower rate. The interest rate on your credit card is the biggest factor in how much you will have to repay.

Two Cents

Financially literate people are aware of how much interest they pay and understand how interest rates affect their bottom line.

The Cost of High Interest Rates

It is important to understand just how insidious these incredibly high interest rates are to your economic health. Let's say that you have five cards on which you owe about $2000 each and that have an average interest rate of 16.9 percent. Between interest payments and fees, your total yearly cost for these cards would be about $2400. This amount is not what you charged, your principal; it is just what you would be charged to borrow $10 000 from your credit cards.

If your interest rate were, say, 8.9 percent, your annual

cost would be about $1400; you would be saving roughly $1000. If you had a card with something like a 5.9 percent rate, your annual savings would be about $1300. Multiply this amount by each of your cards, and you will begin to see some real savings.

Negotiate Like a Pro

Where can you find cards with low interest rates? We suggest that you begin with the cards that you already have. Call your existing card issuers and ask for a lower rate:

Two Cents

One thing creditors look negatively upon when reviewing a credit report is potential credit, that is, accounts that are open. Close all accounts that you are not using and don't plan to use.

➤ Tell them that you are a loyal, existing customer and that you therefore deserve a lower interest rate.

➤ Find out what your existing card issuer offers as an introductory rate and go up from there: "You offer new customers 5.9 percent; I am paying 17.9 percent, and I have been with you for six years. I think 7.9 percent is a good idea if you want to keep my business."

➤ Explain that if they agree to a lower rate and increase your credit limit, you will transfer your other balances onto their cards. This negotiation then becomes a win-win situation; you get a lower interest rate, and the credit card issuers get to make more money off of the higher balance.

➤ Finally, tell them that if they cannot agree to a new, lower interest rate, another card has offered you an incredible introductory rate and that you will be transferring your balance from this card to the new card.

Asking for more than you want is a basic tenet of any good negotiator, so ask for a rate lower than what you hope to get. If you want to get all of your debts onto one card with a 7.9 percent interest rate, ask for 5.9 percent to begin with. If this tactic does not work, then we suggest that you find a new card with a lower interest rate that really wants your business.

Introductory Rates Are Best

Locate a card that you do not have yet that offers a low introductory rate. When you get the new card (need we say), do not charge with it. Transfer your high balances onto it and use its introductory rate to your advantage.

What you have to be especially conscious of is how long the rate is good for; this fact is often buried in the fine print. Sometimes these teaser rates can last up to a year; other

Cheque It Out

A **teaser rate** is an introductory interest rate offered by a credit card issuer to get your business. Some teaser rates are indeed very good, but you must be sure to check the terms and conditions. If the rate sounds too good to be true, it just may be. Beware, also, that teaser rates will rise. In July 1999, four of Canada's major banks bumped their low-rate credit card interest rates up a notch or two, citing higher loan losses due to bankruptcies, fraud, and default.

Over Your Limit

Before applying for a new card, check to see whether there will be any charges for balance transfers. If so, find another card. You should also double-check the limit on the card and be sure not to transfer more than that amount onto the card. It is also important to understand what the annual fees will be.

cards may only offer them for three months. Make sure that when the card comes in the mail, the rate you will be paying is the one you agreed to.

Azriela was offered a card once with a great rate and a $4000 limit. She accepted the offer, got the card, and transferred $4000 from a different card with a higher rate onto this new card. She was shocked when the transfer cheque bounced. It turned out that the new card charged a $4 transfer fee, so she was over her limit by $4. The card issuer assessed her a $25 bounced cheque fee to boot!

About a month before the introductory rate is set to expire, call up the company and see whether they will extend it another six months. Many will. If not, plenty more cards out there offer introductory rates that you can use. A few phone calls and a couple of simple forms to fill out can save you thousands of dollars a year.

Fee, Fi, Foe, Fum

If you do what we tell you to in this chapter, the big, bad giant of a credit card company can be tamed. One way credit card issuers get away with murder is with their beloved fees. Card issuers make a lot of money off of late fees, over-the-limit fees, and the like. Let's say that you are late one time or that your spouse used the card without telling you, thereby putting you over your limit. Can you do anything about it? Absolutely.

Pick up the phone and complain. The discussion will be much like the one when you requested a lower interest rate. Tell the credit card issuer:

➤ You are a loyal customer and have been for some time.

➤ The fee is outrageous, and you won't pay it.

➤ You will transfer your balance elsewhere and cancel your account if it does not reverse the charge.

Especially if you have no consistent history of being charged fees, this tactic should work when you need it.

A Real Grace Period

Understanding what the grace period is and how it works can help you stay out of debt. Remember that a grace period is only available on cards with a zero balance. Using a card with a zero balance and timing your purchase correctly can mean that you will never have to pay interest again on any major purchase; in effect, the credit card company will be loaning you money interest-free if you play the game correctly.

Say that you want to buy a new washer and dryer. You are billed on the first of the month, and your payment is due on the 25th. That means that you have 25 days to repay the debt without getting charged interest. It is quite possible, however, to effectively double that interest-free time.

If you buy the washer and dryer on the second of the month, you won't even receive a bill until the first of the following month. You then won't be charged interest until the 25th of that month. Thus, just by timing your purchase correctly, you can avoid all interest payments for the washer and dryer and still have almost two months to pay it off (or transfer the balance to another card if absolutely necessary).

Over Your Limit

Between 1997 and 1998, the number of credit cards (Visa and MasterCard) increased from 31.9 million to 35.3 million. The outstanding balances increased accordingly, from $20.5 million to $23.9 million.

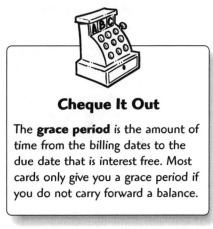

Cheque It Out

The **grace period** is the amount of time from the billing dates to the due date that is interest free. Most cards only give you a grace period if you do not carry forward a balance.

When Disputes Arise

Credit card billing errors do occur, but they can easily be resolved if you know the rules according to your card issuer. Most advise to always check your bill carefully, and if you notice a charge on your statement that you are pretty sure you didn't make (or any other inaccuracy, for that matter, such as a charge amount), notify your card issuer immediately. Some may even require you notify them within 30 days of the statement date of issue.

Call the toll-free number on your statement and give the details of the transaction. For your own files, record the full name of the customer representative who helped you. Your card issuer may request a copy of a sales receipt from the merchant in question. If so, your card issuer will mail a copy to you, along with an accompanying letter confirming your request. This can take up to 60 days. If you are still certain you never made the charge and it doesn't belong on your account, sign the back of the letter and send it back, according to the instructions from your card issuer. Visa or MasterCard will deal with the merchant directly to correct the disputed charge on your behalf.

Merchants are ultimately responsible for checking the customer's signature against the one on the back of the card. Purchasing via telephone and Internet makes this difficult to do if someone else has stolen your credit card, for example.

Credit Card Fraud

Credit card fraud is a major issue in Canada. It's the reason credit card interest rates are so high—to cover the losses (to the tune of $162 million in 1999) split between the issuers of Visa, MasterCard and American Express, according to the Canadian Bankers Association.

Credit card fraud breaks down into the following categories: counterfeit cards, 34 percent; lost / stolen cards, 32 percent; no card (usually perpetrated when a bogus telemarketer gets a credit card number from someone, then uses it), 23 percent; non-receipt fraud, where the newly issued card is intercepted en route to the owner, and then used, 5.5 percent (notably, a 10 percent decline from 1991–92); fraud applications, where someone applies for a credit card by impersonating as someone with a good credit rating, 1.5 percent.

To avoid being a victim of credit card fraud:

Over Your Limit

According to a Canadian Bankers Association statistic, in 1999, the average credit card interest rates for standard cards issued by the six largest banks have dropped by 3.4 percent since their peak in October 1990.

➤ Never give your credit card number over the phone to someone who has called you.

➤ Don't leave your credit card unguarded. A study in Eastern Canada found that cards were most commonly stolen from the workplace, car glove compartments, and health clubs or golf courses, presumably, the locker rooms.

➤ Rip up carbon receipts.

➤ Check your monthly statement for inaccuracies.

➤ Report a lost or stolen card immediately.

➤ Don't lend your credit card to other people, even family members. Ultimately, the card is your responsibility.

Bankruptcy

A final way to get out of credit card debt is to file for bankruptcy protection. Bankruptcy completely wipes out unsecured debts such as credit cards. You could owe $100 000 on your credit cards and have that entire amount wiped clean. Almost all consumers who have filed bankruptcy in the past few years have done so to get rid of excess credit card debt.

The Smart Way to Use Credit Cards

You can do several things to make sure that you do not fall for the "buy now, pay later" ruse again. The most important is to begin to use credit cards properly, to use them as the financially literate do.

These suggested proper uses of credit cards won't get you further into debt:

Pay the bill in full every month. This is the first rule for a reason. Every time you allow your balance to carry forward to another month, you are giving your credit card issuers more of your hard-earned money. If you can't afford to pay for the charge, then you shouldn't be charging it.

Borrow when it costs you nothing. As we said earlier, charging something at the right time of the month allows you to go almost two months without paying any interest.

Budget for an emergency. As we discussed in earlier chapters, you should have some money set aside for a rainy day. Some of that money ($3000 is a good amount) should be earmarked for credit card emergencies. Credit cards come in most handy in a crisis. If you need a tow truck or have to go on a sudden trip, charging it makes a lot of sense. Just remember to use your emergency stash to pay off the card when the bill comes and then replenish your emergency fund.

Budget for pleasure. Credit cards are a necessity when you travel for fun. Use them all you want, but be sure that you won't be breaking the first rule by doing so.

Toss solicitations in the trash. Throw away, unopened, all credit card offers you are receiving in the mail. You don't need more credit.

Cut up cards you are no longer using and cancel the accounts.

Credit cards are great. They are easy to use and allow you the opportunity to buy and do things you would otherwise normally not be able to. In fact, they are too easy to use. That is how you fell into the trap in the first place, and it is a difficult trap to get out of. It will take time and effort on your part.

The Least You Need to Know

➤ Don't make getting out of the credit card trap harder by continuing to do what you have always done.

➤ Get better terms, either from your existing cards or from a new one.

➤ When all else fails, complain.

Chapter 12

Talking to the Lion: Dealing with Creditors

In This Chapter

➤ Cutting a deal

➤ Understanding your legal rights

➤ Getting creditors to leave you alone

➤ Cleaning up your credit report

➤ Avoiding scams

What we want to do in this chapter is show you some tactics you can utilize when it is just not possible to pay the full amount you owe. At that point, your creditors will be harassing and threatening you. Here, we show you how to force creditors to leave you alone and how to negotiate a reduced payoff. Fear not. Relief is in sight. Creditors can be tamed, if you know what to do.

Dealing with the Original Creditor

The first thing to ask yourself is whether you are dealing with the original creditor or a collection agency. As a general rule, original creditors are not nearly as difficult to deal with as collection agencies.

Who you are dealing with usually depends on how late you are with your bill. After a debt is more than say, six months old, the original creditor will probably sell it at a discount or give a percentage of any recovery to a collection agency.

The Payment Plan

Your chances of settling your problem reasonably and with a modicum of dignity are best when you deal with the original creditor. The department store or dentist, for example, will usually try to work with you to settle your outstanding debt. The plan usually means that you make regular monthly payments for an amount you can afford. If you do make a concerted effort to pay your bill, even at something like $25 a month, the original creditor will usually accept the payment, albeit begrudgingly. It is when you stop paying altogether that creditors become upset.

We Can Work It Out

When you cannot pay your bills in full, another option is to negotiate with your creditors and see whether any of them would be willing to accept less than full payment. Here is how to do it: Write a letter explaining to your creditor that you would like to settle your account in full, but that you are unable to do so. Your letter should go on to offer a settlement for an amount less than you owe.

Why would a creditor accept such a proposal? Because, you explain, if it does not, you will have no choice but to declare bankruptcy, in which case, it will probably get nothing. Fifty cents on the dollar starts to look like a pretty good deal.

Although you can try to get your creditor to accept monthly payments for the reduced sum, we think you will have a much better chance of success in your negotiations if you can offer to pay the reduced sum in full.

It is important to realize that if this letter does not work, or you otherwise ignore your creditors, you will end up with a very negative credit history, not to mention the fact

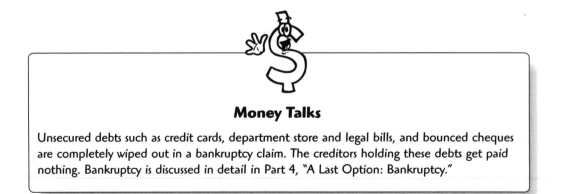

Money Talks

Unsecured debts such as credit cards, department store and legal bills, and bounced cheques are completely wiped out in a bankruptcy claim. The creditors holding these debts get paid nothing. Bankruptcy is discussed in detail in Part 4, "A Last Option: Bankruptcy."

ABC Creditor
2734 Queensway
Saskatoon, Sask.

Re: Account No. 2727

Dear Customer Service:

As I have told you over the phone, I am unable to pay my debt to you any longer. I am writing today to see whether you would be interested in settling my account. I have learned that I could completely erase all of my debts by filing for bankruptcy. I would like to avoid that if at all possible. Therefore, I make the following offer:

1. In consideration for immediate payment of $ _____ (the "Settlement Amount"), which is 20 percent of the outstanding balance I owe your company I, _____ ("Debtor"), and your company, _____ ("Creditor"), agree to fully, completely, and forever compromise and settle this debt. *(Start your offer low, at 20 percent or so, so that you can negotiate a bit higher if necessary later on.)*

2. Creditor agrees to accept the Settlement Amount as payment in full for all possible obligations Debtor may have with Creditor. *(Once your creditor accepts this offer, or something similar, this "Settlement Amount" is all you will owe.)* Creditor further agrees to cease all collection activities regarding this debt, to cease all legal proceedings against Debtor, and to fully release and hold harmless Debtor from any further obligations arising from this debt. *(These points are negotiable. What you really care about is settling your debt for an amount substantially less than you owe.)*

3. Within five days of receipt of a signed copy of this letter, Debtor will forward to Creditor the Settlement Amount via certified cheque or money order. This settlement will only take effect after both parties have signed this letter and the Creditor has received the Settlement Amount. *(If you fail to pay, the settlement will be of no effect.)*

Considering the fact that I could pay you back nothing by declaring bankruptcy, I think that this settlement offer constitutes a quick and equitable solution to this problem for both parties. If you agree to the terms of this settlement, please have the appropriate person sign below, return this letter back to me, and I will immediately forward the Settlement Amount to you. Thank you for your consideration in this matter.

Very truly yours,

Dated _____ *(Your name)*

AGREED AND ACCEPTED

Dated _____ *(Your creditor)*

that you will lose peace of mind and future credit. If you can settle these debts before things get out of hand, you are better off.

The Cost of Education

Government subsidies to post-secondary education have decreased an average of 20 percent across Canada since 1993, according to the Association of Universities and Colleges of Canada. It was well under $7000 per student in 1998, down from a high of $11 500 per student in 1978.

As a result, post-secondary education costs in Canada have doubled between 1993 and 2000, says the Canadian Federation of Students, to an average of roughly $6000 to $7000 a year in tuition costs alone. So it's no coincidence that student loans, dispensed by both provincial and the federal government, are also on the rise. For so many graduates, landing a job after school takes a while, and sometimes another degree is necessary to increase the graduate's chance at getting a job. Next thing you know, you owe tens of thousands of dollars.

Statistics Canada reported in 1999 that students in community college and undergraduate university programs between 1990 and 1996 borrowed more money than ever and found it increasingly difficult to pay it back. While one in five students graduating in 1990/1991 found it difficult to meet loan payment requirements, that number increased to one in three for graduates in 1995/96. What's more, the 98 878 borrowing students who graduated in 1990/91 owed on average $6810. In 1995/96, 148 731 students owed on average $7725. In total, the 1995/96 students consolidated more than $1.1 billion in loans, representing a 70.6 percent increase from the beginning of the decade.

Paying off Student Loans

Payments for Canada Student Loans, granted by the federal government, start six months after you cease being a full-time student. As of 1998, you are allowed to claim a 17 percent tax credit on the interest portion of the amount paid on your student loan each year. StatsCan reported that 21.8 percent of the students graduating in 1995/96 defaulted on their loans within the first year, up from 17.6 percent from five years earlier. If you default on the loan, the government can take the same steps of any creditor to collect its money, first by reporting you to a credit agency, by hiring collection agencies, or even taking legal action. (Changes to the Bankruptcy Act in 1998 made student loans non-exempt in the case of a bankruptcy, unless the loan was more than ten years old.)

The Interest Relief Plan

If you're having trouble making your student loan payments, the government may give you a break by paying the interest on your loan. Interest Relief is usually limited to three-month periods to a maximum of 30 months throughout the lifetime of the loan. To be eligible for interest relief, your total family income must be below a level determined by the size of your family and size of your monthly payment. Other unexpected emergency costs may also qualify you for interest relief.

Extended Interest Relief

If, after 30 months, you still cannot make payments, ask your lending institution to extend the loan repayment period to 15 years. If they agree, your monthly payments will be lowered by 25 percent.

Debt Reduction

If your annual payments exceed a given percentage of your income, the government may just give you a break entirely, and lop off a maximum of $10 000 or 50 percent of the principal of your loan, whichever is less. The loan must be at least five years old, and you must have exhausted all previously mentioned options before qualifying for debt reduction.

Discuss your situation frankly with your lending institution, in the hopes that your lender will revise the payment plans to be more manageable.

Pay No Attention to That Man Behind the Curtain

If you are unable to pay your dental bill, for example, at some point the dentist will sell your debt to a collection agency. Most original creditors would rather sell the debt at a steep discount than continue to try and pry money from you if you don't have it.

An important thing to realize about collection agencies is that their bark is usually far worse than their bite. Yes, they can threaten you, seemingly harass you (which is illegal, as you'll find out later in this chapter), and cause you to stop answering your phone. But that is about it.

Empty Threats

There is much collection agencies cannot do. Can they garnish your wages? No. They may threaten to if you do not pay that bill, but the truth is that they cannot do it. There are only three instances when a creditor can garnish your wages:

➤ If you owe on a student loan, special rules allow the government to garnish your wages. The government can garnish your wages, but more commonly, they will garnish your income tax refunds, and they don't have to warn you either.

➤ If you owe child support, your monthly payment can be garnished from your paycheque.

119

➤ Any other creditor can garnish your wages only when it has sued you, won the suit, and received permission from the court to garnish. You will know if this is happening to you.

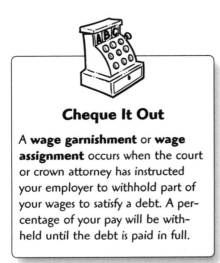

Cheque It Out

A **wage garnishment** or **wage assignment** occurs when the court or crown attorney has instructed your employer to withhold part of your wages to satisfy a debt. A percentage of your pay will be withheld until the debt is paid in full.

If none of these situations applies to you, you should understand that when a creditor threatens to garnish your wages, he is blowing smoke.

Can collection agencies have you thrown in jail? No. Can they threaten you? Sure, but they're not allowed to. But so what? Most of their threats are hollow. They tell you that if five post-dated cheques are not received by the next day, a suit will be filed. Or they might say that if $500 is not in hand by Friday, your bank accounts will be seized. Baloney.

The truth is, most of their threats are empty, and there is no deadline. They make it all up. If the deadline passes, nothing happens. The threat and deadline are nothing more than tactics they use to try and get some money out of you. Do not fall for their threats.

Will the collection agency sue you? Probably not. Lawsuits for consumer debts happen in a surprisingly small number of cases. Depending upon the size of your debt, it is normally too expensive for the original creditor or the collection agency to file suit. And even if it did win a judgment, what is the likelihood that it will ever collect on it? These lawsuits are usually just not cost-effective. That is why collection agencies prefer to make threats: They're cheaper.

Turn the Tides

Knowing that a lawsuit is unlikely, you can turn the tables and demand that the debate be held on your terms. The key thing to remember when dealing with a collection agency is that, believe it or not, you have all the power. You control the chequebook. If you decide not to pay, the collection agency doesn't get paid. If you tell the agencies to leave you alone, they have to leave you alone. Most collection agencies are nothing more than bluffing bullies.

Know Your Rights

Debt collection is governed provincially from the office of consumer and corporate affairs (each province has one, although the names are a little different from province to province—a list appears in appendix C). Debt collectors must be licensed in the province in which they work. If they move to another province, they must obtain their licence in that province too. Though each province and territory's legislation differs slightly, their gist is the same: to protect your rights. For instance, in Ontario, collection agencies are forbidden from:

➤ **Calling at the wrong place or the wrong time.** A collection agency rep cannot call before 7:00 A.M. or after 9:00 P.M. He or she can't call on a Sunday or a statory holiday, and can't call you at work if you have asked them not to.

➤ **Making inappropriate threats.** A collection agency rep can't swear at you or threaten you with violence, repossession, or jail time.

➤ **Misrepresenting itself.** A collection agency rep has to identify himself, the name of the creditor, the name of his company, and the amount of money owing, every time he contacts you. In other words, he can't fish for information without you knowing what's going on.

➤ **Giving misleading information.** A collection agency rep can't give any false or misleading information about you to anyone, such as an employer, that might be harmful to you or your family.

Knowing what is acceptable creditor behaviour can pay tremendous dividends. If an annoying creditor persists in calling you at work, tell him to stop. If he threatens to have your car sold to pay the debt, tell him such threats are illegal. Make sure that when you speak with an annoying creditor, you use the words "Pursuant to the Collection Agencies Act you cannot ...." This phrase lets him know that you know what you are talking about. (See appendix C for the correct legal title in your province.)

If a collection agency continues to violate the law after being told to stop, you have two options:

1. **Contact the proper authorities.** Industry Canada, through its provincial consumer affairs departments, polices collection agencies. See the list of provincial departments in appendix C. Ask them to send you a complaint form. Fill it in, send it back, and keep a copy for yourself.

2. **Contact the police.** The collection agency might be liable for charges ranging from extortion, to assault, to making harassing phone calls.

3. **Contact the community legal clinic near you.** Legal Aid helps people with low incomes.

Do Nothing

A final option is to merely take no action at all. If you ignore your creditors' threats, they may make a lot of annoying phone calls and threaten to sue you, but, as we have said, if the debt is not too large, they usually eventually forget about you. If you live month-to-month and have few assets, you are what lawyers call an "empty pocket" or "judgment proof." No creditor would waste money suing you because the likelihood of ever getting any money back is remote.

Over Your Limit

If you are ever sued for a debt you did not pay, the suit will likely occur in small claims court. Though each province is different, the maximum a creditor can collect in small claims court is usually $5000. You cannot have a lawyer defend you in small claims court.

In most cases, your creditor will probably write off your debt as uncollectable and get a tax break for it. After six years, the bad debt will fall off of your credit report.

Credit Reporting

As you know too well, everyone has a credit history. The two largest companies who keep track of your bill-paying habits are Equifax Canada Inc., and Trans Union Consumer. Each company has a file on you. Credit reports are valuable to new creditors because they show your past financial patterns.

Credit reports include your

> ➤ Name, marital status, and date of birth
> ➤ Social Insurance number

➤ Address

➤ Where you work, including previous employers, positions held and duration of employment

➤ Credit information, including your current financial situation, how much money you owe and to whom, who you've borrowed money from in the past, and how regularly you paid them back

➤ A list of people who have made credit inquiries about you

➤ Public information: Any of your financial affairs that have made it into the public record, including bankruptcies, judgments against you, and tax liens.

Any information about political affiliations, race, colour, religion, or information about criminal charges that did not result in a conviction is not allowed in your credit report. Negative credit information can only sit on the file for six years.

A lot of incorrect information shows up on a lot of credit reports. How? You could be cross-referenced with another person with the same name, or it's possible that the incorrect information was submitted by the lender. Everyone makes mistakes.

What is Your Credit Rating?

Your credit profile is assigned a number based on the following:

R0   Too new to rate; approved but not used

R1   Pays within 30 days of billing, or pays as agreed

R2   Pays in more than 30 days but less than 60 or one payment past due

R3   Pays in more than 60 days but less than 90 or two payments past due

R4   Pays in more than 90 days but less than 120 or three or more payments past due

R5   Account is at least 120 days past due but is not yet rated R9

R6   No rating exists

R7   Paid through a consolidation order, consumer proposal, or credit counseling debt management program

R8   Repossession

R9   Bad debt or placed for collection or bankruptcy

Common Errors

Common errors on credit reports include the following:

➤ **Outdated information.** Any derogatory information can stay on your report for only seven years. If something older than that is on your report, it can and should be removed.

➤ **Inaccuracies.** Credit agencies make many mistakes. An incorrect mark showing a late payment, a repossession that never occurred, or a mistaken tax lien is not unheard of.

Money Talks

One study found that nearly half of all Canadians believe they do not have a legal right to see their credit bureau report.

In order to rid your report of any mistakes, the first thing you will need to do is to get a copy of your report. Make sure you get a copy from both of the two major

Money Talks

Do you even have a credit rating? If you are not the primary holder of a credit card, or the first signator on a joint bank account, it's possible you do not even have a credit file. Many women, in particular, find after years of managing a household and paying bills on time, that once widowed, they have to apply for credit as though they were 18 years old. Ask to have a credit file established for you.

credit-reporting agencies; there could be mistakes on either one of them. A credit report normally costs about $10. If you have recently been denied credit, insurance, or employment because of a credit report, you can also get a free copy from any of the credit-reporting agencies.

Correcting the Report

After reviewing your report, you may find several items that you feel are incomplete or incorrect and should not be on your credit report. Credit reporting is regulated provincially by the ministries responsible for consumer protection. In British Columbia, for example, the legislation is known as the Credit Reporting Act, though the name varies across the country.

Write a certified letter to the agency in question (so you can verify when the letter was received) and explain the nature of the dispute. Give the agency the required proof of identification. Explain the problem with the report and attach a copy of the report to your letter. Provide a written explanation of the charges in dispute. You are allowed 300 to 500 words to state your case, depending on the province in which you live. This is handy if you refused to pay for an inferior product, for example.

If you can prove that an item is in error, the problem will be easier to fix. For example, Muriel had bounced a cheque to the local hardware store, but she cleared up the debt a few months later. When she reviewed her Equifax credit report, she saw that the debt was listed as unpaid. Muriel found her receipt for the payment, photocopied it, and sent it along with a letter to Equifax, demanding that the item be corrected. It was.

The credit-reporting agency must investigate any item that you dispute, even ones that you cannot prove are false. The agency must then report back to you the results of its investigation within a month or so. If the agency cannot verify that its version of the disputed item is correct, then, by law, the agency must remove it from your credit report.

If an agency refuses to remove an item that you think should not be on your report any longer, then you have a couple of options:

Two Cents

The Collection Agencies Act also prevents a creditor from talking to your boss or co-workers about your debt.

1. You can always go back to the original creditor and see whether it will delete the item. But, unless you have paid the debt in full, removal using this method is unlikely.

2. You can contact the proper authorities. File a complaint with your provincial department of consumer affairs. This option requires time and patience in order to get the item(s) removed and your credit cleared.

Two Cents

To order a copy of your credit report, write to one of the following companies. (They'll likely have the same information, so just order from one company.)

Equifax Canada Inc., Box 190, Jean-Talon Station, Montreal, Quebec, H1S 2Z2, or call 1–800–465–7166. You may also be able to order your report on-line from www.equifax.ca. Written requests require two pieces of signed, photocopied identification (your driver's licence, birth certificate, or passport), plus a letter stating your current address, previous address, date of birth, and a phone number that you can reached at during the day.

Credit reports from Trans Union of Canada can be obtained by writing Trans Union, Consumer Relations Department, P.O. Box 338–LCD1, Hamilton, Ontario L8L 7W2, or calling 1–800–663–9980.

3. For larger damages, you could consider filing a suit in small claims court, though waiting lists are notoriously long (about 18 months). This option should be considered a last resort.

Beware of Credit–Repair Scams

You may have seen classifed ads selling credit-repair services, whereby a company will claim to "fix" your bad credit report and give you a clean slate. There's a fee, of course, and you have to pay it up-front. By now, the warning bells should be going off loud and clear.

There is no way to fix a bad credit report; no one can compel a credit reporting agency to remove a correct negative item before the legal time is up. There are no "loop-holes" that these so-called credit repair companies can use to get such changes made. In short, a credit-repair service isn't doing anything that you couldn't do yourself. The only thing that will repair a negative credit history is good credit practices over a period of time, advises Industry Canada. Don't fall for the moneyback guarantee either, since the company probably won't be in business long enough for you to collect.

There are other credit-repair scams that involve creating a new credit identity, using false information such as name or social insurance number and address, or omitting bad credit information on applications for credit. All of these example are dangerously illegal, and you should stay away from anyone advising you to take any of these steps.

The Least You Need to Know

➤ Credit collectors love to make empty threats.

➤ You have the right to be left alone.

➤ You may be able to negotiate a lower payment if you can come up with a lump-sum settlement.

➤ If you are judgment-proof, doing nothing may be a fine solution to creditor problems.

➤ You can have incorrect items removed from your credit report.

Chapter 13

Revenue Canada Folks Are People, Too

> **In This Chapter**
> ➤ How Revenue Canada really works
> ➤ Filing returns
> ➤ Payment plans
> ➤ Audits
> ➤ Audit appeals

Taxes are a special breed of debt problems. All of the techniques and tools that have been offered so far in this book are inapplicable to tax problems because Revenue Canada (now known as the Canada Customs and Revenue Agency or CCRA) is, as you probably know all too well, an animal unto itself. In order to get out of your current tax situation, you must adhere to CCRA's special rules and regulations.

You can have a variety of problems where taxes are concerned. Filing returns, creating a payment plan, and dealing with an audit are discussed in this chapter.

What Happened to Revenue Canada?

On November 1, 1999, Revenue Canada became the Canada Customs and Revenue Agency. Though the organization's mandate is the same—"to promote compliance

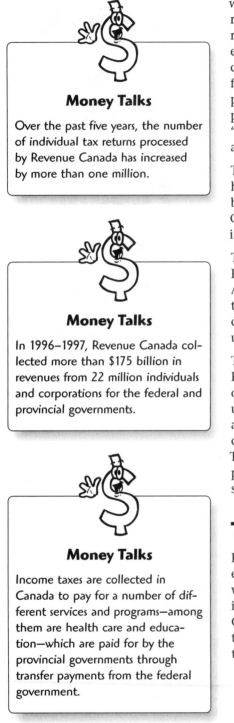

Money Talks

Over the past five years, the number of individual tax returns processed by Revenue Canada has increased by more than one million.

Money Talks

In 1996–1997, Revenue Canada collected more than $175 billion in revenues from 22 million individuals and corporations for the federal and provincial governments.

Money Talks

Income taxes are collected in Canada to pay for a number of different services and programs—among them are health care and education—which are paid for by the provincial governments through transfer payments from the federal government.

with Canada's tax [trade and border] legislation and regulations through education, quality service, and responsible enforcement, thereby contributing to the economic and social well-being of Canadians"—it claims that being structured as an agency gives it the flexibility to improve its services to the Canadian tax payer. As an agency, it says it can explore new partnerships with the provinces and territories to "streamline the collection of taxes and premiums" for an estimated savings of $116 million a year.

The CCRA still aims to provide quality service and help clients pay their taxes and receive their due benefits. A newly drafted fairness policy outlines the CCRA's willingness to use its discretion in assessing individual tax situations and penalties.

The CCRA is accountable to the Minister of National Revenue, Parliament, and the Canadian public. Although it promotes and ensures the collection of taxes, it has nothing to do with how the taxes collected are spent in Canada. Those decisions are left up to the Department of Finance.

Though the American tax collection office—the Internal Revenue Service—is well-known for its reputation as an organization fraught with bureaucrats and tax form upon tax form, the CCRA is somewhat different. Taxes are becoming increasingly complicated to file, but you can still get somewhere with a simply written letter. There are not hundreds of forms for myriad requests and procedures. Having said that, the CCRA does follow a set of rules, as it must lest chaos reign.

The Fairness Provisions

In 1991, 1992, and 1993, the fairness provisions were enacted, which allow the CCRA to cancel, reduce, or waive, on a discretionary basis, certain penalties and interest payments. The fairness provisions allow the CCRA to resolve problems that are not the fault of the taxpayer, and which have prevented them from paying their taxes, such as:

➤ natural or human-made disasters, such as flood or fire;

➤ civil disturbance or disruptions in services,

such as a postal strike

➤ serious illness or accident

➤ serious emotional or mental distress, such as the death of an immediate family member

To make a fairness provision request, simply writer a letter to your local CCRA office, whose addresses are available on the Web site www.ccra-adrc.gc.ca, or listed in the appendix.

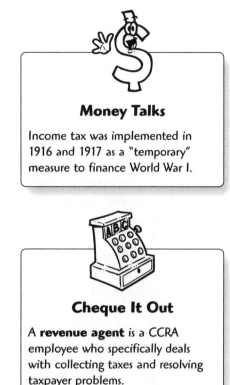

Money Talks

Income tax was implemented in 1916 and 1917 as a "temporary" measure to finance World War I.

The First Commandment: Thou Shalt File Thy Taxes

The first thing to understand about taxes is that even if you don't have the money to pay them, your return—if you owe money—should be filed on time. Not filing on time, even if you do not have the money to pay the amount due, is just plain dumb. The penalty for not filing your tax return on time is 5 percent, plus a further 1 percent a month to a maximum of 12%. If you file late a second time, then the penalty doubles to 10%, with a 2 percent monthly charge to 20 months. On the other hand, you file on time, but fail to remit payment, you will be liable for

Cheque It Out

A **revenue agent** is a CCRA employee who specifically deals with collecting taxes and resolving taxpayer problems.

interest on the unpaid amounts, but there is no other monetary penalty. File on time, even if you can't pay a penny. Just send in the forms without a cheque. Failing to pay taxes can rack up costly penalties as time goes on, and can even land you in jail.

For example, assume that Marty owes the CCRA $10 000. If he files on time and doesn't send a cheque, he will owe the CCRA interest on the $10 000 (based on the average

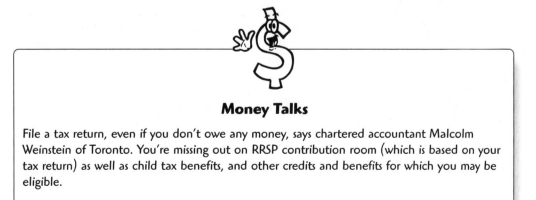

Money Talks

File a tax return, even if you don't owe any money, says chartered accountant Malcolm Weinstein of Toronto. You're missing out on RRSP contribution room (which is based on your tax return) as well as child tax benefits, and other credits and benefits for which you may be eligible.

Money Talks

Settle matters with the CCRA as promptly as possible. As a university student, John owed less than a hundred dollars to the government in taxes one year because he calculated his return incorrectly. Instead of paying it off, or discussing the amount with the agency, he let the payment slip year after year. The interest charges outgrew the actual amount he owed, to the point where he owed the CCRA hundreds of dollars.

interest rate on 90-day treasury bills, which can be as high as 15%), so let's say, $150. If he does not file at all, he will owe the CCRA an additional $500 (5 percent of $10 000) plus $100 a month (1% of $10 000).

In Canada, you must pay income tax to the federal and provincial governments. Residents of Quebec must file two returns.

Voluntary Disclosure

The CCRA is a reasonable body. If you have never filed (or stopped filing) income tax returns (assuming, or course, that you owe money), or if you have never filed (or stopped filing) GST/HST returns, you can volunteer to provide the information and the owed funds. In doing so, you will only have to pay what you owe plus interest. There will be no penalty, and the CCRA will not prosecute or impose any other civil penalties, as long as you beat the CCRA to an audit, investigation, collection, or other enforcement action, including a request to file a return. Don't get caught behind the eight ball. Take proactive measures to minimize your payments.

Two Cents

If you have a computer and an Internet connection, you can download almost any CCRA form from its Web site. You can reach the CCRA by going to www.ccra-adrc.gc.ca.

Filing for an Extension of Time

If you cannot file your taxes by April 30, you should ask for an extension of time, in writing, with which to file. Every year thousands of taxpayers request the CCRA for an extension of time to file and/or pay.

Contact your local District Taxation Office and inform them why you cannot file or pay, and the appropriate agents of the CCRA will give consideration to your request.

Failing to File

The Canadian income tax system is a self-assessing system. If you owe money, the CCRA will file a return for you and make its own calculations, but it is obviously not in your best interest to let this happen. The agency will not concern itself with tax deductions for which you may be eligible, not will it calculate your expenses and/or tax credits.

The CCRA has several methods of finding out whether you have filed a return. The most common are the following:

➤ **T4s.** These wage statements are filed by employers. If an employer declares in a T4 that he paid you $2500 last year, and the CCRA computer fails to find a return by you stating the same thing, you are caught.

➤ **T5s.** These are income statements. If your financial institution reports that you earned $100 on an investment last year, for example, and those CCRA computers find no corresponding return, you're caught.

If You Do Not Have Records

If you do not have records for the year(s) in question, you can request that the CCRA give you a copy of its records. Request in writing, and the CCRA will send you a computer printout of the information it has—T4s and T5s, for example.

Over Your Limit

If you fail to file your income tax return, you could face fines (besides the interest and penalties) of up to $25 000 or up to 12 months imprisonment.

Keep Your Paperwork in Order

Each year, Canadians pay too much tax because they do not have their paperwork in order. According to Revenue Canada the five most common errors found on personal income tax returns filed by Canadians are:

➤ Mathematical errors made in calculating tax credits, surtaxes, and total taxes payable

➤ Improper Registered Retirement Savings Plan deductions

➤ Taxpayers who fail to claim certain tax credits that can be transferred between spouses or between a parent and his dependant child

➤ Taxpayers who neglect to claim provincial tax credits, where applicable

Two Cents

Self-employed individuals have until June 15 to file their taxes.

➤ Taxpayers who do not claim certain interest expenses and other "carrying charges" incurred in the year.

What Happens to Your Return

Once you file your tax return, the CCRA computers begin what is called a desk audit, whereby the agency checks to make sure you've calculated your taxes correctly. Every return, whether filed manually or electronically, is checked to see that there are no obvious errors in calculation.

The next step is to check that the information on the return matches the information given by employers. Approximately 70 percent of Canadians have employers who send T4 slips to the government. It is easy to check that these amounts correspond. If they don't, then the CCRA will follow-up.

Next, the CCRA checks supporting material such as T5s, which record any investment income, or RRSP receipts, charitable receipts, or medical expense bills which have been claimed on the return. If any of these items are missing, the CCRA will contact you. If you file electronically, these supporting documents are often also requested.

If you are among the 30 percent of self-employed Canadians, then your returns are more complicated and involved. The desk auditors have to cross reference a wide variety of supporting documents from several sources. If you have a number of inconsistencies in your return, the CCRA will develop a "taxpayer profile" and flag your file, increasing the possibility that you will be audited in the future.

Money Talks

Self-employed people making more than $30 000 gross income must apply to register for the Goods and Services/Harmonized Sales Tax. But even if you don't make that much, it's in your best interest to get a number and collect GST. First of all, a GST number says to clients that you are a serious business, and they will assume you have a certain level of income. Second of all, you are entitled to the many GST credits that allow you to get money back on GST you paid on business expenses.

You Made It

If everything looks in order, the CCRA will send you a Notice of Assessment. This form will tell you if you filed correctly, and include the appropriate adjustments either in or out of your favour. (This form also tells you how much RRSP contribution room you have for the coming year, so keep it on file.) Most tax filers calculate the correct amount, or come fairly close.

This notice is non-binding, however, and there is nothing preventing you from being reassessed, any time within three years of the date of mailing the original Assessment. On the other hand, if you find you have overpaid tax, you only have 90 days from the mailing date of the Assessment to file a Notice of Objection, or one year from the due date of the return, whichever is later.

You Didn't Make It

If the Notice tells you you filed incorrectly, the first thing the CCRA will request is further information. This doesn't necessarily mean you'll have to pay more tax.

If the CCRA thinks you filed incorrectly, you will receive a form letter describing the discrepancy and be given a certain amount of time to pay up or file a Notice of Objection. Do this by writing a letter to the Taxation Centre to which you mailed your return. Be sure to include your full name, address, identification number or Social Insurance Number, plus the amount owing according to the notice, and the reason you believe that number to be incorrect.

Unless you file an objection promptly, you are still bound to the 90-day payment deadline for the reassessed amount. Filing the Notice of Objection stops the clock for the payment deadline, but not for the interest accruing.

Payment Plans

When you file your return, you may not be able to afford to pay the taxes due. When this is the case, the best course of action is to pay as much as possible and request a monthly payment plan for the balance. Do this by enclosing a letter proposing your payment plan or a series of post-dated cheques. This is usually enough to keep the CCRA happy.

Over Your Limit

Besides banks, the auditor can get records from employers, ex-spouses, friends, government agencies, motor vehicle departments, and public records.

If You Refuse to Pay

The CCRA has limited rights when it comes to collecting disputed amounts, but remember, once the assessment is issued, the interest

clock starts ticking. It may be better to pay the disputed amount to avoid paying interest in the event that the CCRA is right; if you come out the winner, you can recover the disputed funds, as well as the interest. But wait, the interest will be taxable.

If the CCRA gets an idea that the stalling of collection is going to make it harder to get the amounts due, it can start collection proceedings immediately. Also, if it gets wind that the appeal or Notice of Objection was filed simply to delay the payment of assessed taxes, the agency can elect to charge a 10 percent penalty. If you fail to voluntarily pay amounts the CCRA is entitled to collect, the agency will collect the unpaid amount through garnishing, or the seizure and sale of assets. And you foot the bill.

The CCRA may collect delinquent taxes by garnishing wages, other income, or bank deposits, or by seizure and sale of assets. And finally, if the CCRA determines that a taxpayer is wilfully evading taxes, he or she is referred to the Department of Justice, where he or she faces criminal prosecution, the penalty of which can be from two months to five years in jail.

The Taxman Cometh

You may at some point in your life be one of the unlucky few to whom the CCRA issues a notice of reassessment for the purposes of a tax audit. The time limit given to the CCRA to audit a taxpayer is three years from the original filing of the taxes. If the CCRA suspects you of purposely defaulting or of fraud, the three years can be extended indefinitely, until the CCRA is satisfied.

Audits are "triggered" by any one of the following circumstances, says chartered accountant Malcolm Weinstein:

1. **Reporting certain deductions.** In certain years, the agency looks for hot deductions. In the past, this group has included taxpayers who have reported losses on rental properties and allowable business investment losses.

2. **Reporting certain types of income.** The agency decides to audit taxpayers who report income from a particular source, for instance, salespeople who work on commission are frequently investigated.

3. **A tip.** The agency hears from a third party that the taxpayer in question is taking advantage of a tax-free benefit to which he or she is not entitled.

4. **Past history.** The taxpayer has not kept good records when claiming all income and deductions on his personal income tax return and fails to show any improvement in his or her filing methods.

Money Talks

Although your chance of being audited in any given year is only about 1 percent, the chance of being audited sometime in your life is more like 45 percent The more money you make, the greater your chances are, and if you are self-employed, your chances are greater still.

Types of Audits

Most audits are conducted at a tax office. Before beginning an audit, the auditor will contact you to arrange a convenient time to start the audit. Before you arrive, he or she will have spent some time studying your return(s) and claims(s) for rebate. You may be interviewed about the general nature of your business.

The CCRA is probably looking for one or more of the following:

➤ Under-reported income

➤ Excessive expenses

➤ Improper exemptions

➤ Improper deductions

Auditors are overworked and, despite what you might think, will probably not pore over every aspect of the return in question. Far more likely is an audit that covers a few main areas of concern and lasts no more than a few hours. Cooperating with the auditor will help the process go ahead more smoothly and quickly.

Less likely are field audits conducted at your place of business. This type of audit is becoming more common, however, due to the administration and collection of the Goods and Services Tax/Harmonized Sales Tax. Field audits are more common for small business owners and are much more likely to result in additional money being owed. You are therefore advised to hire a tax professional to assist you with your field audit. And make sure you see an identification card from the auditor when he or she arrives at your premises.

The field auditor will be interested in the following:

➤ Verification of business expenses.

➤ Unreported income, especially if you have a cash business.

➤ Bank deposits. An auditor can easily tell if you underreported your income by checking to see how much money you deposited in the bank that year.

Preparing for an Audit

When you get the dreaded audit notice, take a deep breath. The experience will probably not be as bad as you fear. Although you will probably owe additional taxes as a result of your audit (most audits end that way), you can minimize the amount you will owe by making a good impression. You do so by being informed, organized, and confident.

The first thing to do is to go over your return for the year in question. You need to understand how and why you listed things as you did. You must be able to answer the auditor's questions intelligently.

You also need to locate all records for the year in question. Get receipts, canceled cheques, books, records, logs, invoices, and calendars. Make a set for you and a set for the auditor. Not only will this save time, it will also make you look professional.

Money Talks

Never rely on advice you get from the Canada Customs Revenue Agency, unless it's in writing. CCRA agents have been known to be wrong, and if you make a claim or deduction based on verbal misinformation, it doesn't matter who the source was.

It is equally important to act appropriately at your audit. Be neither a meek mouse nor a loud lion. Stay cool. It is akin to a job interview; you want to act your best. Be polite, respectful, and confident and speak clearly. In the process, heed these warnings, too:

➤ **Do not say too much.** Offering too little information is always better than offering too much.

➤ **Do not be too helpful.** You should not volunteer to answer questions not asked and should not do things not requested.

➤ **Do not be a jerk.** The revenue officer is only doing his job. You don't have to like it to respect it.

After the audit is over, the auditor can make an assessment or reassessment until he or she is satisfied that the tax return is accurate. Once you receive the proposed assessment, and if you agree with it, or simply want to get the matter over with, you can either pay the amount due or request a payment plan.

It's Appealing

If you disagree with the proposed assessment, you can try to informally work out an agreeable solution with the auditor or his manager, or you can file a Notice of Objection, within 90 days of the new Notice of Assessment. (These rules are similar to the Notice of Objection mentioned previously.) The Notice of Objection must be in writing, outlining why you think the assessment is incorrect or unfair. Your letter should also be accompanied by a T400A, a Notice of Objection form, available from your local taxation office. Address your letter to the Chief of Appeals of your District office or a Taxation Centre of the CCRA (where you originally sent your return).

Once the District Office Appeals Officer receives your Notice of Objection, you'll be contacted, and possibly asked to make representations either in writing or at a meeting. The District Chief of Appeals may decide to settle the objections based on a mutual agreement with you.

If you cannot reach an agreement, the Chief of Appeals will either confirm the assessment or change it. If he or she confirms it, you'll receive notification via registered mail. If the Chief decides to change the assessment, you'll receive another notice of reassessment, also via registered mail.

Take the CCRA to Court

If the assessment is unsatisfactory, you have another 90 days to file another Notice of Objection, or, appeal the assessment to the Tax Court of Canada. To file an appeal, send a written appeal to: The Registrar of the Tax Court of Canada, Centennial Towers, 200 Kent Street, Ottawa, K1A 0G5. Consult form TLA7, available from your District Tax office, for the options available to you.

You do not need a lawyer to file an appeal or go to Tax Court. You can represent yourself, or have an accountant or someone else represent you.

The Least You Need to Know

➤ The CCRA claims to be a reasonable organization open to payment proposals and negotation.

➤ When dealing with the CCRA, act professionally; do not treat the agency as an adversary.

➤ The biggest mistake you can make with the CCRA is failing to file your tax returns.

➤ If you cannot pay all taxes due, a payment plan is a fine option.

➤ Audits are a game that can be won.

Chapter 14

Handling Business Debts

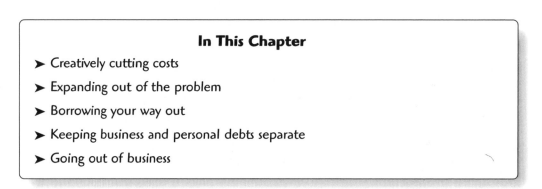

In This Chapter

➤ Creatively cutting costs

➤ Expanding out of the problem

➤ Borrowing your way out

➤ Keeping business and personal debts separate

➤ Going out of business

If you own your own small business, money and debt may be a constant issue. For many small businesses, money tends to come in the door in waves. When surf's up, all is well, but when things die down, you may feel stuck in the middle of an ocean with no land in sight. When you have serious business debts, you have a few basic alternatives. You can cut back, expand, or go out of business.

Reduce Your Overhead

First, you can cut your overhead and scale back. These are the same concepts we have discussed throughout this book, and they make sense in this situation, too. Sometimes you have to scale back a little; sometimes you have to scale back a lot. There are several ways to make sure that you are running a lean ship:

➤ **Control labour costs.** Labour is probably your highest business expense. Whole books are written on such management issues; all we suggest here is that you be sure that you are not overstaffed. Ask yourself whether you could further reduce labour costs by making an employee an independent contractor, thereby taking insurance, benefits, and tax withholding out of the labour equation. Use voice mail instead of having a receptionist. Be creative.

➤ **Reduce overhead.** Cut entertainment and other perks, compare insurance costs, and cut back on travel expenses.

➤ **Reward efficiency.** Make it profitable for employees to point out potential cost savings that you may have overlooked by giving them a bonus for any cost-saving ideas of theirs that you implement.

Although we do recommend running a tight ship, we do not recommend running a ship so tight it cannot sail. Scaling back your business, if done incorrectly and with too much zeal, can mean scaling back your primary source of income. Do not get rid of employees you will need again later. That is going too far.

We would never recommend that you work fewer hours (and thereby make less money) to get out of personal debt, and we do not recommend scaling back your business to the point of making less money as a way to get out of business debt. We understand that there are times that a radical scaling back of the business is necessary. That is fine and should definitely be explored. The important thing to remember is that you need to make more money right now, not less; although tightening the belt is good, doing so to the point of cutting off all circulation is bad.

Begin with the Right Attitude

Your second option is to make more money. Instead of constricting your business, consider expanding it instead to solve your cash crunch.

In order to expand your way out of your problem, you are going to have to return to

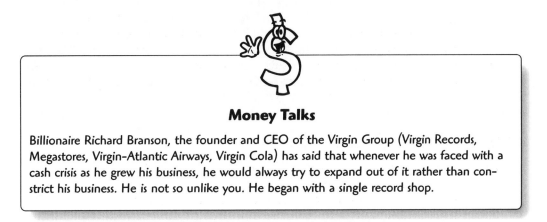

Money Talks

Billionaire Richard Branson, the founder and CEO of the Virgin Group (Virgin Records, Megastores, Virgin-Atlantic Airways, Virgin Cola) has said that whenever he was faced with a cash crisis as he grew his business, he would always try to expand out of it rather than constrict his business. He is not so unlike you. He began with a single record shop.

your roots and think like you did when you first started your enterprise. When you began your business, you were undoubtedly creative when it came to initial financing. Maybe you used your life's savings to start your business. Maybe you financed it with credit cards. Maybe you took out a business loan. A family member could have helped. Possibly you used a variety of sources to get started.

The important thing to remember, and the mindset you have to get back to, is that nothing stopped you. Those who start their own businesses are passionate, driven people. It is trite, but true: You would not take no for an answer. Otherwise, you never would have been successful enough to worry about business debts in the first place.

If you have lost that mentality, you must regain it. (If you cannot regain it, then you must seriously consider shutting down the business or scaling it back to a part-time operation.) Humans are creatures of habit. What you must do is break some bad habits and try something new. How do we know that? Because if what you have been doing was working, you would not be reading this.

Two Cents

Friends and family finance 25 percent of all new business startups.

Two Cents

Banks used to require three guarantees, three years of tax returns, and 30 days to process a loan application. Today, if your business has a decent business credit history, banks lend up to $50 000 with no guarantees, no tax returns, and answers within 48 hours.

Take, for example, Omar. He and his wife immigrated to the Canada from Poland with nothing more than $50 in their pockets. A craftsman by trade, Omar began a small construction company, doing all the work himself initially. Within 10 years, he was grossing more than $1 million a year. Then his accountant embezzled $400 000.

Omar's business went bankrupt, and he had to start all over again. The problem was, he had no working capital. In construction, the bills come due as the job proceeds, but payment is not made until the project is completed. A lack of operating capital severely restricted his ability to run, let alone expand, his business.

Omar could not get a loan. Finally, after a year, he asked his bank for a line of credit. He was denied. He then took his banker out to lunch and asked again, and again he was denied. At the end of the lunch, he told his banker that he was going to be writing cheques against his account that he would not be able to cover for a few weeks and that the banker better figure out a way to cover them. He did write those cheques, sometimes for as much as $11 000 over his balance. The bank covered every one. Omar was then able to rebuild his company, and his relationship with his bank continued to prosper.

The moral? What one person can do, another can do.

If Omar can do it, you can, too. Think creatively. Do not take no for an answer.

Time for Some New Sources of Income

Aside from being creative financially when you started, you were probably pretty darn flexible when it came to making money. You were not sure what would work and in all likelihood tried a number of different methods for bringing in customers, clients, and cash. It is time to do that again.

After much trial and error in your business, you finally figured out what worked. In all likelihood, you then did that same thing over and over again. It could have been an ad that worked, a sale that brought in customers, a seminar, a location, or a stall at the Saturday public market.

In essence, you figured out your recipe for success and money. That is why money is called dough. You make your business dough by utilizing a recipe, a money-making recipe. Think about it. Isn't that what you did?

All successful businesses do the same. The entertainment industry does it. Hollywood has several recipes for movie-making success. They are called the romantic comedy, the teen-slasher pic, and the action adventure. Producers use these recipes over and over and over again. Stephen King's recipe is to scare the heck out of his audience. Television's favourite recipe is called the sitcom.

Microsoft, too, has a recipe (no, it's not called "protect your crappy product by creating a monopoly"). The recipe is to put out a new edition of Windows every few years. Ben & Jerry's Ice Cream's recipe is to create a great-tasting different flavour every so often and give it a cool name.

One way to expand out of your cash crisis is to create or learn a new recipe, a bigger and better recipe. This does not mean that you have to throw your old recipe away. It does

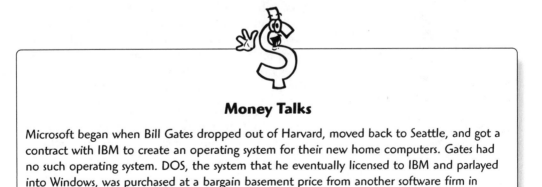

Money Talks

Microsoft began when Bill Gates dropped out of Harvard, moved back to Seattle, and got a contract with IBM to create an operating system for their new home computers. Gates had no such operating system. DOS, the system that he eventually licensed to IBM and parlayed into Windows, was purchased at a bargain basement price from another software firm in Seattle.

mean that it may be time to learn a new one in addition to the one(s) you already have, as in the following examples:

➤ A lawyer may want to begin to handle probate and divorce cases, in addition to his regular bankruptcy practice.

➤ An antiques dealer may want to start selling his wares on an Internet auction site in addition to selling from his store.

➤ A writer can start writing newsletters for big corporations in addition to the books she writes.

➤ A housekeeper can try to get some commercial clients in addition to her residential clients.

➤ A locksmith can start up a mobile service in addition to his shop.

Remember: A new recipe means more dough.

Alternate Sources of Income

Here is a revolutionary concept: You may want to get a job or start a second business. Stay with us here. Your probable problem is that you do not have enough income to cover your expenses. Finding a new recipe for your existing business is one way to create income. Another way is to create a second source of income.

The idea here is to create enough additional revenue to cover your overhead. A new income stream means more money for your business. Although we understand that you want to work for yourself, taking a job for a short-term infusion of cash is a way to keep the business afloat. It is not a sell-out if it allows you to keep the dream alive.

By the same token, starting another business is also a way to bring in more money. Azriela is a good example of this strategy. Besides a successful writing career—she writes books, has a nationally syndicated column, three online biweekly newsletters, and an entrepreneurial coaching practice (four recipes)—she is also a professional speaker. She does not rely solely on one occupation to bring in the money. You may want to consider the same thing.

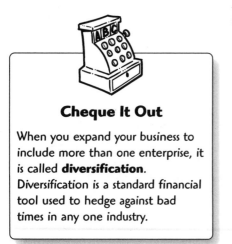

Cheque It Out

When you expand your business to include more than one enterprise, it is called **diversification**. Diversification is a standard financial tool used to hedge against bad times in any one industry.

A smart stock investor knows not to buy just one stock. That stock may go up, but it may go down. Having more than one stock ensures that when one stock does go down, the likelihood of taking a big financial hit is remote. Diversification is a good tool to use to adapt to changing financial situations.

As a savvy entrepreneur, you may want to do the same thing. Think in terms of multiple income sources instead of just one. This way of doing business has multiple advantages. All businesses have cycles. When one of your businesses is slow, it is unlikely that another will be as well. Instead of suffering a cash crisis, you are still able to keep money coming in.

Large businesses do the same thing. Amazon.com began selling books online. Now it sells CDs and gifts, conducts auctions, and has an interest in a pharmacy business.

Money Talks

Apple Computer, Dell Computer, Intuit (makers of Quicken software), and The Learning Annex all began as home-based businesses.

Give Yourself a Raise

Robyn runs a day-care business out of her home. She loves her kids and loves what she does. She is also always strapped for cash. Does she need a new recipe or another business? No. Robyn's problem has a far simpler solution. Robyn has not raised her prices in 10 years.

Because you are your own boss, you set the prices. When is the last time you raised your prices? Although you should be concerned that you will drive away clients if you do, it is still worth a shot. If your fears are valid, you can always lower your prices again. But if your fears are ungrounded, you will be giving yourself a well-deserved raise.

Azriela coached a professional who was very concerned about "inflicting" higher prices on her clients until she was able to see that it was also for their benefit. The woman was burning out and was unable to give her clients the service they deserved because she was taking on too many clients in order to pay the bills. By raising her prices, she was able to say no to some new clients and better serve her existing ones.

You will never know until you try. People who buy apartment houses for a living are always looking to purchase units where rents are too low for the area because they can raise rents upon completion of the sale. Such units are quite easy to find. If many landlords are charging too little, you certainly could be as well.

Receive Your Receivables

When you allow someone to buy your product "net 30" (that is, payable 30 days after the purchase), you are essentially lending that person money. Permitting these people extra time beyond 30 days to pay for a purchase is a commonplace, yet easily correctable, mistake. Would your bank allow you an extra 60 days to pay your loan? Of course not. Your business should be run the same way.

Always remember that accounts receivable (AR) are the lifeblood of your business, representing your business's cash flow and liquidity. Getting your receivables current, therefore, has two advantages:

It will bring in immediate cash.

It will make your business look better to potential lenders.

Here is how to get those friendly deadbeats to pay up:

➤ **Assign someone the task of contacting all AR over 30 days old** (or if you are a sole proprietor, you must prioritize this task for yourself). Get a specific date as to when the debt will be paid and call again on that day if the money is not received. You must remember this: a vow is just a vow. Begin with a friendly reminder but get increasingly aggressive as time goes by. Once an AR is more than 60 days old, you have a real problem.

➤ **Add interest.** Institute a new policy of at least 10 percent interest on all AR over 30 days old.

➤ **Stop all shipments.** Inform your repeat customers that all outstanding balances must be made current before any new product will be sent out.

➤ **Hire a professional.** As a penultimate resort, hire a lawyer or a collection agency to commence collection activities.

➤ **Sell the debt.** The money owed to you is a commodity and can be sold like one. Collection agencies buy bad debt every day, for a sharply discounted price. Expect bidding to begin at 50 percent of what you are owed.

Cheque It Out

Your **accounts receivable** is the total amount you are owed by all customers who have not yet paid you and is a great source of income in hard times.

Cheque It Out

Money is a **fungible** item. That means it is easily exchanged for other things, making it highly desirable. Accounts receivable, bad debts, and money owed are also fungible goods and also can be exchanged for money or services.

Business Loans

It's highly ironic: One way to get your business out of debt is to go into more debt. Sometimes business owners just need a short-term infusion of cash to get things moving again or maybe a long-term note or a line of credit might help.

Then again, a loan may be nothing more than a band-aid cure. Take Stephen, for example. He ran a consignment furniture store and got into the bad habit of not paying some consignors after he was paid. He ended up $10 000 in the hole, so he took out a loan and solved the short-term crisis, but he never changed his ways. He was finally forced out of business a few years later. Make sure that your loan will not fortify bad business practices, but will instead enable you to get through an unusual money crunch.

Several different types of business loans may be right for you:

1. **Accounts receivable financing.** This revolving line of credit is based upon your accounts receivable. Depending upon how much you are owed and the likelihood of repayment, this type of loan can speed cash flow to meet current obligations. As cash needs vary, the borrower is able to increase or reduce the loan amount without renegotiations, and the ability to borrow grows directly with accounts receivable.

   A typical program enables a client to borrow a predetermined percentage of accounts receivable, usually 80 percent. You would then receive periodic advances, upon request, deposited directly into your bank account. Interest is charged only on the amount funds advanced to you.

2. **Purchase order financing.** Say that you have a purchase order for $50 000 worth of widgets, but you need capital to service the account and get everything shipped. Using this method of financing, a borrower can obtain advances on designated purchase orders that can be repaid directly by the borrower's customer. This method of borrowing can be particularly convenient for large projects or when you only need to borrow money occasionally (only when you receive unusually large orders, for example).

3. **Inventory loans.** These funds are usually short-term and are used to take advantage of attractive purchasing opportunities or to support seasonal increases in inventory.

4. **Fixed asset loans.** These loans are based upon fixed assets (such as machinery you own) and can be used to acquire additional equipment and to improve a company's financial position by increasing working capital, consolidating debt, and reducing monthly payments.

5. **Business loans.** Banks have a history of being interested in financing loans for small businesses. In 1999, 93 percent of small- and medium-sized businesses who approached one of the seven chartered banks for financing reported that their loan applications were granted. According to an independent survey commissioned by the Canadian Bankers Association, loans were granted on the basis of the business case and how it is presented, rather than on the applicant's gender, visible minority, region, or type and size of business operation.

6. **Personal loans.** Mom and dad or other relatives may lend you money.

Keeping Business Debts and Personal Debts Separate

You may be tempted to dip into your personal pocket to help out your business. Maybe you want to use your credit cards to finance your business during a rough stretch, or you are being asked to personally guarantee a business loan.

Although we understand the desire to do this, we do not recommend this course of action. Yet we also know that it is commonplace. Indeed, two of your authors have broken this rule and mixed personal and business debt in order to keep their respective businesses going. If you do mix these debts, the important thing is to keep the debt manageable.

Caren made the mixing mistake. She helped found a nonprofit AIDS awareness organization and ran it for six years. Every time fund-raising slowed down, Caren took an advance on her credit cards to keep the organization afloat. After 10 years, it finally folded, and Caren was $40 000 in debt and unemployed. She was forced to file for bankruptcy.

One great way to keep your business and personal money lives separate is to incorporate your business. Although expensive (roughly $1000 for lawyer and provincial filing fees), incorporation has tremendous financial advantages.

The main one is that once you incorporate, you are personally off the hook insofar as liability goes. A disgruntled customer could sue your corporation, but not you. A creditor could legally go after the business, but not you personally. Incorporating protects your personal assets, your home, and your spouse's income from your creditors. To learn more about incorporation, talk to a certified accountant who specializes in small business incorporation.

Closing Up Shop

Going out of business, although unpleasant, is not the worst thing in the world. If your business debts are so bad that keeping the doors open is too difficult, closing up shop may be more a relief than a failure.

When shutting down a business, remember to do the wrong thing. You may be tempted to do the right thing, namely, borrow from yourself to pay off your business creditors (even though we already told you not to!). For instance, you might be tempted to take out a second mortgage to pay off everyone and close the doors with nothing owed. It would feel good. It would be dumb.

First, you will be unemployed. You do not know where you will be working or how much you will be making. Taking on additional debt at this point is the complete antithesis of everything we have been trying to teach you in this book. There are other ways to solve money problems besides incurring additional debt.

Second, you will be trading unsecured debt for secured debt. If you fail to pay some vendors, there is not a whole lot they can do. They surely cannot repossess your house. But if you pay them by refinancing your house, and then cannot pay the new mortgage, the bank can take your home. Never trade unsecured debt for secured debt.

You may have to go to the court of last resort. Although it is not our favourite solution, bankruptcy is one way to close a business, wipe out the debts (at least legally), and start over. We discuss this option in more detail in Part 4, "A Last Option—Bankruptcy."

The key point to take away from this chapter is this: There are many ways to get out of debt. Use your imagination and figure out what will work for you.

The Least You Need to Know

➤ Cutting back your business is okay; cutting into it is not.

➤ Expanding out of the problem is your best solution, if you can figure out a way to do it.

➤ Getting a loan to get out of debt may be oxymoronic, but it just might work.

➤ If you do mix business and personal debts, do so with caution.

Chapter 15

Credit Counselling

In This Chapter

➤ How it works

➤ Assessing your options

➤ Consolidation Loan

➤ Debt Repayment Program

➤ Is bankruptcy a way out for you?

Every year in Canada, tens of thousands of people seek credit counselling from their local Credit Counselling Service. There are several not-for-profit CCS offices, and other not-for-profit as well as for-profit credit counselling agencies. (Look for not-for-profit agencies that charge nothing or a token fee for their services. Remember, you want to save money, right?)

The Credit Counselling Service of Metropolitan Toronto, for example, helped 21 000 people in 1999. These individuals were looking for various levels of financial help, from basic budgeting skills and debt repayment, to advice on whether to declare bankruptcy. People seeking credit counselling are from all walks of life, income level, gender, and race.

The ultimate goal of credit counselling is to prevent a bankruptcy (or, if you've already declared bankruptcy, to make sure the same mistakes don't happen twice).

See appendix C for a list of credit counselling services near you.

How Does It Work?

The CCS is funded through payments from creditors, such as financial institutions, department stores, and collection agencies. In exchange for helping the creditors get paid, the creditor voluntarily pays CCS a percentage of the payment—anywhere from 22 percent for banks, to 10 percent for some retailers, such as Zellers. Smaller creditors, such as dentists or other health care professionals not covered under health insurance, or even family members or friends who made a personal loan, will usually agree to stop interest, but rarely contribute to the CCS.

Though creditors depend on the CCS to recover a lot of unpaid debt, and the CCS depends on creditors for their support, neither side is beholden to one another. Most creditors support CCS, because, ultimately, they don't want to see people go bankrupt, and they recognize that they were the ones who issued the credit card in the first place. They want to support the program, and want to have a positive, caring corporate image.

To creditors, the CCS represents a better way to recover unpaid debts than, say, collection agencies, who purchase the debt at a deep discount. The CCS does not buy debts from its clients, but rather, engineers their payment. Credit counselling is completely confidential.

Assessing Your Options

Once you've made an appointment with a credit counsellor, you're on your way to financial health, though it may be a slow recovery at first. The first visit with a credit counsellor is free, and carries no obligations. Most of the remaining counselling will also be free, depending on your particular situation. You may be asked to make a donation, or pay some small fee that is within your means.

First, the counsellor will want to hear your story and you may be asked to fill out some forms. Try not to be embarrassed about your financial situation. Just as your doctor has seen everything there is to see on the human body, a credit counsellor has seen just about every maxed-out credit card statement, and heard every collection agency horror story there is. Part of your "therapy" in learning to better manage your

Two Cents

When a credit counselling service starts helping you pay your debt, collection agencies have to stop harassing you.

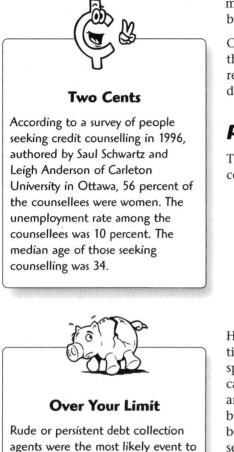

Two Cents

According to a survey of people seeking credit counselling in 1996, authored by Saul Schwartz and Leigh Anderson of Carleton University in Ottawa, 56 percent of the counsellees were women. The unemployment rate among the counsellees was 10 percent. The median age of those seeking counselling was 34.

Over Your Limit

Rude or persistent debt collection agents were the most likely event to prompt people to seek credit counselling, according to the 1996 survey.

money, is learning how to talk about money and not be afraid of it.

Credit counselling has two arms: one, a preventive arm that focuses on budgeting and education, and two, a remedial arm that helps people dig themselves out of debt.

Preventive Counselling

The credit counsellor will go over many of the topics covered in this book, for example:

➤ developing a realistic budget that helps reduce expenses;

➤ increasing income through a second part-time job or overtime hours;

➤ freeing up cash by parting with assets such as a second car, or moving to a smaller house or cheaper apartment.

He or she will try to see if there is a way that you can tip the balance in your favour so that you are not spending more than you earn every month. Through a careful analysis of your spending habits, your debts and assets, the counsellor will help you come up with a budget that is within your monthly means. You may be able to get rid of some of your debts just through self-discipline and hard work.

Remedial Counselling

For others in more dire situations, there is no amount of self-discipline or hard work that can help. The CCS offers two options here: the debt consolidation loan, and the debt repayment program. Both of these will nip the collection agencies in the bud; they will no longer be able to contact you, an immediate benefit.

Debt Consolidation Loan

A debt consolidation loan through the CCS is different than a bank consolidation loan. Through CCS, you are paying the creditors; through a bank, the bank is paying the creditors. However, the gist is the same—one lower monthly payment that stretches out the loan over a longer time period, but is easier to maintain. You make the payments to the CCS, and the CCS distributes the monthly payment for you to your creditors.

Bank consolidation loans are difficult to arrange if you are already behind on your bills. And increasingly, banks are insisting on loan collateral or a cosignor to guarantee the loan. Credit unions may be more flexible. And bank consolidation loans don't come with counselling. Unless you are prepared to cut up your credit cards and stop the pattern of overspending, debt consolidation will not likely work, except to get you into more debt.

A Debt Repayment Program

Many people who have already had contact with collection agencies enter into a Debt Repayment Program, comprising roughly one in five people who are seeking counselling. Here, the CCS intervenes on your behalf and asks your creditors to stop interest and reduce monthly payments, based on what you can afford with your newly conceived budget. If you've tried this approach with creditors to no avail, you may have more success with the CCS backing you up. According to the Credit Counselling Service of Metropolitan Toronto, the CCS has had better success in getting creditors to stop interest than their American counterparts. Creditors in Canada would appear to be more socially conscious.

A typical debt repayment program might cover a credit card debt of, say, $10 000. The monthly payment for a card like this might be $500. The CCS will try to reduce it by about 50 percent to $250 a month. You may be asked to pay about 10 percent of that amount to cover some administrative fees, but the actual amount is up to the discretion of the credit counsellor, who is ultimately looking after the best interest of the cash-strapped client.

Making Payments

In both a consolidation loan or a debt repayment program, individuals send the CCS a certified cheque or money order once a month, for the agreed-upon amount, or, in some offices, may transfer the money through telephone banking, which is the most cost-effective method of the three. The CCS places the money in a trust account and cheques are then mailed to your creditors every month. CCS offices that are "sanctioned" by Industry Canada are registered and licensed, so you need not fear your money is being siphoned into an off-shore account in the Grand Cayman Islands.

Money Talks

The Heart and Stroke Foundation of Canada's Annual Report Card, released in February 2000, revealed that one in five Canadians suffered stress due to finances. The foundation warns that too much stress can lead to heart disease and stroke.

Over Your Limit

More than half of the counsellees surveyed in 1996 rated too much borrowing or credit card use as a "very important" reason for seeking credit counselling.

Your Credit Rating

As your accounts are slowly being paid, your creditors may report to a credit bureau that your accounts are being paid. Even though the money is coming in slowly, the credit bureau still notes that you are making a sincere effort to resolve your debt problem.

Is Bankruptcy the Answer for Me?

Bankruptcy is like a financial death. We'll go into further detail of declaring bankruptcy in the next section, but suffice to say, it is the right decision for some, and not the right decision for others. Qualified credit counsellors can help you determine the pros and cons of declaring bankruptcy, and will direct you on your way if you decide to pursue bankruptcy.

Money Talks

Secured credit cards—which offer credit secured by a cash deposit—are not widely available through most financial institutions in Canada. But the CCS, through CIBC Visa, offers a secured credit card, with a minimum $500 deposit for $500 credit limit, to a maximum $5000 deposit for a credit limit of $5000.

The Least You Need to Know

➤ Choose a credit counselling service that is not-for-profit, and available at no cost or low-cost to you.

➤ A credit counsellor will help you work out a reasonable budget to make ends meet.

➤ A credit counsellor may suggest making some lifestyle changes to free up more cash to pay off debts.

➤ A credit counsellor can help you consolidate your debts into one lower, monthly payment.

➤ A credit counsellor can also speak to your creditors on your behalf and stop interest and reduce monthly payments to be in line with your budget.

Part 4

A Last Option—Bankruptcy

Sometimes you need to file bankruptcy to beat debt. Many people feel that bankruptcy is shameful (an indication of incompetence) or wrong (that people have a moral obligation to pay back all debts, even those charging 17 percent or more). Bankruptcy is an option you should consider. It's the law, and you're allowed to do it. Once you've done it, you cannot be discriminated against on the basis of your bankruptcy filing. And once you've gone through bankruptcy, your debts are gone, subject to some special exceptions explained in detail later in the section. Bankruptcy is complex; if you decide to file for bankruptcy, you will need a trustee in bankruptcy. This section contains a lot of information about bankruptcy. The decision is yours.

Chapter 16

Will Bankruptcy Help You?

In This Chapter

➤ What kind of debts do you have?

➤ Wiping out your debts

➤ What kind of assets do you own?

➤ Protecting your assets

Throughout this book, we have endeavoured to give you a variety of methods for handling your money problems. If budgeting better doesn't work, then maybe rethinking your relationship with money might. If negotiating with creditors has not worked, then possibly credit counseling is the answer. Then again, maybe none of these strategies is the answer. Maybe it's time for a fresh start. Maybe it's time to consider bankruptcy.

Luckily, we live in a country that believes in second chances. With regard to debt, the federal government provides that second chance in the form of the Bankruptcy and Insolvency Act (BIA).

The BIA grew out of the Poor Debtors' Assistance Program, created in 1972 to help people across the country who were trapped in impossible financial situations, with no way out. Prior to 1972, the bankruptcy level in Canada was quite low, especially

Money Talks

The highest bankruptcy rate in Canada in 1998 (by region) was in Quebec, at 3.4 per thousand. The lowest was British Columbia, at 1.9 per thousand.

for an industrialized country. In 1968, for example, according to BankruptcyCanada.com, there were just six bankruptcies per 100 000 people, significantly lower that the U.S. rate of 90 per 100 000.

Once the Poor Debtors' Assistance Program was in place, the bankruptcy rate began to climb, as more Canadians took advantage of the ability to declare bankruptcy more easily. During the recession of the early '80s, the bankruptcy rate rose by 33 percent in just one year. Once the economy began to pick up again by 1985, bankruptcies declined slightly. But since then the rate rose steeply, hitting record highs in 1997. In 1998, the bankruptcy rate in Canada was 2.6 per 1000, exactly half the rate as in the United States.

Take a deep breath. Although bankruptcy sounds scary, for many people, it is nothing short of a blessing.

But before you even begin to seriously consider filing for bankruptcy protection, you need to understand if it will help. The Bankruptcy Act sets standards and limits; if you don't meet these requirements, there is no use in filing. Either your case will not go through, some of your debts will not get discharged, or you will lose some assets that you don't want to lose. None of those are desirable outcomes, so you need to understand what is required, what type of debts are discharged, and how to best protect your assets.

How Much Do You Owe?

To be eligible to declare bankruptcy a person must be "insolvent". This means you must:

➤ owe at least $1000

➤ not have any way of paying your debts

All Debts Are Not Created Equal

There are two primary categories of debt: secured and unsecured debts. There are also other types of debt that you may have that don't fall into these broad categories, such as taxes, student loans, child support, and alimony. The important thing to figure out right now is whether declaring bankruptcy will get rid of your particular debts.

Secured Debts

Again, a secured debt is one that is attached to some sort of collateral, such as a car loan. A bank will happily lend you money to buy a car as long as the car is used as collateral to secure the loan. If you fail to pay back the loan, the bank will repossess the car and sell it to pay back the loan. The car secures the loan.

There are many other sorts of secured debts:

➤ **Mortgages.** Any time you borrow money against your home, a mortgage is created. All mortgages are secured against the house.

➤ **Judgment liens.** The holder of a judgment can file a lien against the property of the one who owes the judgment. That is called a judgment lien. When the property is sold (usually a house or car), the lien is paid before the defendant receives any money.

Cheque It Out

A **lien** is a document filed with the county recorder. It attaches to the property and must be paid off before title to the property is transferred to a new owner. Liens usually involve mortgages.

➤ **Big-ticket items.** Some electronics or computer items may be registered by the retailer or manufacturer with the provincial government (in Ontario, it's the Personal Property and Securities Act, but the name varies from province to province). This means that the product bought on credit is secured, but if you surrender the property back to the retailer during a bankruptcy, its resale value is considerably less. The retailer can file as an unsecured creditor for the difference.

The important thing to understand before filing bankruptcy is that **secured debts** are not automatically discharged in a bankruptcy. If you want to get a break on your mortgage payments, for example, bankruptcy will not help you. You'll have to talk with your mortgage holder, state your case and hope to make an alternate payment arrangement. Although your personal liability for the debt will be discharged, the security interest survives the bankruptcy. Stay with us here; this is a very important (albeit very difficult) concept to grasp. We'll try and make it simple.

A secured creditor essentially has two methods of collection if a debt is not repaid (before the debtor is bankrupt). The first is to take back the property securing the debt by repossessing the car or foreclosing on the house. But what if the resale of that property repossessed is not enough to cover the debt? Then the lender can always sue you for the difference. Why? Because of the second method ensuring repayment: your personal liability under the contract.

Jillian was sued for this very reason. She still owed $10 000 on her car when she was laid off from her job. She was unable to continue to make her car payments and thus her lender eventually repossessed her 1997 Honda Accord. The lender sold the car at a wholesale auction for $4000 and then sued Jillian for the $6000 balance she owed on her contract.

Had Jillian filed bankruptcy, she could not have been sued. Why? Because bankruptcy wipes out your personal liability for your debts. No liability means there is nothing to

159

Cheque It Out

When you buy an item on credit like a house or a car, the lender has two methods of being repaid. The first is the right to **repossess** the property and sell it again if you don't pay. The lender can do this because it has a stake in the property, called a security interest. The second method of repayment is the right to **sue** you for the money owed, because of your personal liability under the contract.

sue you over. Debts in bankruptcy are wiped out because the bankruptcy court issues an order stating that your personal liability for all debts has been discharged. Thus, for example, when a credit card debt is discharged, the credit card company can no longer come after you.

That is not true for secured creditors. In a bankruptcy, the security interest survives the bankruptcy even though your personal liability does not. What that means is that after a bankruptcy, a lender holding a security interest can still take the property back, but because your personal liability for the debt has been discharged, it cannot sue you for the difference. In Jillian's case, had she filed bankruptcy, the entire $6000 balance on her car loan would have been wiped out because she would no longer have had any personal liability for the debt.

The key point, then, when contemplating bankruptcy is that it is only your personal liability, not the security interest, that is discharged in your bankruptcy. If most of your debts are secured ones, bankruptcy may not solve your problems, although the option to get out of a bad contract still makes it attractive to some people.

Because the idea here is to get rid of debt, you might want to consider the surrender option. With a surrender, you simply give the car back to the lender. Because your personal liability will be wiped out with the bankruptcy discharge, and because your giving back the property means the lender already has its collateral back, your responsibility for the debt will be completely wiped out by the discharge. Your personal liability is gone, and the property is returned, so the lender has no more tools to get at you.

Unsecured Debts

Unsecured debts are not associated with any sort of collateral. Most of us have a lot of unsecured debt. The typical example is a credit card. When a credit card company issues you a credit card, it normally does not ask for any sort of collateral and so any debt you incur is considered unsecured debt.

Besides credit cards, the following are other types of unsecured debts:

➤ Dental or chiropractic bills

➤ Legal bills

➤ Utility bills

➤ Unsecured lines of credit

➤ Bounced cheques

The advantageous thing about unsecured debts (where bankruptcy is concerned) is that these debts are completely wiped out by a discharge. You could owe $75 000 to 10 different credit card companies, $3000 in dental bills, and another $2000 in other bills and have all of this debt discharged in your bankruptcy. In a bankruptcy there is no limit as to how much unsecured debt you can have discharged.

If you are having a difficult time figuring out whether a certain debt you have is secured or unsecured, the key question to ask yourself is this: Have you pledged any sort of collateral to secure the debt? If the answer is no, then the debt is unsecured. Most people have a lot of unsecured debts (credit cards mostly) and a couple of secured debts (car and home loans).

If you have a lot of unsecured debts, then filing for bankruptcy protection will help you a lot. Unsecured debts are the easiest type of debts to get discharged in a bankruptcy.

What Debts Are not Wiped out by a Bankruptcy?

Other than secured and unsecured debts, you may also owe student loans, past-due child support, or taxes. Should you file bankruptcy if you have these sorts of debts? Are they dischargeable? Probably not.

➤ Child support and alimony payments are not wiped out in a bankruptcy.

➤ Student loans can only be discharged if they are more than 10 years old. (This was changed in 1998; before that, they only had to be 2 years old.)

➤ Fines imposed by a court are not wiped out.

➤ Money owing for stolen goods is not wiped out.

➤ Things obtained by misrepresentation are not wiped out.

➤ Award of damages by a court for intentionally inflicting bodily harm or sexual assault.

➤ Taxes, in most cases, are discharged, providing the person did not wilfully evade taxes or is not a tax protestor.

What Can You Keep?

Aside from figuring out whether your debts are dischargeable, the other major consideration before filing bankruptcy is whether you will be able to keep your property. One of the great fears people have about bankruptcy is that they will lose their property.

Depending on the size of your debt, and the province you live in, you will be able to keep a good deal of your property. However, unless you rely on your car for your work

Two Cents

The surrender option is very powerful. If you own a car in which you owe more than it's worth (say you owe $10 000, but it is worth $4000), you can surrender the car to the lender during your bankruptcy, get out of the contract, and owe nothing more on the vehicle. Where else can you unilaterally get out of a bad contract? Answer: nowhere.

Two Cents

Bankruptcy is a topsy-turvy world. In real life, lots of unsecured debt is a bad thing, but in bankruptcy it is a fine thing. No matter how much unsecured debt you owe, it will be wiped out. In real life, creditors can harass you if you do not pay, but in bankruptcy, they cannot do a thing.

(that is, you need to drive for your work, not to get to work), it will probably be the first thing to go. When you go to file for bankruptcy with your trustee, in Ontario for instance, prepare to leave the car with them.

The items on each province's list are somewhat arcane—(it would seem in some provinces you can keep your pet, others don't specify; in Quebec you can keep family photos and medals...) You are entitled to keep the equity in your principal residence, up to a value of $40 000 in Alberta, $9 000 to $12 000 in British Columbia, and $32 000 in Saskatchewan (for non-farmers.) As indicated, some provinces are very generous when it comes to real estate, and others are not. We've listed the provincial exemptions in appendix B.

What Don't You Keep?

Any assets valued at more than the exemption allowed by your province, that are your property, such as real estate, cars, and boats, on the date of the bankruptcy or acquired during the bankruptcy, go toward the creditors. This includes windfalls such as lottery winnings and inheritances (if someone in your family dies during the bankruptcy), as well as anything bought with any surplus income, the term used to describe your disposable income during the bankruptcy. Tax refunds outstanding, as of the date of the bankruptcy, also go toward your creditors. Tax refunds receivable from your post-bankruptcy tax return (you are required to file two returns in the year of a bankruptcy, see chapter 17), may have to go to your creditors as well.

Protecting Your House

You may be concerned that your mortgage holder will foreclose on your house if you file for bankruptcy, but that is usually a groundless fear. If you are current with your mortgage payments when you file and stay current throughout the case, then your lender cannot foreclose. It would be illegal. When your case is over, you will continue to make payments as if nothing has happened.

Things are a bit different if you are behind on your mortgage payments and you want to file for bankruptcy. In that case, you will need to make up the past-due amount within about a month or two from the date you file, as well as keep current throughout the entire case. If you remain in arrears after filing bankruptcy, your lender will eventually go before the bankruptcy court and ask for permission to foreclose on your house.

As we've said previously, if you want to keep your house, you must make arrangements outside the bankruptcy with your mortgage lender. Your trustee, the person who helps you file for bankruptcy, may advise you to move to a less expensive living arrangement, but if renting is just as costly as paying the mortgage, this is unlikely.

Can you Exempt Your House?

To figure out whether you will be able to fully exempt your house, you will need to do two things:

1. Figure out how much equity you have in your home. Subtract the amount you owe your lender(s), and that is your equity.

2. Look up your equity limits and see whether you fall under the limit for your province.

Two Cents

Remember, it is just the equity in your property that you need to exempt.

While Alberta's Homestead Act makes it a very generous province in which to go bankrupt, with a $40 000 home equity exemption, Ontario has no limit on real estate exemptions. This means in that province it doesn't matter how much equity you have in your home. It falls outside of the bankruptcy and to keep your home—if that's really the most economical thing—you'll have to make arrangements with your mortgage holder. However, if you and your trustee determine selling your house is the best way to go, that is not the end of the world. Houses are money-suckers, and many people find they just simply can't afford the inherent costs of maintaining a property. For example, Sherrie owns a house in London, Ontario, in which she has a $30 000 equity. If she absolutely had to keep her house (some people want to stay in the same neighbourhood for the sake of children and other support), she would have to come up with the difference between her equity (her downpayment plus principal mortgage payments) and what her trustee has determined to be the market value, based on market valuations, property taxes and comparable property prices. With the home being valued at $150 000 , she would then have to come up with $120 000 to cover what the trustee would get if he sold her house. Well, if she could come up with $120 000, she probably wouldn't be declaring bankruptcy, right? In most cases, the trustee will individually assess the best course of action; in some cases, selling the house is the best thing.

In provinces where there is a principal home exemption, market value isn't important, but the amount of equity you have in your home is. Remember, your equity is the purchase price minus the current amount of your mortgage. For example, Spencer lives in Victoria, British Columbia, where the home equity exemption is $9000. His home is worth $200 000, in which he has $20 000 equity. If he wants to keep his house, he needs to put forward $11 000 ($20 000 equity – $9000 equity exemption). If you are over your exemption, that is, say you have $60 000 in equity in your Alberta home that you are desperate to keep, then the trustee will ask you to pay back $20 000 into the bankruptcy estate. In essence, you are buying the trustee's interest in the asset.

The Least You Need to Know

➤ A bankruptcy wipes out your personal liability for your debts, but it doesn't wipe out any security interest.

➤ If you have a lot of credit card debt or other unsecured debt, bankruptcy makes sense.

➤ Make sure you will be able to exempt and protect your assets before you file your case.

➤ Do not lie on your paperwork, but be sure to value your assets as low as is reasonably possible.

➤ Don't forget to deduct the cost of sale from your home equity analysis.

Chapter 17

Bankruptcy Basics

In This Chapter

➤ How does bankruptcy work?

➤ Advantages and disadvantages of bankruptcy

➤ Last chance alternatives to bankruptcy

In 1996, 79 361 Canadians declared bankruptcy. The following year was a record-breaking year, and it has caused some concern. Levels have stabilized since then, due in large part to a change in 1998 to making student loans dischargeable in a bankruptcy only if they are older than 10 years.

Bankruptcies in Canada are handled through Industry Canada's Office of the Superintendent of Bankruptcy. There are 14 offices across Canada, all offering services in English and French. The Office has a number of responsibilities besides handling bankruptcies, chief among them, handling consumer proposals (a last-chance effort before bankruptcy, which we'll talk about further in this chapter), ensuring that insolvency practices are on the up and up, and licensing the trustees who carry out bankruptcy proceedings. The Office also makes sure debtors get the advice and counseling they need, and make sure their licensed trustees remain competent. While the law is a federal one, bankruptcy rules and regulations differ from province to province. For the complete list of provincial offices, as well as the text of the code of ethics for trustees, see appendices A and C.

Money Talks

Every bankruptcy case is administered by a trustee in bankruptcy. This person is licensed by the Superintendent of Bankruptcy to administer proposals and bankruptcies. The trustee is an officer of the court and ultimately, represents your creditors. However, the trustee also helps and advises you and ensures that your rights are respected too. See the Trustee Code of Ethics in Appendix A.

Who Is Declaring Bankruptcy?

An extensive research paper done in 1998 by Saul Schwartz and Leigh Anderson of Carleton University in Ottawa identified three groups—the self-employed, unmarried women, and people under 30—who seemed particularly vulnerable to financial hardship. The paper reports that the problem is getting worse. Since 1977, the number of self-employed people has risen by about a million. The divorce rate and number of single-mother families is increasing, widening the pool of potential bankrupts. While there are not more young people than before, what has changed, according to the study, is young people's likelihood of borrowing—credit cards, student loans, car loans, and lines of credit. The volume of government student loans almost tripled from $768 million in 1989–90 to $2.13 billion in 1994–95. These numbers are only poised to escalate further, as governments continue to cut funding to post-secondary institutions.

Two Cents

The average number of debts by people declaring bankruptcy (as declared by the bankruptcy trustees surveyed) was 8.6. That means that most people had about eight or nine different debts hanging over their heads.

Why Do People Choose Bankruptcy?

Schwartz and Anderson identified a number of events of debts that "triggered" bankruptcy. The two most-heard responses were loss of job or reduced income, and credit cards. Credit counselors also cite divorce as being hard on a family's finances—some people may have to pay for two homes on one salary. And other unforeseen events such as an accident to the person declaring bankruptcy or to a family member, which prevents the bankrupt from working and paying the bills, can also lead to financial ruin.

While government-funded health care goes a long way in preventing people from mortgaging their homes to pay for medical bills, it can't cover the costs of lost work time.

Think of people with sick children who fly half way across the country to wait for an organ transplant for months; or parents who have to quit their jobs to look after a child who has become disabled in an accident. If they can't rely on the benevolence of their extended family or community, bankruptcy may enter into the picture.

It's Not So Bad

You have valiantly tried to do everything in your power to fix your money problems. You are determined to handle money differently in the future, but nothing you do now can seem to get you out of the huge hole you have put yourself in. There comes a point for some people where they just want to raise the white flag over their money ship, give up, and start over. They do not want explain their situation to even one more unsympathetic creditor. They do not want to even answer their phone at all. Their ship is sinking.

One of Steve's clients, John, had a successful career as a BMW salesman and made a fine living. Then his wife left him one day, and he grew despondent. A short time later, he was fired. He lived off of his credit cards for a few months, sure that he would be able to get a new job and repay the debt in no time.

His depression was getting worse, so he finally decided to ride his bike across the country as a kick-start for a new life. The night before he was to leave on his adventure of renewal, he tripped over his bike and shattered his leg. John was in the hospital for two weeks and in rehab for three months. By the time he was finally able to get a job and go back to work, he had been unemployed for almost eight months. His credit card debt had gone from a manageable $35 000 to an unmanageable $60 000. What was he to do?

His massive debt was enough to put him over the edge. John never thought he was the type to file for bankruptcy, but he had few options left. No amount of fancy letter writing or negotiating would ever get him off the hook. Eventually, his creditors would sue him and win. This is called getting a judgment against a defendant.

For many people, the threat of a lawsuit or a wage garnishment is what finally forces them to seriously consider bankruptcy. But far less desperate circumstances can also hasten a bankruptcy. You merely have to be at a place where you feel you need a new financial beginning and see no other viable solution.

The bankruptcy act does not ask why a person is in debt. Losing a job is equal to getting divorced is equal to binge-shopping is equal to illness is equal to poor money skills. You could owe your creditors $1000 to $100 000—it does not matter. The decision to file bankruptcy is strictly a personal decision based upon individual circumstances.

In the right circumstances, bankruptcy can be a safe harbour in the financial storm. It is

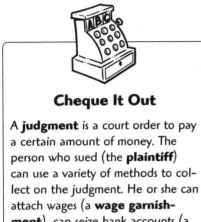

Cheque It Out

A **judgment** is a court order to pay a certain amount of money. The person who sued (the **plaintiff**) can use a variety of methods to collect on the judgment. He or she can attach wages (a **wage garnishment**), can seize bank accounts (a **levy**), or can file a lien against the debtor's real estate.

a place that can stop all creditor harassment, allow for a new beginning, and forgive your debts.

Forgiveness, doesn't that have a nice ring to it? Almost all of the law is about the opposite of forgiveness, namely retribution. Lawsuits are all about retribution. The entire criminal justice system is about retribution. The truly amazing thing about bankruptcy laws in this country is that they are founded upon the idea that sometimes, just sometimes, people need a break. Bankruptcy is about forgiving your debts, forgiving your mistakes, and letting you start over, at least financially. Take a deep breath. That last option is not so horrible.

Your Creditors Will Survive

Of course, you would rather pay your debts if you could. But if you are reading this, then maybe you cannot. Although it is certainly understandable that you might feel bad for your creditors, it also might be helpful to know that most of them will be just fine.

Do you think that the people who service your Visa account go home and worry at night about the fact that if you pay the minimum on your card you will owe more next month due to penalties and interest? Of course not. Furthermore, these companies are in the business of making money and have made a fortune off of you already. They will get by just fine without your $119 payment every month. That is one of the costs of capitalism. Do not fret. Your creditors will survive.

Money Talks

Ever wonder why you have been paying 18 percent on many of your credit cards? One reason is that credit card companies know that a certain percentage of their customers will never be able to fully pay all amounts due on the card (either because of default or bankruptcy). Thus they charge everyone a higher interest rate than necessary to offset these losses. You have been subsidizing other people's bankruptcies for years.

Know this, too: Bankruptcy is a legal right that has been part of civilized societies for thousands of years. You may notice that corporations file for bankruptcy protection all the time. Like you, sometimes they need help. Even the Bible says that creditors should forgive debts every seven years.

So if you are feeling ashamed and despondent over your need to file bankruptcy, get over it. You are in good company. Of course, you should learn your lessons and not get in this pickle again. But both bankruptcy and this country are about second chances. If you need to, take yours.

My Legal Rights Trump Yours

Right now you are probably feeling very defensive. Creditors are probably calling you at all hours of the day and night. You may be getting threatening letters, possibly even lawsuits and threats of foreclosure. What to do? Bankruptcy to the rescue!

The moment your bankruptcy trustee files the authorized forms with the Official Receiver, you are legally bankrupt. This is the first step in your redemption. Once you are legally bankrupt, your creditors are the ones put on the defensive. (Doesn't that sound nice?)

Two Cents

In 1998, 75 465 Canadians sought bankruptcy protection. You can, too.

Money Talks

In the past few years, many famous people have taken advantage of bankruptcy protection, including Burt Reynolds, Kim Basinger, Donald Trump, and MC Hammer.

The bankruptcy immediately puts a halt to all collection activities. It stops lawsuits. It stops wage garnishments. It stops all phone calls and letters. It stops auto repossessions. Your house could be on the block, ready to be sold by your bank at a foreclosure sale tomorrow, and if you file bankruptcy today, the sale will be stopped. No matter what action a collector is about to take against you, you hold the ultimate trump card: bankruptcy.

The bankruptcy continues for nine months (for first-time bankrupts) until it is absolutely discharged. Or your trustee will have to discharge the bankruptcy with conditions, if a) you didn't pay the agreed amount of surplus income, or b) you filed for bankruptcy instead of proposing a viable repayment plan. This is called a Proposal, which we will go into in more detail later on.

How Is the Bankruptcy Discharged?

➤ Your debts will be wiped out if your trustee recommends an Absolute Discharge, which is usually the case for first-time bankrupts.

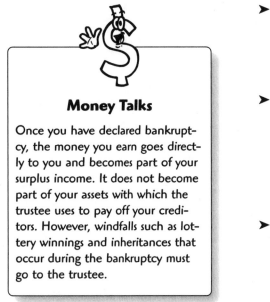

Money Talks

Once you have declared bankruptcy, the money you earn goes directly to you and becomes part of your surplus income. It does not become part of your assets with which the trustee uses to pay off your creditors. However, windfalls such as lottery winnings and inheritances that occur during the bankruptcy must go to the trustee.

➤ Your trustee may also recommend an Order of Conditional Discharge, where the court orders you to meet certain conditions before your debts can be wiped clean, such as paying the trustee.

➤ An Order of Suspended Discharge could also be recommended, perhaps because there is an ongoing criminal investigation or some sort, or you did not perform all your required duties as a bankrupt during the nine months, which are basically to hand over all assets, property titles and deeds, as well as cancel credit cards.

➤ It's possible, but unlikely, that the bankruptcy will not be discharged, due to a disagreement between two of either the bankrupt, the trustee, or the creditors. In this case, the bankruptcy proceeds to Bankruptcy Court.

Bankruptcy Benefits

The discharge occurs at the end of your bankruptcy and states that your debts have been wiped out (discharged) and your liability for those debts has been forgiven (there's that word again). You could owe $60 000 to six different credit cards, and the entire debt will be forgiven at the conclusion of your case.

Suppose you pay $800 a month in credit card bills. The filing of the bankruptcy means that you need never pay that money to your creditors again. The opportunity to get rid of $800 a month in payments produces a lot of disposable income.

The last benefit of bankruptcy is peace of mind. Few things in life cause more marital strife and personal stress than money problems. Bankruptcy, with its chance to start anew, get creditors off your back, wipe out debts, and create disposable income, will help you to get along better with your mate and sleep better at night.

Although many people think of bankruptcy as a horrible last resort, many people have the exact opposite experience. Take our friend John, who we mentioned previously. Through bankruptcy, he was able to wipe out all his credit card debt. After that, he got a job at another BMW dealership, and he eventually remarried. Bankruptcy was the tool that gave him the chance to start over, both financially and emotionally.

The Dark Side of Bankruptcy

Of course, filing bankruptcy has its downsides, including the following:

Money Talks

Boomers may be getting a bad rap for taking advantage of the economic upturns, leaving their succeeding generations with enormous bills, but there's one thing they didn't plan for: the rising cost of a university education. Many boomers with children entering post-secondary education find themselves in the position of having no means to help their children pay for tuition, while younger parents are bombarded with Registered Education Savings Plans.

➤ **The effect on your credit report.** A first-time bankruptcy, like any other negative credit item, stays on your report for no more than six years.

➤ **The effect on future credit.** Filing for bankruptcy does not mean that you will never get credit again. What it does mean is that the credit you do get will be more expensive. For example, although you might be able to get a car loan at 10 percent interest today, that same loan will cost around 20 percent after you file. Although people routinely get mortgages about two years after their discharge, they will definitely pay higher interest. Credit cards will be difficult to get for a few years.

Money Talks

Bankruptcy, for the most part, can be kept fairly quiet. If you have significant assets and numerous creditors, an ad may be placed in the "Legals" section of the newspaper alerting creditors to the date of the first meeting. But most personal bankruptcies are smaller in scale, and the creditors are notified by mail.

➤ **Loss of property.** In a few cases, a person may lose some of his property to the bankruptcy trustee.

➤ **Employment.** You may have trouble getting bonded, a requirement for certain jobs. Your trustee can tell you more about this.

➤ **Stigma.** Although there used to be a great stigma attached to filing bankruptcy, that is far less true today. With so many people doing it, and so many notable businesses and celebrities doing it for good or ill, there is not much of a social stigma left.

Cheque It Out

Unsecured debt is debt that has no collateral attached to it. **Secured debt**, on the other hand, is debt that is tied to collateral, such as a car loan. If you don't repay the loan, the car is repossessed; the car secures the loan. Unsecured debts have no such collateral. Unsecured debts include credit cards and dental bills.

Although there are certainly some negative aspects to filing bankruptcy, the truth is, for those who are seriously contemplating it, the benefits of bankruptcy usually outweigh the burdens.

Other Alternatives to Bankruptcy

But wait, there are a couple of other possible solutions to your financial crisis before you declare personal bankruptcy.

A Consolidation Order

If you live in British Columbia, Alberta, Saskatchewan, Nova Scotia, or Prince Edward Island, you may apply for a Consolidation Order through the Bankruptcy Court. The order determines the amounts and due dates for payments to the court. The court then distributes your payments to your creditors. You have three years to pay off your debts, during which you are freed from creditors and wage garnishment. You will not lose any of your assets in a consolidation order.

Voluntary Deposit Scheme

Better known as the "Lacombe Law", residents of Quebec can apply for this process, which functions the same way as a consolidation order. The monthly payment, however, is based on your income and number of dependents. Your local courthouse usually offers this service.

Consumer Proposal

The last possible step before declaring bankruptcy is to make a Consumer Proposal, sometimes called a Personal Proposal, available to people with less than $75 000 in debt, (excluding a home mortgage). Since creating this option in 1992, then further amending the Bankruptcy Act in 1998 (to provide more of a disincentive to declaring bankruptcy), the rate of consumer proposals his risen steadily in Canada. According to the Office of the Superintendent of Bankruptcy, the rate of consumer bankruptcies to proposals in November 1999, for example, was roughly six to one (6523 bankruptcies versus 1029 proposals). Most trustees do their utmost to make sure that a proposal is not an option (i.e., if there is sufficient cash flow to make payments) before going ahead with a bankruptcy.

Cheque It Out

Any property that you would lose in a bankruptcy is **nonexempt**. Each province has its own rules regarding exempt property.

Just as you may have been writing your creditors to ask them to reduce the amount of your debts, the amount of your monthly payments, or to give you more time to pay them, a Consumer Proposal does the same thing under the auspices of the Bankruptcy and Insolvency Act. Your creditors may be more likely to go for this over your letters asking for patience. Now they know you are serious about getting rid of your debt, and they should know they'll get more in a proposal than they would if you went bankrupt.

During a Consumer Proposal, your unsecured creditors cannot come after your property or garnish your wages. Collection agencies must stop calling you. This gives you some breathing space to approach your creditors again and explain your situation and ask for support.

You Should File a Proposal if You

➤ are prepared to pay a premium for a quick resolution.

➤ think you might not get an absolute discharge from a bankruptcy, and conditions may be imposed.

➤ find bankruptcy unacceptable.

➤ are in business and will be negatively impacted by a personal bankruptcy when dealing with clients and other third parties.

➤ have professional accreditation that may be jeopardized by a bankruptcy.

➤ are someone for whom bankruptcy will result in a secured creditor acting on its security and therefore repossessing property, such as a home or car.

➤ wish to retain some key asset, such as property or an impending inheritance.

➤ have previously declared bankruptcy.

To make a proposal, you must meet with an administrator who may be a bankruptcy trustee or a person appointed by the Superintendent of Bankruptcy. The administrator will ask about your financial situation, assess it, and advise you about what kind of proposal will be best-suited to your needs and the needs of your creditors.

The proposal must give your creditors, at a minimum, more than what they would get if you declared bankruptcy. For example, if you own $30 000 equity in your home, the proposal must say you'll pay back $30 000. If the proposal is for less money, there is no incentive for your creditors to accept the proposal, because they know if you sold the house, they'd have access to more cash.

Before filing the proposal, your trustee will talk to your creditors and see just what they will accept. In some cases, you might just need more time to pay off your debts in full. In other cases, you need a break on the amount owed. But if you can pay more than the creditor would receive if you go bankrupt, you have a good chance.

You will sign specific forms that the administrator will file with the Official Receiver. Within 10 days, the administrator will send the Official Receiver a report saying whether or not the administrator thinks you can realistically meet the conditions laid out in the proposal. The report also contains a list of your assets and debts, as well as a list of your creditors. Copies of your proposal are sent to your creditors, along with the administrator's report. The creditors have 45 days to accept or reject the proposal. If the creditors do not respond, then they are considered to have accepted the proposal. If enough creditors (2/3) accept the proposal (or decline to reject it) with 50 percent plus one of the eligible creditors having voted, then the proposal is binding and you will have to meet its terms.

If the proposal is rejected, the Act can no longer protect you, and your creditors are free to go after you within five days of the rejection. If, on the other hand, the proposal is fully accepted and you manage to pay off the debts as described in the proposal, the administrator will give you a certificate of full performance (as well as to the Official Receiver) and you will be relieved of the debts in the proposal.

If you fail to make the payment plan laid out in the proposal, the proposal can be annulled. You then go back to owing your creditors the full amount before you made the proposal (minus whatever you may have paid to them during the proposal). You will be considered bankrupt on the date of the annulment.

There is a filing fee and an administrator's fee when you file a proposal. These fees are determined by the Bankruptcy and Insolvency Rules. Visit the Office of the Superintendent of Bankruptcy Web site at http://osb-bsf.ic.gc.ca for more information.

The Least You Need to Know

➤ Bankruptcy is not such a bad option when all else fails.

➤ You have paid your creditors a lot of money, and they will survive just fine without your money.

➤ There are some last-chance options to bankruptcy, such as a consolidation order, or a voluntary deposit scheme, if you live in certain provinces.

➤ A Consumer Proposal is administered under the Bankruptcy Act, and is one last attempt to get your creditors to agree to a reduced payment plan.

Chapter 18

How a Bankruptcy Case Proceeds

In This Chapter

➤ Getting the case filed

➤ Understanding your paperwork

➤ The first meeting of creditors

➤ Amendments

➤ The discharge

The process of going through a bankruptcy is surprisingly easy for most people. Life before bankruptcy is usually quite unpleasant: creditors are calling, money is tight, and people are stressed and worried. But once you enter the bankruptcy process, all that changes. Almost magically, the phone stops ringing, and extra cash reappears.

Relief Is in Sight

The phone stops ringing because once you file bankruptcy, it stops all creditor collection activity. You don't have to worry about dealing with nasty creditors ever again.

Even better, money shows up. How? Because the money you previously spent servicing your dischargeable debts every month is now yours to keep. If you have been paying $500 a month servicing your credit card debt, there is no need to pay that ever again once your bankruptcy case is filed. Voilà! The $500 a month is now yours to keep. It does not go into your bankruptcy estate, which we'll talk about further. You will pay some money each month for the nine months of the duration of the bankruptcy, called the surplus income. This is based on your monthly income and payments.

You will also find that, unlike your life today, life in bankruptcy is surprisingly nonadversarial. Throughout the process, you will be treated with respect and courtesy. Besides the fact that your creditors can no longer harass you, you will soon discover that civility is the rule in court.

Over Your Limit

In 1998, Canadians charged more than $84 billion on bank-issued credit cards (not including cash advances). Those cards carried $23.9 billion in outstanding balances for the same year, representing 16 million card holders.

Steps in the Process

There are basically five steps to the process: hiring a bankruptcy trustee, filing your paperwork, possibly meeting with creditors, attending two mandatory credit counseling sessions, and obtaining your discharge.

"If it pleases the court ... "

The first thing to do is to choose your trustee in bankruptcy. Visit www.bankruptcycanada.com for a list of trustees near you. Or, consult your local yellow

Two Cents

There are several fees to know about when filing bankruptcy. An ordinary administration bankruptcy costs $150. A consumer proposal costs $50. Your trustee has fees, and the two required credit counseling sessions during bankruptcy costs $75 each.

pages or credit counseling services. Choose your bankruptcy trustee like you would hire any professional—on a strong recommendation or through word of mouth. Choose someone that you like, above all, since you will be spending some time with him or her during the bankruptcy.

If you cannot find a bankruptcy trustee, the Office of the Superintendent of Bankruptcy (OSB) will help you find one through its Debtor Assistance Service, as long as: your debt it mostly personal rather than business-related; you have tried at least twice to find a trustee; and you are not in prison.

Getting Your Case Filed

The next step is also the most time-consuming. Because the court requires a lot of information from you before it will discharge your debts, you have to sit down and organize this information with your trustee.

Among the things you will need to organize, and eventually list in your paperwork, are the following:

➤ **A list of all major assets.** This list includes everything of substance you own. All furniture? Yes. Every piece of silverware? No.

➤ **A list of all unsecured debts.** This list must include to whom the debts are owed, their addresses, and your account numbers (bank credit cards, retailer credit cards, unsecured lines of credit, personal loans).

➤ **A list of all secured debts.** This list would also include an indication of what property secures the debt (your house, car, cottage, boat). Make a note of any property you wish to keep, so you can determine how much you will have to pay to do so.

➤ **A list of income and expenses.** This list would comprise all sources of income and a list of average monthly expenses.

A bankruptcy case is officially commenced when your trustee files the information with the Official Receiver. Once you do that, the trustee does the rest of the work. Bankruptcy courts are divided into geographical districts and are normally located in the provincial building of each particular district. The filing fee is the same whether you are filing alone or jointly with a spouse. After your case is filed, a stay is issued and remains in effect for the duration of your case. This is a stop sign for all creditors and collection agencies. Peace in our time!

The Duties of a Bankrupt

Once you've declared bankruptcy, you may be off the hook from your creditors, but you have a lot of responsibilities to make the road to being discharged a smooth one. Here's a list, according to the Bankruptcy Act:

➤ Itemize and deliver the property you own or control to the trustee (or someone he authorizes).

➤ As specified by the Superintendent, deliver all credit cards to the trustee for cancellation.

➤ Deliver to the trustee all paperwork pertaining to your property and assets, including title papers, insurance polices, tax records, and returns.

➤ Attend a meeting with the Official Receiver, under oath, discussing the causes of the bankruptcy and disposition of your property.

Money Talks

By and large, a personal bankruptcy is filed independent of a spouse. You could be married to a gazillionaire, but he or she is kept out of a bankruptcy proceeding.

➤ Within five days of the bankruptcy (unless otherwise extended by the Official Receiver), prepare and submit to the trustee (in quadruplicate) a statement of your affairs in the prescribed form (verified by affidavit), which shows the your assets and liabilities, the names and addresses of your creditors, the securities held by them respectively, and the dates when the securities were respectively given. (If this proves too complicated for you to reasonable handle, the Official Receiver may authorize using another qualified person to help, at your expense.)

➤ Help the trustee in making an inventory of your assets.

➤ Tell the trustee if you sold anything during the 12 months before and up to the date of the initial bankruptcy, how and to whom, and if it was under extraordinary circumstances.

➤ Tell the trustee if you gave anything away without receiving adequate valuable consideration, during the five years before, up to and including the date of the bankruptcy.

➤ Go to the first meeting of your creditors (unless you're sick or have some other good reason for not going).

➤ Go to any other meetings of your creditors or inspectors as required.

➤ Submit to any other examinations under oath, with respect to your property or affairs as necessary.

➤ Help as much as possible in the selling of your property and distributing the proceeds to your creditors.

➤ Execute powers of attorney, conveyance, deeds, and instruments as may be required.

➤ Verify all proofs of claims filed, if required by the trustee.

Money Talks

Income Tax law requires you file two tax returns for the year in which you declare bankruptcy. The first covers the period from Jan. 1 to the date of the bankruptcy, which can probably be filed soon after the bankruptcy. The second covers the period starting with the date of the bankruptcy to Dec. 31 of that year. This will be filed the following year.

➤ Tell the trustee if someone has knowingly filed a false claim.

➤ Tell the trustee is your financial situation has suddenly changed.

➤ Do whatever the trustee reasonably requests you to do, in regards to your property and distribution of the assets.

➤ Keep the trustee advised of your current address at all times, until you've been discharged.

The First Meeting of Creditors

After your petition and schedules are prepared and filed, the court, if it decides one is necessary, sets a time for the first meeting of creditors. If 25% of your creditors ask for a meeting, then a meeting is held and you must attend. You may even have to go to the Official Receiver's office and answer questions under oath pertaining to your financial situation. That meeting usually occurs about a month or two after your case is filed. At the meeting, your trustee will give a report about your assets and liabilities, and the creditors will vote to confirm the trustee's appointment, or substitute a trustee of their choice. The creditors will then vote for the appointment of inspectors, who further verify the trustee's estimation of your assets' worth. The creditors may also make requests to the trustee regarding the administration of your estate.

What Does the Trustee Do?

After you've filed your paperwork, and you've attended the first meeting of creditors, your trustee gets to work on seeing what amount of your assets he can liquidate into the bankruptcy estate, for the benefit of the creditors. (Your trustee should go over all of this when you are considering bankruptcy, so none of this will come as a surprise to you.)

Your trustee will contact the holders of any RRSP investments and look into the merits of collapsing them (for which you will have to pay the income penalty) or of cashing in other investments; he or she will determine the cash value of any life insurance policy, and see about taking a loan against it. Your car, if you don't use it for your livelihood, will have been picked up and put into storage, and it will eventually be turned over to an auto dealer. Unfortunately, you have very little say in the matter.

All the moneys collected go into your bankruptcy estate, and earn interest until they are distributed to your creditors. Even though your bankruptcy will be discharged in nine months, the Trustee's discharge of your bankruptcy estate could take as long as three years. Your creditors may be waiting that long to see their money.

Over Your Limit

Bankruptcy fraud is a federal crime. Be sure to be thorough when you fill out your paperwork. Be sure to list all assets, even if doing so will put you over the exemption limit. Losing a car is preferable to going to jail.

What the trustee rarely does is go into a bankrupt's house and look for hidden assets. He or she is unlikely to rip an engagement ring off your finger. While their responsibility is to get your creditors as much of their owed money as possible, trustees doesn't really go looking for it.

During the nine months of your bankruptcy, you are required to pay a monthly sum depending on your surplus income. This amount is derived from the Superintendent's "standards" and is based on your cash flow and family situation. In general, bankrupts with $100 to $1000 in monthly surplus income are required to pay 50 percent of that sum spread out over the nine months. High-income earners with more than $1000 a month must pay between 50 percent and 75 percent.

The Web site of the Office of the Superintendent of Bankruptcy provides the following example, based on a family of two:

Bankrupt's net monthly income: $1800

Spouse's net monthly income: 1000

Total net family income: 2800

Total Family Surplus Income as per Appendix "A" $936

(standards based on Statistics Canada information plus a 1.2% adjustment to standards due to 1998 Consumer Price Index, plus a 1.6% adjustment reflecting Superintendent's projection for the 1999 CPI.)

Bankrupt's portion of family income

$1,800 \div 2,800 = 64.3\%$

Payment required from bankrupt

$((936 \times 64.3\%) \times 50\% = 300.92)$ $301

Money Talks

Be above board with your trustee. If you try to hide an asset, such as a commission payment that is not on a pay stub, it will eventually be found out and discredit you in the end.

Consult a bankruptcy trustee for the Superintendent's Standards, or visit http://osb-bsf.ic.gc.ca. The standards are listed in the Index of Directives (post-1992), under the Bankruptcy and Insolvency Act Regulations.

Bankruptcy Mediation

In 1998, the Bankruptcy and Insolvency Act was amended to include the right for the bankrupt to ask for mediation. Mediation brings in an independent third party, or mediator, to help settle bankruptcy disputes regarding the surplus income, or the conditions of discharge. The mediator is either an employee from the OSB, or someone with experience in mediation approved by the Superintendent. The mediator helps the two sides, usually the bankrupt and the creditors, communicate. The mediator will help both sides explain their point of view, but does not get involved in deciding what the settlement will be. That's for the two parties to decide. During a mediation, the trustee's role is to provide guidance.

The trustee, mediator, and bankrupt all attend the mediation session, as well as any creditor who requested the mediation, a friend or spouse of the bankrupt, and legal counsel for any of the parties if necessary.

Surplus Income Mediation is available to first or second-time bankrupts, and happens if:

➤ You do not agree with the amount of surplus income, the trustee has to request mediation.

➤ Any of your creditors disagree with the amount of surplus income, they may submit a written request for mediation.

Discharge Mediation is available to first-time bankrupts only, and can be requested by any of the following three parties:

➤ You, if you disagree with the conditions imposed;

➤ The trustee, if he or she opposes the discharge because you failed to pay the agreed amount of surplus income, or if you've filed for bankruptcy when you should have filed a consumer proposal (i.e., you had the cash flow to make a proposal).

➤ The creditors, for the same reasons as the trustee.

If the mediation is successful, then all parties agree, and a mediation settlement agreement is drawn up and signed. You will have to comply with any provisions in the agreement.

If the mediation is not successful, then the whole matter will be turned over to the courts.

Understanding Your Paperwork

Bankruptcy paperwork may look intimidating, but it is quite easy to understand. A bankruptcy is made up of a statement of personal data, a list of monthly income and monthly expenses, a list of debts, general information about your assets (including investments, life insurance, and RRSPs), and a specific inventory of household effects.

Money Talks

Some of the most vigilant creditors are family members. Do not get into formal loan agreements with family members if you can help it!

Bankruptcy Application Checklist (from BankruptcyCanada.com)

Make sure you have all of the following when you meet with your trustee to file for bankruptcy.

1. Bankruptcy application.

2. Vehicles. Bring a copy of the vehicle registration and keys.

3. Agreements. Bring copies of debentures, mortgages, separation agreements, alimony and child support documents, leases, sales contracts, judgments, fines, wage assignments, court orders, etc.

4. Credit cards. All of your credit cards must be turned over to the trustee, including those with a balance of zero.

Two Cents

Although bankruptcy information must be thorough and correct, here is an important tip: budgets are flexible, and you want to come up with a budget that roughly equals your income, if at all possible, and stays within the bounds of truth and reasonableness.

5. Life insurance. Bring a copy of all policies.

6. Stock/Bonds/Securities/RRSPs. Provide all pertinent documentation and statements.

7. Pay stubs. Offer the most current one available, plus any Employment Insurance Compensation (EIC) stubs for the current year if applicable, and the address of the EIC office where application was made.

8. Tax information. You will need a copy of your last return filed, plus information from previous years if you are not up to date; a list of employers with gross earning and deductions made for tax, CPP, EIC, union dues, and any child support or alimony payments; and spousal earnings.

9. Initial payment to the Bankruptcy Estate to cover filing fees, mailings, etc.

10. Post-dated cheques totaling the surplus income amount.

Over Your Limit

Don't lie to the court. The penalty for perjury can include jail time and a fine of up to $500 000.

The Discharge

The final step in the bankruptcy process occurs about two months after the creditors' meeting when your discharge comes in the mail, thereby ending your case and officially discharging you from your legal liability to repay the debts listed in your schedules. This entire process, from filing to meeting to discharge, normally takes about nine months. That's it! Your case is over, your debts have been discharged, and you get your fresh start.

As one wise bankruptcy trustee once said, bankruptcy is like surgery. If your doctor said to you, "You need an operation, it might hurt a bit, but your prognosis is excellent," you'd say "Let's do it."

Money Talks

The first bankruptcy statute in England dates back to 1542. In biblical times, ancient Israelites celebrated the Year of Jubilee every 50 years, whose provisions, among others, included the forgiveness of all debt.

The Least You Need to Know

➤ From start to finish, a first-time bankruptcy in Canada lasts nine months.

➤ If you cannot find a suitable trustee, the Office of the Superintendent of Bankruptcy will appoint one.

➤ Bankruptcy mediation is a process that helps resolves disputes between the involved parties.

➤ It's in your best interest to help the trustee and perform the duties of the bankrupt as prescribed by the Act.

Part 5

Getting Ahead of the Game

It's not over when the debt is gone! Remember everything you went through at the beginning of this book? Remember the lessons you learned, the ideas that you read about that seemed obvious when you learned them, but which were new to you nonetheless? Here's one more obvious idea: Just because you've beaten the debt you had does not mean you will never be in debt again.

We discuss ways of using debt in a positive manner, and ways of avoiding bad debt. We talk about maintaining your vigilance and planning for the future. Maintain you freedom! Invest for your future!

Chapter 19

Getting Credit Again

In This Chapter

➤ Credit cards

➤ Auto loans

➤ Other bank loans

➤ Home loans

It will be difficult for you to reestablish a good credit rating and get credit again after a bankruptcy. That is a fact. But getting credit is not impossible; there are many creditors who still want your business. Credit will just be more expensive this time around. You will pay, literally, for your mistakes.

A Credit Card Society

As you near the end of the debt tunnel, you may never want to see another credit card again. Although we understand, appreciate, and empathize with that sentiment, living without a credit card in this world is difficult and almost unrealistic. Be that as it may, either through voluntarily cutting them up, having them canceled, or because of a bankruptcy, many people have no credit cards whatsoever when they teeter back from the brink of bankruptcy or when they emerge from the bankruptcy tunnel.

Money Talks

Do not apply for dozens of credit cards in the hopes that one will come through. Instead, talk to the card issuer (your local branch) and discuss your situation honestly. The branch manager is more likely to come up with a solution for you. Applying and re-applying for credit shows up on your credit report, and has a negative impact on your credit rating.

Over Your Limit

Credit card scams usually start with a telephone call, a postcard, or a letter offering, for a small fee (usually $30 to $50), a preapproved credit card. If you have poor credit, be especially wary of offers for pre-approved credit cards with no credit check. Also, make sure that you don't end up with a store or catalog credit card.

As you know (only too well), our society is dependent upon credit cards. To do something as mundane as cash a cheque or rent a car while on vacation in some places, you must have a credit card. You probably need to get a credit card again. This time, though, you will use it differently.

What if you don't want a credit card? In that case, it still is possible to travel. Most large hotel chains will allow you to prepay for your hotel room, thereby obviating the need to reserve a room with a credit card. Many car rental companies will rent you a car without a credit card if you leave a hefty deposit (about $500).

Getting a credit card again can be a very positive step in your journey toward financial solvency. Getting a new card and not abusing it is a sign that lessons have been learned. The trick is in getting a new card.

Choosing a Credit Card

Though it will be difficult for you to get a credit card again for quite a while, you will eventually be granted a card again—if that's what you really want! Choose a credit card based on these criteria:

➤ **The grace period.** You need to become more familiar with this concept if you are going to become a more money-savvy individual. The grace period is the amount of time you are permitted to repay your balance without paying an additional finance charge. These time periods can range from 0 days to 30. More is obviously better, and we recommend finding a card with a 25- to 30-day grace period.

➤ **The interest rate.** Interest rates on secured cards can range anywhere from 10 percent or so to 20 percent and even higher. Go for the lowest rate you can find.

One thing you need to be sure of with any card you choose is that the issuing bank reports your payment history every month to the credit reporting agencies, Equifax and TransUnion. If it does not, you will not be reestablishing a new, good credit history.

The following financial institutions issue Visa and MasterCard credit cards:

Visa: Bank of Nova Scotia, Bank One International, Caisses Populaires Desjardins, CIBC, Citibank Canada, Citizen Bank of Canada, Laurention Bank, Royal Bank, TD Bank (now owner of Canada Trust); Vancouver City Savings Credit Union.

MasterCard: Alberta Treasury Branches, Bank of Montreal, Credit Union Electronic Transaction Services Inc., G.E. Capital Corp., MBNA Canada, National Bank of Canada, Wells Fargo.

A Tiger in Your Tank

Another way to reestablish credit is by getting a gasoline credit card. Normally, this would be difficult to do without good credit; however, there is a small loophole that you can jump through.

The first thing to do is to find an oil company that is publicly traded that has a gas station near you. The trick is that you must buy stock in the gasoline company you want directly from the company. Call the company and say that you want to join its dividend reinvestment plan (DRIP). Do not say that you are applying for a credit card. You must buy at least $250 worth of stock to enroll in the company's DRIP.

Cheque It Out

DRIPs get their name from the fact that they use dividends to purchase more stock. Thus "Dividend Reinvestment Plan." Whether or not you have to reinvest the dividends depends on the plan. A **dividend** is an annual payment to shareholders from company profits. You might make money through dividends and through a rising stock price.

You will then get a packet in the mail explaining how to buy stock straight from the company. You will need to send in $250, and the company will enroll you in their DRIP and buy $250 worth of stock for you.

After about six months, the oil company will send you an application for a gas credit card. In essence, your stock will be securing your gas card. Not only will you be getting a new credit card, but you will also be starting your investment portfolio.

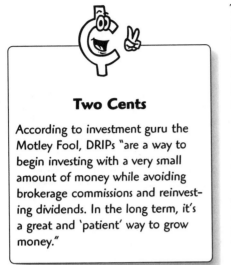

Two Cents

According to investment guru the Motley Fool, DRIPs "are a way to begin investing with a very small amount of money while avoiding brokerage commissions and reinvesting dividends. In the long term, it's a great and 'patient' way to grow money."

The only oil company in Canada currently offering DRIPs with stations in many places is Imperial Oil (Esso). To invest in Esso's DRIP, contact the Trust Company of Bank of Montreal at 1-800-267-9515, or write the Trust Company of Bank of Montreal, "B" Level North, 129 Saint-Jacques Street, Montreal, Quebec, H2Y 1L6.

Debit Cards

Debit cards have become extremely popular in Canada since their introduction in the '90s. According to a recent study by the Strategic Counsel, in 1999 38 percent of surveyed Canadians preferred Interac direct payments over other forms of payment, representing $1.36 billion in purchases. (Cash purchases declined to 39%. Using credit increased to 19%, and cheque-writing dwindled to a mere 3%.) Using your ABM card and PIN number, you can buy many goods and services from retailers with the corresponding technology.

The only drawback to debit cards is that you still have to track your spending. While the old-fashioned chequebooks prompted you to write down which cheque went to whom, debit cards do not. However, some Internet banking services do record where the money goes, be it to pay a bill, grocery store, restaurant, or whichever. And some banks are now offering slightly more detailed descriptions of Interac payments when you update your bankbook.

On the downside, because you are not using credit, you are not reestablishing any credit.

Have We Got a Deal for You!

Another way to reestablish credit after a tough time is by getting a loan for a used car. You see ads all the time that say "Bad Credit? No Problem!" Of course it's no problem when you are charged 23 percent interest. Nevertheless, whether you filed bankruptcy or are just trying to reestablish a good credit file, a car loan is a good way to show that you can pay a bill on time.

There are three ways to get a car loan. First, you can go to your bank and try to get a loan. Second, you can buy from the dealer and have it locate financing for you. Lastly, you can buy from a dealer and finance it through that dealer.

No Money Down

Getting a loan from a bank is the best way to go, but of course, this only works if your credit rating is fairly good. The advantage of a direct bank loan is twofold. First, you will

Money Talks

By comparison, a $10 000, 6 percent auto loan, if it were to be paid back in three years, would cost you $11 800 (6 percent of $10 000 equals $600; $600 multiplied by three years equals $1800; $10 000 added to $1800 equals $11 800). The same loan, at 23 percent payable over three years, would cost $16 900.

get a lower interest rate than you could find almost anywhere else. Second, you will be in a stronger bargaining position when you go to buy, because you can either buy from a private party (which is cheaper) or do without the dealer's help financing the car you like.

If you are unable to get a bank car loan, the next best option is to buy from a dealer and have it attempt to find financing for you through one of its sources. Depending upon your credit rating, your loan could run anywhere from 6 percent to 23 percent.

Although getting credit again is nice, be wary of falling into the same trap you were in before when you probably cared little about interest rates. It is that type of financial illiteracy that helped get you into debt in the first place.

Everyone Is Approved!

The last and worst option is a dealer-financed car loan. The key phrase to look for is "we carry our own papers." That means that the dealership does not use a bank to finance its used car loans. Instead, it finances the car itself. If you stop paying, they start repossessing.

The problem with dealer-financed auto loans is the extraordinarily high interest rate you will pay. But such loans are also an opportunity for people with bad credit to get a car and reestablish themselves financially.

After you have paid back the car loan faithfully, it will be far easier to get a loan in the future. Not only will the interest rate be lower the next time, but more dealers will be interested in selling you a car.

Two Cents

Want to pay cash for a car? A fine idea, but consider too that many car buyers prefer taking out loans to paying cash because 1) it builds credit; 2) cash may be better used for other purposes; 3) saving the cash enables them to build a cash cushion; or 4) the money might be needed for emergencies.

Insurance

A final thought about cars and money: The higher the deductible is on your car insurance, the lower your monthly payment. The monthly payment on a $100 deductible policy is far higher than on a $1000 deductible policy. Considering the few times that you use your insurance and have to pay the deductible, you could pay for the $1000 in a few months by getting the cheaper policy and banking the difference.

This decision would show real financial literacy. Say that your insurance with a $100 deductible is $200 a month, but that with a $1000 deductible it would be $100 a month. If you purchased the insurance with the higher deductible, you could bank the extra $100 a month and in 10 months have enough to cover any future deductible. On top of that, you would earn interest on your money.

Bank Loans

Getting a bank loan will also help you reestablish credit.

To get a bank loan, take a fair amount of money, $1000 for example, and open up a savings account at a bank. Add money to the account every so often for a few months. Then, ask the bank for a loan for an amount less than what is in your savings account and secured by that account. The bank will loan the money to you because the loan is secured by the savings account.

Right off the bat you have convinced a major financial institution to give you a loan. Anyone reading your credit report will be far more likely to extend you credit when he or she sees that a conservative institution like a bank was willing to take a risk on you and lend you money.

Cheque It Out

If you can come up with a hefty down payment, say 25 percent or more, the bank will ignore your past credit problems. The bank does not document your credit history for this type of loan, which is why it is called a **no-documentation loan**.

A Mortgage?

As strange as it may sound, you can get a mortgage after you have cleaned up your debt problems or received a discharge in bankruptcy. It usually takes about two years of clean credit to get one.

The reason you can get a mortgage is that it is usually quite a bit easier to pay bills in a timely manner after you have gotten out of debt. A record of paying bills on time again is the key to getting a home loan after debt. You need to have established a new history of good credit, instead of your old history of bad credit. Paying bills on time and rebuilding your credit with the techniques outlined in this chapter will help make you a more attractive candidate to a lender.

How Much House Can You Afford?

Lenders will pre-approve a loan based on two formulae: the gross-debt service ratio or the total service-debt ratio. The gross-debt service ratio compares your total monthly housing expenses to your total pretax family income. Your expenses cannot exceed 30 percent to 32 percent of your income. The total debt-service ratio includes, as the name suggest, all your debts, such as credit cards, car loans, and personal loans. Housing costs plus all these other financial obligations cannot add up to more than 37 percent to 42 percent of your pretax income.

For example, 30 percent of $50 000 in annual pretax income would result in a loan payment of about $1500 per month. A 20 percent loan, however, results in a more manageable monthly mortgage payment of only $833 a month. In your post-debt era, less may be more.

Keeping Costs Down

Because you are cash-strapped and haven't been able to save much for a down payment, you want to put as little money down and pay as little per month as possible on your new house. Canada Mortgage and Housing Corporation will insure a mortgage with as little as 5 percent down payment, for a fee of course.

Two Cents

Want to keep your credit outstanding? Follow these rules: 1) Pay all of your bills on time. All of your bills. You would be surprised at the kind of bills that might show up on a credit report if you pay them late. 2) Once a year, get a copy of your credit report and make sure that there are no errors on it.

Over Your Limit

Remember: The financially savvy earn interest; the financially illiterate pay interest.

The two main things to consider when looking for a mortgage are the points you will pay for the loan and your closing costs (things like land transfer taxes, real estate agent fees, and lawyer's fees). A point is 1 percent of the loan value, so the lower the points, the better. Closing costs can be outrageous, but here are some tips for savings money on other hidden fees:

➤ Negotiate with your lender to cover the appraisal and/or inspection fee. The lender will conduct its own appraisal to make sure the house is not overvalued (and that in the event that the bank has to foreclose, it will get its minimum investment out of the house.) An inspection is done for your purposes, and you should have one, even if you think the house is perfect. A qualified home inspector will tell you if you need updated electrical wiring or amperage service, plumbing, a new roof, or have dreaded termites or wood rot. Both of these services cost

Money Talks

The CMHC is a crown corporation that administers the federal government's National Housing Act (NHA). Its primary objective is to assist in providing housing opportunities for low- to moderate-income families who cannot come up with more than 25 percent down payment on a home. The agency does not generally provide the funds for the mortgages directly, but rather insures home mortgage loans made by private lenders such as mortgage brokers and banks.

Cheque It Out

Do you think you may have some money kicking around in an old bank account? Or perhaps a long-dead relative does, on which you might eligible to make a claim. The Bank of Canada offers a free service on their website (http://www.bank-banque-canada.ca) for searching unclaimed bank balances. You can also write to Unclaimed Balances Services, Bank of Canada, Ottawa, K1A 0G9 or send your request by fax at (613) 782-7802.

anywhere from $150 to $300, and the bank will usually waive its appraisal fee if you ask.

➤ Get a tax rebate on your land transfer fees. This will take some foresight, but if you think you might be in the market for a home, you can buy a home-owners savings plan from a chartered bank. (The plans go by different names from province to province.) When you purchase the plan, you get a tax rebate for that year, and then, when you buy your home (it has to be your first home, principal residence), you use the money in your plan and receive a substantial break on land transfer fees, depending on the purchase price of the home, and on how much you deposited into your plan.

Finding Money for a Down Payment

Even with CMHC-insured mortgage, you will need to come up with at least a few thousand dollars for a down payment, which can be difficult. Here are two ways to get the money:

Withdraw money from your registered retirement saving plan (though you probably don't have much there if you're reading this book). The government allows you to "borrow" from your retirement savings without paying the income tax penalty in order to buy a principal residence. The only catch is that you have to pay back what you borrowed within 15 years. (You can now take advantage of this a second time, as long as you have paid back the "loan" from the first purchase).

Buy the house with a lease-option. In this scenario, you lease the house from the seller for a year or two and the seller agrees to earmark part of the money for your down payment. If you pay $1000 a month for two years and the seller agrees to utilize 50% of that as your down payment, then after two years you have put $12 000 down on the house. This is how one of your authors bought their first home. This plan isn't ideal in a seller's market—most people would rather have the purchase be a done deal, but if the market is sluggish, a seller is more likely to go for this sort of plan.

Whatever you do with your new credit, do not make the same mistakes you made before. Make sure that any debt you acquire is manageable.

> ### Two Cents
>
> It really does pay to be nice. An Anglican priest living in British Columbia retired in his 60s. He and his wife, having lived in Church-owned houses all their lives, had never had a mortgage to deal with. During his retirement, the priest had driven one of his old parishioners to her hair appointment once a week, and in her will, she stipulated the priest's outstanding mortgage was to be paid off—an amount of close to $70 000!

> ### The Least You Need to Know
> ➤ Car loans are also a good way to get credit again, but they can be very expensive.
> ➤ You can get a mortgage even with a few black marks on your credit report.

Chapter 20

What the Rich Know That You Don't

In This Chapter

➤ Assets versus liabilities

➤ Investment basics

➤ Investing versus speculating

➤ Determining long-term goals

➤ The 10 percent solution

Becoming intelligent with money requires more than just getting out of debt. It also means making your money work for you instead of you working for it. It means earning interest instead of paying interest. It means buying assets instead of liabilities.

All of these things are true even if you are not out of debt yet. Even if you are diligently repaying your debts, it is still time to begin to think and act like the rich do; not because being rich is the goal (it may or may not be), but because rich people understand money.

Beginning with this chapter, and for the next few chapters, we will show you how money works for the wealthy and how you can begin to make more of it. Not only will this enable you to get out of debt more quickly, it just makes life easier. As John Lennon once said, "I'd rather be rich and unhappy than poor and unhappy."

Start Now

It is easy to say that you can't begin to invest until you are out of debt. That is commendable. It is also wrong. If we are looking at how wealthy people treat money, do you think that they don't have debts or that they don't have bills to pay? Of course, they do. Their bills would dwarf yours by comparison because their overhead is so much higher than yours. But that does not stop them from using their money wisely.

They buy cattle ranches, collect art, invest in businesses, dabble in the stock market, and gobble up real estate because they know that money invested is money returned. Despite mortgages, credit card bills, family members needing help, and huge tax liabilities, most wealthy people make sure to invest at least 10 percent of their income. Investing is how rich people stay ahead.

It doesn't matter what type of investment you pick; you could choose to start your own business or buy some mutual funds. The important thing is to shift your thinking from just getting out of debt to getting ahead.

We are not saying that you have to get rich. You don't. What we are saying is that if you are in debt, then maybe there are a few things you could learn about money, and rich people are the best role models.

Take Jill, for example. A writer and producer for the television show *Cheers*, she made a lot of money and now lives the good life. But she does not just have her money sitting in the bank. Jill owns six in-and-out auto lube franchises. Her money makes money.

You need to begin to do the same. Sure, money is tight, but there are ways for you to create investment capital without changing your life. We explain how to do so at the end of the chapter, so read on.

Money Talks

In 1963, John Lennon and Paul McCartney formed Northern Songs, a corporation that would own the rights to Beatles songs. The company was formed with assets of a little more than $200. In the late 1980s, Michael Jackson gained control of the company, paying more than $60 million for it.

Money Talks

The *World Bank Atlas* estimates that the total value of all assets owned by individuals in the world is between $500 trillion and $1 quadrillion.
(That's 1 000 000 000 000 000.)
This amount does not include assets owned by governments or religions.

Assets and Liabilities

In the movie *The Edge*, Anthony Hopkins and Alec Baldwin played two men stranded in the Alaskan outback. Armed with only a few knives, a book about survival in the wilderness, and

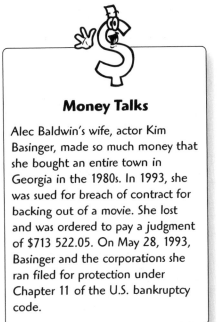

Money Talks

Alec Baldwin's wife, actor Kim Basinger, made so much money that she bought an entire town in Georgia in the 1980s. In 1993, she was sued for breach of contract for backing out of a movie. She lost and was ordered to pay a judgment of $713 522.05. On May 28, 1993, Basinger and the corporations she ran filed for protection under Chapter 11 of the U.S. bankruptcy code.

their wits, the two had to find a way to live and make it out.

At one point a grizzly bear began to stalk them. The survival book had a chapter on how to kill a bear. Baldwin was convinced they could not do it without a gun. Hopkins thought otherwise. His motto was, "What one man can do another can do." He read the book, learned how to kill a bear, believed that what one man could do another could do, and made Baldwin believe it, too. It was not easy, but they killed the bear.

Only a movie, yes, but it's a powerful lesson nonetheless. What one man can do, another can do. If those men can slay a movie bear, you can slay the money bear. What the financially literate can do, you can do, too—if you learn how they do it. Do you want to know how the wealthy became rich in the first place? They bought assets.

Liabilities Are Not Assets

We all think we know the difference between an asset and a liability, but sometimes the most obvious thing is the most difficult. The problem for most people who fall into debt is that they buy liabilities, but think they are assets. The first thing to understand then is the difference between an asset and a liability and how they affect your bottom line.

There are many ways to define what assets and liabilities are. Accountants have definitions, as do business people and investors, but let's keep it simple:

➤ An asset makes you money.

➤ A liability costs you money.

If you want to get rich, or out of debt, you will buy assets instead of liabilities. Let's say that you and your sister Sydney both just inherited $5000. What would you do with that money? If you are like most people, you would buy a liability. Maybe you would use it as a down payment on a new car or use it to take your mate on a nice trip. Those are fine things, but they just don't make you money. They cost you money.

Look at the facts. If you put that $5000 down on a new car, you would be creating more debt in the form of monthly payments. Sure the car would be an "asset" in the conventional sense of the word, but a car and a car loan don't make you any money. They cost you money. The same is true for a trip. These things look like assets, but they are liabilities insofar as money goes, see? (This is not to say that you shouldn't buy a new car when you need one.)

Let's also assume Sydney is a bit more financially literate than you and that she decides to do something different with her $5000. She wants to buy an asset. She might buy some stocks or mutual funds, or she might invest it in some real estate. Maybe she will decide to expand her business with it. She would use the money in such a way that it would make her more money instead of cost her money.

Consider the difference. Even if you got a low interest rate, your new car would end up costing you maybe another $20 000. Five years from today, you would be another $25 000 in the hole (with a five-year-old car to show for it). Conversely, $5000 put in a mutual fund might make Sydney another $3000. Five years later, she would be $8000 ahead. There's a big difference between $25 000 down versus $8000 ahead.

This, then, creates a cycle. With $8000 to use, Sydney might be able to purchase a small rental property and thereby create even more income for herself. You would have an older car with probably 75 000 miles on it that is worth one third of what it cost you and no way to create more money.

Over Your Limit

A $20 000 car loan at 15 percent interest payable over five years would end up costing you over $33 000.

Multiply this time and again, and you will begin to see why the rich do indeed get richer. Assets make money; liabilities cost money. Wealthy people buy assets. The poor and middle class buy liabilities thinking they are assets.

Types of Assets

Of course, you need a new car sometimes (well, maybe you don't need a new car; maybe a used car would do, and you could pocket the difference). The point is, if you are going to get out of debt, get ahead, and make more money, you need to buy some assets; you need to invest some money.

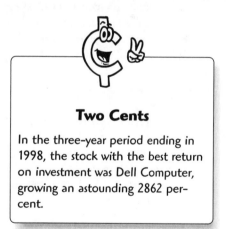

Two Cents

In the three-year period ending in 1998, the stock with the best return on investment was Dell Computer, growing an astounding 2862 percent.

Consider the following investments:

➤ **The stock market**. You can buy stocks, bonds, or mutual funds to make money for now or for your retirement.

➤ **Real estate.** With a mortgage backed by the Canada Housing and Mortgage Corporation, qualifying for a loan is not so far-fetched.

➤ **A new business.** We all know the economy is changing. Home-based businesses and other entrepreneurial activities are the jobs of the future.

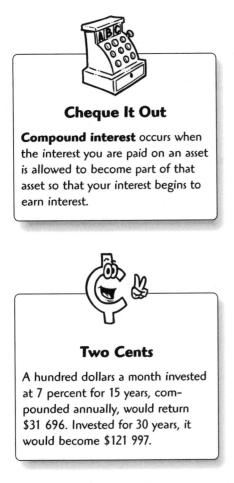

Investing 101

So just what is investing? It is putting something of value into something else with the expectation that the end result will be bigger and better. You can invest your time in a good cause, you can invest your energy in your job, or you can invest yourself in a relationship. When you invest in these things, you expect that something good will come of your effort. Likewise, when you invest your money in stocks, mutual funds, real estate, or a business, you do so because you think your money will grow over time.

The magic in investing is in something called compounding. As you earn investment returns, your returns begin to gain returns as well, allowing you to turn a measly dollar into thousands of dollars if you leave it invested long enough.

You saw this concept in action with the example of Sydney earlier. Her $5000 became $8000. If she continued to invest the $8000, it would soon be worth $12 000, and so on. The more money you save and invest today, the more you'll have in the future. Real wealth is created almost miraculously through investing and the most mundane and commonplace principles of time, patience, and the power of compounding.

Compounding is so magical that you can fairly easily double and triple your money over long periods of time. When you hear someone brag about doubling his money in 10 years, you should know that you only need a 7.1 percent annual return to double your money in 10 years (This is known as the rule of 7.). If the Standard and Poor's 500 (a widely used barometer of the stock market) had gone up 10.6 percent a year, the poor fellow who doubled his money in 10 years underperformed compared to the market.

Investing Is Not Speculating

With compounding, you have to wait patiently for years for your riches to accumulate. But why put your money in slow-and-steady investment vehicles that merely promise double-digit returns when (according to some infomercials) you could have near-instant riches? What if you want it all now?

Then speculating is for you. Speculating is the art of taking your hard-earned money and putting it in a scheme that promises potential amazing returns. The key word is potential. What are the odds of winning the lottery? Probably something like one in seven million. What about Vegas? Your odds of walking out a winner are less than 50:50. These are extreme examples of speculating. Speculating is like gambling.

According to the dictionary, a speculative investment is a "transaction or venture the profits of which are conjectural or subject to chance; to buy or sell with the hope of profiting by fluctuations in price." To invest, though, is to "commit capital in business in order to earn a financial return; the outlay of money for income or profit."

Over Your Limit

You have a greater chance of dying from flesh-eating bacteria (about one in a million) than you do of winning the lottery.

Understanding the difference between speculating and investing is simple once you focus on the difference between two words in the definitions of these concepts. The key word in the definition of speculation is hope. The key word in the definition of invest is earn.

Let's say that you hear your dentist telling a patient about a company that is "going to go through the roof in the next few months." If you call your broker the first thing the next morning and place an order for 100 shares, you've just speculated. Do you know anything about the company? Are you familiar with its competition? What were its earnings last quarter? Are you just hoping that your dentist knows what he is talking about? That's speculation.

Investing, on the other hand, requires research, expertise, and patience on your part. If you do your homework and learn about where and how to invest your money, the

Money Talks

Tulips were introduced in the Netherlands in 1593. In 1636, trading in tulips rapidly increased, and more and more people started speculating. Bulbs of one or two guilders could be worth a hundred a few months later. Fortunes were being made, and people from all walks of life who knew nothing of tulips became swept up in the gamble. "Tulipomania" was in full bloom. In 1637, prices spiraled to a ridiculous level. The market finally collapsed in 1637, leaving many people bankrupt.

chances that you will lose it are quite small. Yes, all investing requires some element of risk. The difference is, real investing takes a lot of the risk out of the equation (but even with investing, there's always at least a little risk, except with guaranteed income certificates, which, coincidentally, usually reap low returns.

Setting Your Investment Goals

Deciding how you are going to become an investor and what types of investments you will make requires planning. You need to answer these sorts of questions:

➤ What do you want to accomplish by investing? Is this money to get you out of debt? A down payment on a house? Your child's education? A home? Income to live on in retirement?

➤ What is your investment time frame? Five years? Ten, twenty?

➤ How much money will you need to reach your goals?

Don't let yourself get away with nonspecific answers, either. In the end, investing is about numbers, and you need to get used to that. That is a good thing. Real numbers let you see exactly what you need in order to get to your financial destination. How much do you need to get out of debt? How much will post-secondary education cost when your child needs to go? How much yearly income is reasonable for your retirement?

After you have a rough idea of how much money you will need, you can start to think about what investment vehicles might be right for you and what kind of returns you can reasonably expect to make from them. Take a look at how various types of investments have performed historically in the United States:

➤ Treasury bills or money market funds have yielded roughly 4.2 percent per year during this century.

➤ Long-term government bonds have returned around 4.0 percent per year since 1900.

➤ Overall, the American stock market has returned an average of 9.8 percent per year since 1900.

The Canadian economy has moved, more or less, in lock-step with the U.S. economy, usually a few paces behind. The Canadian stock market has yet to enjoy the phenomenal growth of the U.S. stock market, that turned ordinary investors into millionaires. But our stock market is strong and healthy and continuing to grow. The point is to remember that all investments accrue over time. Be patient and prepared to keep your money invested for as long as possible.

Investing in real estate can be profitable as well, but it is very complex. Read Chapter 21, "Real Estate Investing," for a more detailed discussion of this topic.

Investing for Retirement

Though the point of this book is to help you get more money now, we would be remiss if we didn't explain a key element of Canadian investing: registered investing. When you decide you want to earmark a particular investment—just about any will qualify—for retirement, you "register" it with the government. This means you are more or less guaranteeing that you will not touch the money until you retire, which is somewhere between 60 and 69 years of age.

In exchange for taking some of the pressure off the government to look after you in your golden years, you get to enjoy three tax benefits:

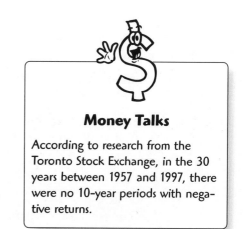

Money Talks

According to research from the Toronto Stock Exchange, in the 30 years between 1957 and 1997, there were no 10-year periods with negative returns.

➤ registered investments are tax-deductible, which means the amount you invest comes directly off your gross income, thereby reducing your tax bill for the investing year

➤ registered investments are tax-deferred, because you do not claim any profits or derive any income from them, therefore you do not pay any income tax on them, until you collapse them upon retirement.

➤ registered investments are, therefore, tax-sheltered, which means the investment is allowed to compound undisturbed.

Taking the Plunge

The two major variables in figuring out your investment plan are your risk tolerance and the amount of time you can dedicate to investing. In our capitalistic society, the biggest rewards are given to those who take the biggest risks—the entrepreneurs.

Rather than being risk takers, most of us have gotten into the habit of putting in eight hours a day working for someone else. At the end of the week, we cash our paycheque and do it all over again. It's called the rat race.

But think about the guy who owns the company you work for. He's not hurting for money, is he? He knows something you are just figuring out: Working for someone else doesn't make you rich. Being the employee just makes you the employee. Being the boss is more risky, but it can also make you rich.

You need to become the boss of your own financial world. It need not be a full-time position, and you certainly do not have to quit your job tomorrow because you have decided to become an investor today. What it will require is learning the entrepreneurial skills necessary to take back control of your financial house. It is going to require taking chances with both your time and money and possibly being told by your loved ones that it cannot be done. But it can.

So what kind of financial investment is right for you? Here are the pros and cons of each possible investment option:

➤ Stocks are fairly risky, but they can easily be done on a part-time basis and have historically given good returns.

➤ Bonds are much less risky than stocks and can also be done part-time, but they give smaller returns.

➤ Real estate can be risky if you buy the wrong piece of property or buy at the wrong time, but generally speaking, it can be a great way to make extra money part-time. For some people, however, the hassles of dealing with tenants are not worth the possible return.

➤ Starting your own business is probably a full-time venture, and both the risks and rewards are high.

The 10 Percent Solution

You are probably thinking that this all sounds well and good, but where will you find any extra money to invest? We are here to tell you that you can create it, but we warn you: It will not be easy.

Over Your Limit

The 1997 savings rate of Canadians who are saving for their retirement was 11.8 percent of income. Though people earning less than $10 000 a year comprised the smallest group of savers, they still saved the greatest percentage of their income, at 19.9 percent, or an average of $1192 that year, according to StatsCan.

Of course, you have lots of bills; that's why you bought this book. You have a list of things and people you need to pay: rent, mortgages, car payments, dad, credit cards, and household goods. Pay them. But you need to add one more category to that list: you. We are not advising you to be irresponsible. Pay your bills. Get out of debt. But as you do, pay yourself first.

First? Yes, first. You need to take a fixed amount of your income every month, put it in savings, and not touch it. Saving 10 percent of your income would be great, but 5 percent would do for starters. Do it every month. As we said, this will not be easy. It will take self-discipline. But it's the best way to be sure you have money to invest.

Say that you bring home $2000 a month. Of that amount, $600 is paid toward rent, $300 goes for the car payment, food takes up another $500, and utilities take another $300. You have $300 left over for everything else. Now, take a percentage of the total, say 5 percent ($100), and stick it in the bank. Besides getting into the habit of saving, you will begin to create a nest egg.

At the end of a year, how much would you have? $1200? Nope. You would have more. Why? Because you would have begun to act like the rich do and you would have been compounding your money and earning interest instead of paying interest. That $1200 might be worth $1300 at the end of the year. It would be a small, but very significant, milestone.

You don't need a lot to get started in the world of investing. You can buy plenty of mutual funds for $1000. A total of $5000 could be the down payment on a duplex in some cities or towns. You could live in half, rent out the other half, and begin a real estate investment career.

The secret, and the hard part, is to put away money every month and to pay yourself before all others. There will be months where you are sure you cannot do it, but who is more important to pay than you? If you don't prioritize your finances, who will? Pay yourself first, and you will thank yourself later.

If you do this, you will begin to act like the rich. You will be creating the means to buy some real assets instead of frittering a measly $100 away on liabilities. You will earn interest instead of pay interest. You will be acting like the financially literate. Remember: What one man can do, another can do.

The Least You Need to Know

➤ Liabilities are not assets if they cost you money.

➤ Compounding your money is the secret to getting ahead.

➤ Investing and speculating are very different.

➤ Saving money every month is how you can get started.

Real Estate Investing

Real estate is one of the best ways to invest your money. Not only does it allow you to use other people's money to get ahead, but it is also generally less risky than almost any other investment. Real estate is one of the least risky investments you can make because you own the entire investment, so you can control almost all of it.

Most other investments are subject to a host of outside factors that affect the investment. Stocks fall because of such silly things as rumour, gossip, or herd mentality. Bonds fall the day a new inflation report hits. If Asia blinks, 200 mutual funds lose 20 percent of their value. Real estate, although certainly subject to market conditions, is just not so whimsical. It does not appreciate or depreciate in a day like some other investments do.

Real Estate and You

With real estate, you have a great opportunity to get ahead. The investments are solid and give very good returns. Many of the richest people in North America, people like Donald Trump and Merv Griffin, owe their fortunes to real estate.

Banks also own real estate. Think about your bank. How big is it? How many branches does it have? Banks make much of their profit by investing in real estate. Consider the buildings they have their offices in. These trophy properties, the furniture, the huge salaries paid to their executives, and the dividends paid on their stock are almost all made possible by real estate investments, both here and abroad.

There are many ways to invest in real estate. You can buy your own home, commercial property, rental homes, or raw land, for example. Of all of these options, buying and selling rental properties stands out for the person who is just beginning to get out of debt, save a little money, and is looking to start investing.

Look around your city. Someone owns all those apartment houses and homes that people rent. Becoming a landlord enables you to invest in a tangible asset, maintain control of that asset, and sell it (usually) for a great profit. The best part is that you don't need a good credit history and lots of cash to get started.

It is important to understand that while real estate is often used to fuel fortunes, it is not an investment without risk. Markets are cyclical, renters fail to pay their rent, tenants move with no notice, buildings get damaged; many things can go wrong. The point is, if you are willing to put up with these types of risks, the rewards can potentially be great.

Money Talks

Bank CEOs are compensated at the same level as other corporate CEOs, of both privately and publicly owned companies. According to *Report on Business* magazine's 1999 ranking of CEO salaries and compensation, Charles Baillie, CEO and Chairman of Toronto-Dominion Bank, is number 8 on the list at $8.5 million, behind such notables as Peter Munk of Barrick Gold Corp., pulling in $38 million (#1); Frank Stronach of Magna International at $26 million (#3); and Ivan Fecan, CEO of CTV Inc., at $8.9 million (#7). CIBC's John Cleghorn, as of January 2000, took home $6.7 million.

Use Other People's Money to Get Rich

Besides good profit, the biggest advantage real estate has over other investments is that the system is set up to allow you to use other people's money. This concept is one of the most important reasons why real estate can make you richer than any other investment you could choose.

Most commodities that you can invest in require that you pay all of the money needed to purchase them. Take the stock market, for example. Unless you are buying on margin (which is rare and risky), you are required to pay for the shares you purchase. There is nobody else's money to use but your own. Other investments, including bonds, mutual funds, bank deposits, coins, stamps, or art, work the same way. If you want to own it, you have to pay for it. That is true everywhere in the world of investments, except real estate.

Money Talks

The top three banks in the country in terms of assets are CIBC, with more than $268 billion; Royal Bank of Canada, with more than $262 billion; and Bank of Nova Scotia, with $232 billion. Their respective international rankings are 55, 57, and 62.

Cheque It Out

Leverage allows others to pay for property you buy.

In real estate, you typically put down 3 percent, 5 percent, or 10 percent of the money necessary to purchase a property. Rarely does an investor put down more than 20 percent for a purchase. The bank (and sometimes the seller) loans you the rest of the money to buy the property. You are using other people's money to buy a great and valuable asset. Remember what we said earlier: The rich buy assets; the middle class buy liabilities.

This ability to use other people's money is called leverage. The advantages of using leverage are twofold. First, because more money is invested, leverage significantly increases the percentage of profit you can make. Second, and more importantly, leverage allows you to purchase a much larger investment than you would normally have been able to.

For example, with $10 000 to invest, you could buy $10 000 worth of stocks or bonds or mutual funds or gold. However, if you used your $10 000 to invest in real estate, you could purchase a $300 000 four-unit apartment building. You put down $10 000, the bank puts down $290 000, and you get to own an asset worth $300 000. That is remarkable.

Banks aren't the only ones who help you buy property using leverage. Sellers will often carry some of the loan to help you get into a property as well. You can even buy property without putting any of your own money down. Much more common, however, is getting banks and sellers to finance 80 to 90 percent of the property. That is the rule, not the exception in real estate.

Why Real Estate Works

Another advantage real estate has over other investments is that it offers many different sorts of profits and financial incentives. The following sections detail the things that make real estate such an attractive investment.

Cash Flow

Cash flow (or income) is the money you receive as a return on your investment and is probably the most sought-after return from any investment. In real estate, your rental income is your cash flow. The more units you have, the greater your cash flow. If you buy the right piece of property, not only will your rental income enable you to pay off your property's mortgage and build equity every month, but you should also have enough extra left over to use as you want.

Tax Deductions

Ordinary and reasonable expenses connected to your real estate business are deductible from your annual income tax. These expenses include interest paid on your loans, utilities, insurance, property taxes, maintenance, supplies, legal fees, dinners with your broker (within reason), office supplies, and a new computer. Even a trip to Whistler can be deductible if you are considering purchasing property there.

Equity Growth

Your equity will grow in your investment property in two ways. The first is due to inflation. Inflation is great when you are a real estate investor because not only will the value of your property increase, but you can also increase your monthly income by raising rents (in accordance with the landlord/tenant act in your province or

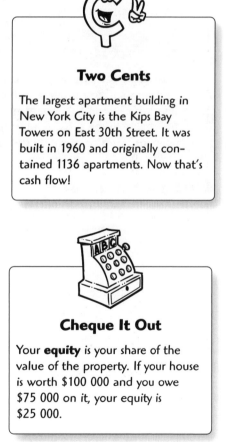

Two Cents

The largest apartment building in New York City is the Kips Bay Towers on East 30th Street. It was built in 1960 and originally contained 1136 apartments. Now that's cash flow!

Cheque It Out

Your **equity** is your share of the value of the property. If your house is worth $100 000 and you owe $75 000 on it, your equity is $25 000.

city). Your equity also grows as you use your rental income to pay off your mortgage. And while inflation has been somewhat stagnant in Canada for the last few years, hovering around two percent, certain rental markets have seen huge growth. In Toronto and Vancouver, for example, lack of housing has forced rents up, regardless of inflation.

Increased equity has another benefit. It gives you increased borrowing power at the bank. Your bank will happily loan you money based upon your property's increased value. You can then use this money to pay off your old loan, and any money left over can go in your pocket. Even better, you can use increased rents to pay any increase in your new loan payments.

The Ability to Grow into Even Larger Buildings

As you get out of debt, you will have more and more money to allocate toward making money. Many real estate moguls began just as you will, with a small property, but with the desire to grow into larger ones. Because tenants pay off your mortgage, getting a bigger property is very possible.

Subsidized Rent

Most provinces, through their department or ministry of housing and municipal affairs, offer rent subsidy programs to people earning little or no income. The government determines what the tenant is able to pay, then agrees to pay you, the landlord, the difference. Some provincial programs, such as the Nova Scotia Rent Supplement Program, are also partially funded by Canada Mortgage and Housing Corporation.

Getting a Loan

The most difficult part of getting started in any business is finding the money to buy the business. When that business happens to be real estate, the government, through the

Money Talks

The only caveat with investing in real estate is that you have to pay capital gains tax on any profit you make from selling real estate that is not your principal residence. And if you sell a rental property at a profit, the Canada Customs and Revenue Agency doesn't stop there. It will also want a portion of your net rental income. Get a good accountant.

CMHC, will step in and help you out considerably. We've mentioned this organization before, but insuring high-ratio mortgages on investment properties is just one of the many services offered. Just as in purchases of individual homes or properties, CMHC works with your approved lender to finance your residential property purchase. Because CMHC is insuring your purchase, you can get a larger loan, up to 85% financing without a maximum dollar amount.

CMHC can also offer lower interest rates to borrowers, and also bundles application fees and premiums into the mortgage loan, which saves you cash at a time when you are no doubt short.

Getting Started

Even with great loan programs, real estate investing requires a large commitment of time and money, so research and planning are critical. The first and most important thing to do once you decide to invest in real estate is to learn all you can about it.

Study Real Estate

There are many sources from which to learn about real estate investing. Many excellent books about real estate are available, and community colleges have courses about real estate taught by teachers with real-world experience. Apartment owners associations offer very practical property management seminars.

Finally, many authors and lecturers offer weekend and evening seminars. Along with the chance to purchase the books and tapes (of course), these individuals usually have plenty of good information and ideas to share.

Besides learning about the subject of real estate and real estate investing, you will also need to educate yourself on the property market in your locale. You must become an expert in your area and understand how it performs before you ever start buying.

Find an Agent

After you bone up on real estate basics, find a real estate agent who specializes in investment property and who would be willing to help you learn about the market. Commercial real estate brokers are the best place to begin your search for one. Just ask around for some names of real estate agents who specialize in selling apartment houses.

After you get a few names and speak with a couple of agents, you will find that most of them will be happy to help you because they will see you as a source of potential future income. When picking an agent, take the following advice:

> ➤ **Demand experience.** The real estate profession is plagued by high turnover and thus it contains a workforce made up of many newcomers. Most new agents are

Over Your Limit

Beware of "get rich quick" real estate seminars that make promises seemingly too good to be true. These seminars are indeed get-rich-quick schemes—for the speaker. Be especially wary of the ones that are free; they are just trying to get you in the door. They will soon try and sell you the real seminar that will cost real money.

Over Your Limit

Before buying any property, consider and analyze the possible downsides to real estate investing. You could have tenant problems, problems collecting rents, and repairs to make.

full of good intentions, but why trust one of the largest investments you'll ever make to someone without experience? Always look for an agent with at least two years of experience.

➤ **Hire a full-time realtor.** Too many real estate agents practise part time. These folks have either retired from some other career, work in real estate seasonally, or are earning a second income for the family. No matter how long they have been in real estate, their lack of full-time commitment makes it impossible for them to fully service your needs. Hire a full-time professional.

➤ **Consider education.** In many provinces, the requirements for real estate licensing are not that difficult. You cannot rely on licensing to indicate competence. Hire someone smart.

➤ **Interview.** Before you hire an agent to help you buy or sell an investment property, speak with at least three agents. Get recommendations from friends, landlords, property owners, family, and neighbours. Look on the Internet and in the local newspaper. Make some brief fact-finding calls to determine which of the agents on your list are full-time, experienced, and educated. Find one you like, explain your goals, and ask him or her out to lunch.

You need to find out things about your area from the agent. Learn how much properties sell for. Ask about good and bad locations. Discover market trends.

Research Rates

Just as important as researching value, you must become equally familiar with the rental rates in your market. Find out what current properties rent for. What does a single-family home rent for? What about a two-bedroom duplex or a four-bedroom apartment? Another source for this information, besides the real estate agent, is the classified ads in your local paper.

Research the historical values in your area to see whether the market is appreciating or depreciating. Obviously, you don't want to invest in an area that has been hit hard by the closing of a factory, for example.

Again, the help of a real estate agent is invaluable, because most real estate agents have access to this information through their local Real Estate Board. If you are fortunate enough to find an agent who specializes in investment property (not all do), he or she may have the data you want readily available. The more data you can get, the better you will be able to make some estimates of the future trends for property in your area.

Begin to read the business section of the paper with new vigour. Business expansion means jobs, jobs mean employees, and that means more people to rent units. Even high inflation becomes good news to the real estate investor because that means you can charge higher rents (although if your adjustable rate mortgage loan goes up, it is not good news).

Money Talks

According to Royal LePage Real Estate Services, Vancouver has consistently reported the highest average home price in Canada since 1990. Regina has reported the lowest. It stands to reason that rental costs follow these same trends.

The goal of all this research is to learn about real estate investments as a business. If you do your homework, you will be able to find a nice little starter unit that will put you on the path to becoming a real estate mogul.

A Plan of Action

After you have learned about real estate investments and understand the product, it is time to put together a plan of how you want to meet your investment goals. One of

Money Talks

If you had invested in real estate in Whistler, B.C. in the last decade, you would have enjoyed the highest real estate growth in Canada in the last century. Property values have skyrocketed since the 1960s, and in early 2000, the average home cost around $900 000. Interestingly, the tourism industry is forecast to expand to maximum capacity over the next seven years, but the lack of affordable housing is making it difficult for local businesses to keep employees.

the most important steps in accomplishing any goal is the definition of the goal itself.

Generally speaking, successful people have very well-defined goals. It's not enough to just say you want to get rich or that you want to find a good deal and make a lot of money. Being specific is the key. Buying a four-unit building or making enough profit in five years to buy your husband a new car are the kinds of goals that can focus the mind.

After you have defined your goal, put pen to paper and decide what type of real estate investment best meets that goal. Analyze the amount you have to invest, market conditions, what type of loan you can get, and the rents you can expect to get, and then figure out how much building you can afford to buy.

If you have researched your neighbourhood well, you should know exactly what a property will cost and how much revenue it can be expected to generate. You can even figure out how long you will need to hold onto it before you build up enough equity to trade into a bigger and better building. This is the kind of information you need to incorporate into your plan.

The right set of personal goals and a specific plan of action will give you the incentive to begin this new business, to do the necessary legwork, and to take a risk and invest your money. In a few years, you will have the payoffs.

Two Cents

With a fixed-rate mortgage, your interest rate stays the same for the term of the mortgage, which normally is three to five years. The advantage of a fixed-rate mortgage is that you always know exactly how much your mortgage payment will be, and you can plan for it. With a variable-rate mortgage, your interest rate and monthly payments usually start lower than a fixed-rate mortgage, but they can change either up or down.

Money Talks

Donald Trump was forced to file for bankruptcy in the early 1990s. By the end of the decade, he had reestablished himself in real estate, gaming, and entertainment. His list of assets in New York includes the Empire State Building, the Trump Tower, and the Plaza Hotel. He also now owns three casinos: the Trump Plaza Hotel and Casino, the Castle Casino Resort, and the Taj Mahal.

Your First Real Estate Investment

Your first property will be a big step. You will be investing your hard-earned money, hoping to make enough extra to finish that debt-repayment plan or to finally get ahead. Accordingly, you will have a strong desire to make a bundle of money all at once.

Don't try to become a millionaire on your first purchase. Many beginning investors make the mistake of purchasing a no-money-down, bank-repossessed, fixer-upper because they think a lot of money can be made doing so. Sure, this is possible, but it takes a lot of work and, very often, takes years of experience. A first property is not the place to take such a chance. Yes, buy a property that won't break the bank, but don't buy a place that is filled with problems.

When a hockey player begins his career, he doesn't go straight to the NHL. He begins in the junior leagues or varsity hockey, perhaps culminating in being part of an Olympic team. He (and increasingly she) learns about teamwork, stick handling, and the politics of sport, and then makes a bid for the NHL. That is what you should do too. Before you know it, you too may have scored a financial hat trick.

The Least You Need to Know

➤ Leverage is the greatest financial secret in the world.

➤ The unique characteristics of real estate as an investment make it a very good investment choice.

➤ CMHC–insured mortgage loans make getting into real estate investing possible for many people.

➤ Finding a good agent is critical.

➤ Start small, but dream big.

Chapter 22

Stocks, Bonds, and Mutual Funds

Do not despair if you were not part of the incredible bull market that rampaged through the '90s (well, you might despair a little bit). Still, you can make money in the stock market, even if it's not a wild bull (when the market is rising, it's called a bull market; and when it's falling, it's a bear market).

Over the last 75 years, stocks have been a basic part of any good investment portfolio. Over the long term, stocks have historically outperformed all other investments, including real estate. From 1977 to 1997, the Canadian stock market returned an average annual 13.5 percent gain. The next best performing asset class, bonds, returned 11.99 percent. Isn't it time that you began to invest that money that you have been paying your creditors and started to earn 10 percent interest rather than pay it?

Stock Market Basics

Stocks are a great investment for someone coming out of debt for two reasons. One, you don't need a lot of money to get started. Two, you can invest in stocks in your spare time, so you need not quit your job.

When you buy stock, you are buying a small percentage of ownership in a company. The company sells the stock in order to raise capital. If the company is run well, it takes the money and uses it to make more money. As a result, its profits and earnings go up. When its earnings go up, its stock's value goes up as well. So if you pick a company that is well run and has the opportunity to make more money, the chances are good that your stock will rise in value.

Like any investment, investing in stocks is a risk. Do not use rent money to dabble in the stock market. You have to decide how much money you can afford to risk, how much you are willing to risk (which may be different), and then figure out which stocks you want to buy.

But before you do, there are some basic rules about the market that you need to understand up front:

➤ **The biggest single determiner of stock prices is earnings, how much money the company is making.** Over the short term, stock prices rise and fall based on everything from interest rates to gossip to news to investor sentiment. But over the long term, earnings are what matters. If a stock's underlying company's earnings rise substantially over the course of five years, so will its share price.

➤ **Risky investments generally pay more than safe ones.** Investors demand a higher rate of return for taking greater risks. That's a basic reason that stocks, which are perceived as riskier than bonds, tend to return more than bonds. That is also why a stock in a new startup company may double in a day or lose 50 percent of its value. It's a risky investment.

➤ **A diversified portfolio is key.** Diversifying among a number of different types

Money Talks

In 1969, an American investing $1000 in the stocks listed in the Standard & Poor 500 stock index (the S&P 500), would have more than $1 million worth of stocks by 1994, according to Lipper Financial Services.

Over Your Limit

Tony inherited $100 000. He took a class given by a well-known stock guru who taught him that buying and selling stocks quickly, often holding the stock for only a day or two, was the way to "safely double his money." He jumped in, never really learned any stock market fundamentals, began trading, and lost $60 000 within six weeks.

of stocks lessens your risk because even if some of your holdings go down, others go up, or vice versa.

➤ **Think long-term.** The market goes up and down. Individual stocks go up and down. Because markets do change, your initial investment may be worth less in any given year than what you put in. If you invest for the long term, you will be unaffected by yearly fluctuations.

Types of Stocks

When you begin to create an investment portfolio, you will want to avoid concentrating all your money in any single stock. You might be tempted to put all your money in one great stock, like Nortel, which has been roundly credited for the TSE's turn-of-the-century ascent (its stocks total roughly 17% of the TSE). But few stocks perform like Nortel, and even Nortel does not always perform like Nortel. What if you invest all $10 000 of your investment capital in Nortel, and it stays stagnant for three years? That's three years of lost opportunity. Diversifying your portfolio is critical.

Cheque It Out

Your **investment portfolio** is all your holdings at any given time. It may contain a combination of stocks, bonds, GICs, and mutual funds.

For every stock like Nortel, BCE (Nortel's former parent), or Corel that sometimes delivers amazing returns, there are thousands that do nothing. So rather than risk plowing all their money into the next high-tech flavour-of-the-month, most people create a portfolio with a variety of different types of stocks.

Obviously, some stocks fit into more than one of these categories.

Here are seven of the major types:

Growth stocks. Nortel is a classic growth stock, but any stock with rapidly rising profits fits the bill. Although growth investing can be highly profitable, it is also risky because the same investors who love a stock when its earnings are expanding bail out if the growth rate slows. That, in turn, can drive the stock's price down rapidly. Holding onto a growth stock a day too long is not fun.

Momentum stocks. Think of the Internet startup boom in the late '90s. Momentum investors will buy a stock simply because its price is going up. The risk is that it is difficult to know when the momentum will end.

Value stocks. Value stocks are stocks that are supposedly undervalued by the market and thus are less expensive. The market is down on them possibly because their earnings have taken a temporary hit because of some bad news, their product line is in a momentary lull, or some other passing event has knocked their price down. A value investor bets that whatever ails these companies will soon end. (For example, when Asian economies ran into trouble recently, stock prices of all Asian companies fell drastically—clearly, there were a few values available.)

Cyclical stocks. Some stocks, like those of oil producers, are cyclical because their services or products are not in constant demand. A cyclical investor might decide that because oil stocks tend to rise in the summer when oil prices rise, buying oil stocks in the spring is a good idea. Steel makers see sales rise when the economy heats up, spurring builders to put up new skyscrapers and consumers to buy new cars. Another cycle is at work in the steel business, too: When steel is expensive, steel makers build more steel plants, and the increased supply of steel causes the price of steel to fall, which then puts some plants out of business. When enough plants have gone out of business, the price of steel begins to rise, and the cycle begins again.

Large caps (capitalization). Also known as blue chips, these companies are the big boys. Blue chips are generally considered a less risky investment because the companies are well known and usually well run. Large caps include stocks like Imperial Oil, Loblaws, Inco, and Canadian Tire. Remember, though, less risk equals less return.

Small caps. An investment that's perceived as more risky, small caps are smaller companies with the potential for large growth.

Cheque It Out

When a stock is performing well, the company may decide to send **dividends** to its shareholders. In essence, a dividend is a cheque from the company to the shareholder paid out of company profits.

Two Cents

Dividends can offer a clue as to where management thinks a company's earnings are headed. A dividend requires a vote by the company's board of directors, so the paying of a dividend means, in essence, that the board has cast a vote of confidence in the long-term earning power of the business. If the outlook were glum, the board would eliminate the dividend and use the precious cash for more pressing needs. However, sometimes a company offers a good dividend to drive up the stock price.

Income stocks. Conservative investors who want a steady stream of cash from their investments generally favour income stocks that produce dividends.

Do Your Homework

You have to become a student of the market if you are going to make money. You need to read the *Report on Business* (ROB) and the *Financial Post* (FP). And because our economy is so influenced by the American economy, you might pick up the *Wall Street Journal* on occasion too. ROB and FP both have monthly magazines, and there are a plethora of other business publications such as *Canadian Business, MoneySense, IE:Money* as well as regional business titles. Popular online resources include Quicken.ca, imoney.ca (which also functions as the personal finance section of sympatico.ca), and the Investor Learning Centre, the non-profit resource arm of the Canadian Securities Institute, at www.investorlearning.ca.

Treat investing in the stock market as a business. In business, you make a profit by selling your product or service for more than it cost you. The same is true for buying and selling stocks. You have to listen and learn in order to buy low and sell high.

"Buy low and sell high" is an easy phrase to remember, but how do you know which stocks are low? The key to investing is to determine what is high and what is low, and then take advantage of that knowledge. To make money in stocks, you must find companies that the market has undervalued. That is how legendary stock billionaire Warren Buffet made his money.

According to Buffet, it is not all that difficult to make money in the stock market if you do your homework. The way to win, he says, is to

> Work, work, work, work and hope to have a few insights. How many insights do you need? Well, I'd argue that you don't need many in a lifetime. If you look at Berkshire

Cheque It Out

Just what is the **Dow Jones Industrial Average**? It is a compilation of 30 of the top blue-chip stocks, plus transportation and utility components. As the Dow goes, so goes the U.S. stock market. Stocks in the Dow Jones industrial average include American Express, AT&T, Boeing, Chevron, Coca-Cola, Eastman Kodak, Exxon, GE, Hewlett-Packard, IBM, McDonald's, 3M, Sears, Wal-Mart, and Disney. The TSE 300, TSE 200, TSE 100, TSE 60 and Toronto 35 are similar indexes, though the Dow Jones is regularly reported here in Canada also.

Hathaway [his investment company] and all of its accumulated billions, the top 10 insights account for most of it.

If you are going to be successful in your stock business, you need to put in the hours, do the research, learn the facts, and thereby reap the benefits.

Mutual Funds

You may not like the idea of having to pick individual stocks. If so, then mutual funds are for you. You can find funds that specialize in just about any type of investment, ranging from technology stocks to bonds to GICs, although stocks are the most common.

Mutual funds offer these advantages:

➤ The mutual fund company hires an expert, a *fund manager*, to pick a variety of stocks for its fund. As such, you are getting the expertise of one of the top stock pickers in the country when you buy a particular fund.

➤ Because the manager picks many different stocks for the fund, you are diversifying your portfolio and reducing your risk by not putting all your eggs in one basket.

➤ There are thousands of funds to choose from. Some are aggressive, and some are conservative. Some invest in high-tech companies, and others only invest in blue chips. You can pick and choose which fund fits your goals.

➤ Because many mutual funds automatically reinvest income and dividends in additional shares of the fund, they are one of the easiest ways to grow investments.

Over Your Limit

According to a graph of the Dow Jones Industrial Average (DJIA) published in 1997 by Value Line, the DJIA does not always go up. In 1928, it first hit 300, rose in 1929, and then fell and failed to reach 300 again until 1954. It first broke 1000 in 1972, rose slightly, then fell, and did not reach 1000 again until 1980.

Two Cents

If you are just starting out as a stock investor, mutual funds may be the way to go. You get the expertise of the portfolio manager and the advantage of picking what sector of the economy and what types of stocks you want, but you do so without the risk of having to pick a single stock.

Mutual funds are considered "near perfect investments," according to Fortune magazine editor Marshall Loeb, who says that they "give you the double-barreled advantages of instant diversification of your investments and professional management of your money." Millions of individual investors agree. Holdings in Canadian mutual funds today total about $389 billion—a dramatic increase from $3.5 billion in 1981—split among 1368 funds.

Types of Funds

Although investing in mutual funds is indeed less risky than investing in stocks, there is still a significant difference in philosophy from one fund to the next. The greater the perceived risk in the fund choices is, the greater the potential return or loss. You need to decide what an acceptable risk level is for you.

What type of fund fits your profile?

➤ **Growth funds** invest in large, well-established companies whose earnings are still accelerating. During the past five years, the average return of growth funds has been slightly higher than the S&P 500, generally considered an overall market indicator.

➤ **Income funds** are designed to generate accessible income for investors via dividends.

➤ **Small cap** funds invest in the stock of smaller companies with, hopefully, faster and higher growth potential than larger or blue-chip companies. As you might expect, these funds are often quite volatile.

➤ **Growth and income funds** look for both growth and dividends when selecting blue-chip stocks.

➤ **Balanced funds** invest in both stocks and bonds, a strategy that tries to balance the gains and losses of these two investments, which perform well under different economic conditions.

➤ **Bond funds** restrict their investments to corporate and government bonds.

➤ **Equity income funds** invest in high-yield common stocks, bonds, and preferred stocks. Their goal is to provide income at the same time that they increase their capital.

➤ **Index funds** are funds that aim to mirror the performance of a market index. Financial institutions such as CIBC, TD, and Canada Trust all offer index mutual funds in their fund families.

➤ **International (or global) funds**, as the name implies, invest in foreign companies. Today there are more than 300 international funds; some of these funds concentrate on emerging markets such as Latin America; others invest in equities from around the world, including the United States.

➤ **Specialty funds** focus on one sector, such as technology, precious metals, health care, or insurance. These funds can be highly volatile.

A common investment strategy when getting started in mutual funds is to select a few funds that pursue different strategies to further diversify your investment. If you invest a portion of your money in a high-risk technology fund, another portion in a moderate-risk international fund, and another portion in a low-risk fund that restricts its investments to government securities, presumably all three funds will not slump at the same time. The funds you select may depend in large part on your age and your investment goals.

A Loaded Question

When you start investigating the world of mutual funds, you will first have to decide whether you will invest in load or no-load funds. A load is a sales commission. A load fund charges a commission when you buy the fund; a no-load fund does not.

Paying a load does not guarantee you superior performance, but plenty of excellent funds charge loads, so you don't want to rule them out entirely. The problem with load funds, as you have no doubt surmised, is that they cost you money. If you are investing $10 000 and have to pay a $500 load, your investment is only $9500. Beware of a financial advisor who recommends a load fund; he is the one who stands to profit from the choice. With over 7000 funds around, it is not too hard to find many good no-load funds.

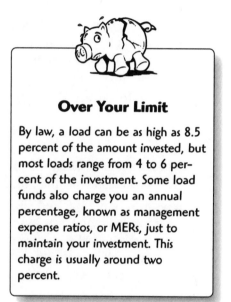

Over Your Limit

By law, a load can be as high as 8.5 percent of the amount invested, but most loads range from 4 to 6 percent of the investment. Some load funds also charge you an annual percentage, known as management expense ratios, or MERs, just to maintain your investment. This charge is usually around two percent.

Bonds, Treasury Bonds

What is a bond? It is an IOU. The people who buy bonds are loaning money to the people who issue the bonds. The bonds are then paid back regularly with interest to the investors. Let's say you invest $1000 in a 10-year U.S. Treasury bond that pays 8 percent. You would receive a cheque for $80 every year, and at the end of 10 years, you would get your initial $1000 back. Overall, you would make $1800 on your $1000 investment.

Although not nearly as glamorous as stocks and mutual funds, bonds are a safer and less volatile investment because they tend to be offered by bedrock institutions like the Canadian government, provincial governments, and large corporations. Because of their perceived (or real) stability, conservative investors who don't like the fluctuations in the stock market favour bonds.

Canadian Treasury bonds are as close to a sure thing as an investor can get because the government is unlikely ever to default on its bonds. For one, the Canadian economy is historically strong, and two, the government can always print more money to pay off the bonds if need be.

However, not all bonds are risk-free. As in the rest of the investment world, the greater the risk, the greater the potential return. Here are your choices:

➤ **Government of Canada Bonds**. The federal government fully guarantees these bonds for terms of 1 to 30 years. These are even safer than GICs or term deposits. Of course, the low risk factor comes with a price—low yields. Interest is usually paid twice a year until maturity, when the face value is repaid. Minimum investment is usually $5000.

➤ **Provincial and Municipal Bonds**. Provincial or municipal governments fully guarantee these bonds for the same 1- to 30-year terms. Usually, these are only marginally riskier than federally-backed bonds, depending on the credit quality of the province or city.

➤ **Strip Bonds**. These are created from government bonds when the interest "coupons" are separated from the principal and sold as different investments. The strips are sold at a discount and by the time they mature, they will be worth the face value. (The longer the term to maturity, then, the greater the discount.) The different between the discounted purchase price and the face value at maturity price represents the interest, which is paid out at maturity.

➤ **Mortgage backed securities**. The CMHC issues "bonds" from their pool of insured mortgages. Mortgage backed securities pay interest monthly, which blends the principal and interest accruing from the mortgages. Though you don't receive as much at maturity (since you've been receiving an income all along), you still can expect to receive 94% to 98% of the face value at maturity.

Finding a Broker

One of the best places to learn about investments is through your broker. Unless you are planning to invest solely in mutual funds, you may want to hire a brokerage house to

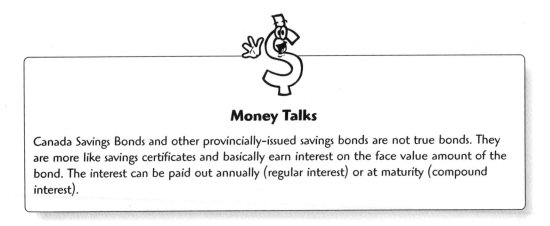

Money Talks

Canada Savings Bonds and other provincially-issued savings bonds are not true bonds. They are more like savings certificates and basically earn interest on the face value amount of the bond. The interest can be paid out annually (regular interest) or at maturity (compound interest).

help you process your buy-and-sell orders. There are a myriad from which to choose—the quality and quantity of help you decide to use is up to you.

There are three types of brokerage houses:

➤ **Full-service brokerages** are the most costly. They offer a wide range of services, research, advice, and personal attention. Although more expensive, the advice of a broker who buys and sells stocks for a living can be very helpful.

➤ **Discount brokers** forego the frills and charge lower commissions. You get the research, but you get little in the way of personal attention, and you get no advice.

➤ **Online brokers** allow you to place orders directly over the Internet at an even lower fee, and they tend to offer plenty of online research and information (but you need to learn how to use it).

The best place to find a broker is through word-of-mouth information. If you know someone who invests in the market, ask about his or her broker. Or call around, speak with a few brokers, find a couple you are comfortable with, interview them, get some references, and then pick one.

A Diversified Portfolio

The savvy investor will mix and match many different types of securities to create an investment portfolio that meets his or her goals. You may want to have some individual stocks, some mutual funds, and some bonds. Younger investors trying to get ahead and with the advantage of time on their side usually take more risks with their portfolio; older investors take fewer risks.

Whatever you do, it is time to get into the game. Sure, you have plenty to learn, but

Over Your Limit

Before selecting a discount or online broker, learn what it has to offer. The cheapest commissions in the world don't matter if you cannot make a trade because you are on hold or the Web site crashes. In fact, recent class action suits have been launched in the U.S. due to faulty technology. Look out for hidden costs. Sometimes discount brokerages offer low commissions by charging for everything else. Ask your friends who they use and how happy they are with the service.

that's half the fun. The other half is watching your money grow. Remember, the financially literate earn interest; they don't pay it.

The Least You Need to Know

➤ There are many sorts of stocks; the important thing is to buy different types and diversify.

➤ Work, work, work, and hope for a few good insights.

➤ Picking a good broker is critical.

➤ Mutual funds take some of the risk out of the process.

➤ Bonds can take even more risk out of your investment.

Chapter 23

Starting Your Own Business

In This Chapter

➤ Is it for you?

➤ What kind of business?

➤ Working from home

➤ A family plan

➤ Money issues

Everyone, at one time or another, dreams about going into business and becoming his or her own boss; and a growing number of Canadians are making that fantasy a reality. A new economic climate is emerging in this country that encourages entrepreneurship. People from all walks of life are striking out on their own, creating a dynamic force that is revolutionizing business in this country.

Creating your own small business, although certainly a big risk, can be one of the best ways of getting out of debt and ensuring that you stay out of debt. Let's be clear about one thing up front: Yes, you may have to go into debt to start your business, but remember, not all debt is bad debt. Creating debt in order to start a business and make more money is far preferable to running up your credit cards with no discernible way to pay them off.

Two Cents

Studies of successful entrepreneurs have found that they take action, don't discourage easily, work long hours, are highly disciplined, and are overly confident.

Is It Right for You?

Unlike the other options we have gone over as ways to make extra money (investing in stocks and real estate, for example), starting your own business is a much riskier undertaking. Not everyone is cut out to be an entrepreneur. It takes a certain kind of person who can put up with the pressures and who has the time, passion, creativity, and energy necessary to create a successful business.

Certainly, the rewards are great. Living without a boss (being the boss!), making more money (hopefully), and being able to implement your own ideas are very gratifying. But to get these rewards, you must be willing to risk failure and more indebtedness. That's the harsh bargain you must make with yourself.

So do you have what it takes? Take the following quiz and see whether you have the entrepreneurial spirit. Be brutally honest here. You will only hurt yourself and your family if you let your ego get in the way.

Part 1

How would you rate yourself on the following?

(4 = excellent, 3 = good, 2 = fair, 1 = poor)

➤ I am able to concentrate.

➤ I can make hard decisions.

➤ I am willing to take risks when necessary.

➤ I have creative ideas.

➤ I am a self-starter.

➤ I enjoy doing things differently from the way other people do.

➤ I can ask for money if I have to.

➤ I am able to handle money.

Total for Part 1:

Part 2

How often does the following apply to you?

(3 = often, 2 = sometimes, 1 = rarely or never)

➤ I feel satisfied with my life.

➤ I have enough money for now.

➤ I generally trust other people.

➤ I think people respect my opinion.

➤ I generally like people.

➤ I think other people approve of me.

➤ I can ask for money.

➤ I like to meet new people.

➤ Life generally treats me fairly.

➤ I can negotiate well.

➤ If I have a problem, I know where to go for help.

➤ I have faith in my abilities.

➤ I like trying new things.

➤ I try to learn about how money works.

Total Part 2:

Part 3

How often does the following apply to you?

(3 = often, 2 = sometimes, 1 = rarely or never)

➤ I like people to help me.

➤ I feel good about my life.

➤ I like the people in my life.

➤ I enjoy spending time alone.

➤ I eat well.

➤ I exercise regularly.

➤ I am grateful for what I have.

➤ I am flexible.

➤ I like myself.

➤ I go places with people.

➤ I am good to myself.

➤ I only spend what I have.

Total Part 3:

Scoring for Part 1

24 to 32: You have the qualities of a successful entrepreneur.

17 to 23: There are areas of weakness that you can work on to improve your chances of success; but with some work, you will do fine.

8 to 16: Unless you are willing to deal with your issues on an emotional level, it will be difficult for you to make a success of a one-person business. But difficult is not impossible if you are highly motivated.

Scoring for Parts 2 and 3

72 to 81: You're in great shape for entrepreneurship. If you also had a high score on Part 1, you have a high likelihood for success if you do your homework.

55 to 71: You have a better-than-average chance of making it, but you can improve your chances if you work on developing more self-esteem and improving your relationships.

41 to 54: Your chances of making a business grow and prosper are a bit low, but you can make it if you improve your self-esteem.

27 to 40: Your chances of success in a one-person business are not terrific. However, if you get help and find out why you feel the way you do about yourself, your chances will improve.

Dell Computer was started by 19-year-old Michael Dell in his college dorm room with $1000. He started by putting together components and then selling his systems at a greatly reduced price. Starting with ads in trade magazines, he then moved into direct marketing, selling to computer stores, and then finally over the Internet. Today, Dell Computer earns more than $500 million a year and Michael Dell is worth $4 billion. Even if your answers pointed toward no, do not despair. If becoming an entrepreneur is your dream, you can learn and cultivate many of the required traits.

Two Cents

We have all heard the depressing statistic that the majority of new small businesses fail in their first year, and 95 percent fail within the first five years. That may be an urban myth. The Canadian Federation of Independent Business reports that more than three-quarters of Canadian businesses are small, employing fewer than five people; also, more than three-quarters of job growth since 1989 has been in self-employment, which has increased by 3.3 percent, while paid employment only grew by 0.2 percent. And, while salaried employees make more money on average, self-employed and those working for small companies report greater job satisfaction.

What Kind of Business?

Once you have decided to start your own business, the next step is to figure out what type of business it will be. It could be anything: part-time, full-time, product, service, retail, wholesale, home-based, mobile, serious, or silly. Some people decide to become self-employed and then search for a business; others have a great idea or run across a great opportunity and decide to take the plunge. If you are in the first category, this section will explain how to find some business opportunities that might be right for you.

In 1980, high school drop-out Chris Haney and a former sports reporter Scott Abbott conceived of a board game that would revolutionize the toy industry, and breathe new life into parlour games. To produce the first 1200 copies of Trivial Pursuit for a test run, they needed money. They sold shares to 32 reluctant friends, relatives, and former colleagues, raising about $60 000.

Despite slow sales at first, word began to get around that the game was worth buying. But the 1200 boxes had been sold, and the company had run out of money. Haney and his wife Sarah were now living on baby-bonus cheques and Sarah, expecting another baby, went back to work as a nurse part-time to bring in some much-needed cash.

Banks turned them down for credit, and savings were the only thing the couple could live on. Finally, they managed to get a line of credit from a bank in St. Catharines, Ontario with some loan collateral from Abbot's father, and they produced another 20 000 games. It was enough to justify turning an old boat-works in Niagara-on-the-Lake into their assembly plant.

Today, the phenomenon of Trivial Pursuit has become the stuff of legend. Just about everyone knows someone, who knows someone who was one of those 32 original investors, and that someone laughed his way to the bank. Shareholders' investments reputedly increased about 25 times in just the first few years. Chris and Scott and their partners became millionaires and have since set their sights on other entreprenurial projects.

What Do You Love?

Begin with your passion. What do you love to do? Do you see other people making a living at it somehow? Larry always wanted to go into business for himself, and when he inherited $10 000, he decided to make the jump. He asked himself the questions you need to ask yourself:

➤ What makes me the most happy?

➤ If I could do anything, what would it be?

➤ Would I like to do that all day, every day?

➤ What am I best at?

➤ What skills do I most like to use?

Two Cents

You can also find a wealth of good ideas for a new business in just one day if you attend a trade or industry show, an entrepreneurial expo, or a business convention.

Larry grew up near an old train station, had always played there, grew up with every possible train toy imaginable, and answered these questions by deciding that he had always loved trains the best. So he quit his job at Xerox and opened up a store that sold everything he could find that had to do with trains: electric trains, wooden trains, engineer hats, railroad-crossing signs, you name it. As odd as it might sound, he now has a store at a major mall, pays a huge rent, and makes a ton of money.

Look around. Do you know anyone who has a job you like? Do you see people doing things during the day that intrigue you? Take them out to lunch and interview them, even if you don't know them. People love to talk about themselves.

You should also have a brainstorming session. Start with ideas that you have some familiarity with and branch out from there. Consider your work experience, your hobbies, business trends, technology, and social change. Are there opportunities somewhere in this list that would satisfy a market need and support a business?

Successful businesses have many characteristics, but one shared by all is that they fulfill a need. If you can figure out a business that fulfills the needs of consumers, you are a long way toward starting your own business. Who knew there was a need for a toy train centre? Larry did.

Lucy started her small business out of desperation. She had left her husband, needed to support her six-year-old daughter, and knew her job as a bank teller would not cut it.

Money Talks

According to a study by IBM Canada Ltd., and the Women Business Owners of Canada in 1999, women entrepreneurs are the growing force in the Canadian economy, leading 31 percent of firms and one-third of self-employed businesses. (Notably, women are not making the same inroads in male-dominated corporate Canada. Only 3.4 percent of the top posts in corporate Canada are held by women, and half of the top companies in Canada have no women in high-ranking positions, according to a recent study from New York-based Catalyst.)

Always interested in holistic health and exercise, Lucy decided to become a massage therapist. She could go to school part-time, it was not expensive, and she thought she could make a good living at it.

Six months later, she had her certification. Her health club then hired her, and she began to make $40 an hour. A year later, with a strong clientele, she went off on her own, began to make $60 an hour doing something she loved, and worked four days a week. What about you?

Other Considerations

You must consider other things too if you want to start your own business:

➤ **What is the competition?** Is your community large enough to support another business like the one you are considering? You can go to your local chamber of commerce to get some statistics or simply open the phone book to see how many similar businesses there are.

➤ **Who are your customers?** How will you reach them? How much do they pay for your goods or service?

➤ **How much do people make who do what you want to do?** If you know people in the business (and even if you don't), you must find out how much you can reasonably expect to make in a year.

These are just preliminary considerations. There is so much to think about and do in preparation of starting your own business that we can only cover the highlights here. Whole books are written on the subject (Azriela has written several—you can check them out in her author bio inside the back cover of this book).

Choose carefully, but with a sense of anticipation. If all goes well, you will spend more time at your new business over the next five years than almost anyplace else.

Over Your Limit

For a legitimate tax write-off, you must be able to show that your home-based business is run solely from home in a space that is dedicated to the business. For example, a desk in the corner of a bedroom doesn't cut it. You need to create a real home office or workshop space.

Home-Based Businesses

An especially attractive option for someone just emerging from debt is to start a business out of a home. This strategy drastically cuts down on overhead and makes the business much more affordable and possible to do, and the potential of success is therefore greater. Home-based businesses also open up a slew of tax write-offs, for example, a portion of your utilities and mortgage interest can be deducted as business expenses, as well as some home improvements (necessary to the business), as long as they are proportionate to the amount of space your business occupies in your home. You may wish to consult an accountant when you're setting up your business to make sure you are taking advantage of all the write-offs you can.

There are pros and cons to working from home. It affords you the opportunity for independence and freedom and the chance to make a lot more money. Best of all (and maybe worst of all), you get to work from home. Although it is certainly nice not to have to commute and to go work in your sweats if you want, it is sometimes too easy to goof off or be distracted when you work where you live and play.

Yet despite potential distractions, working from home allows people to combine the

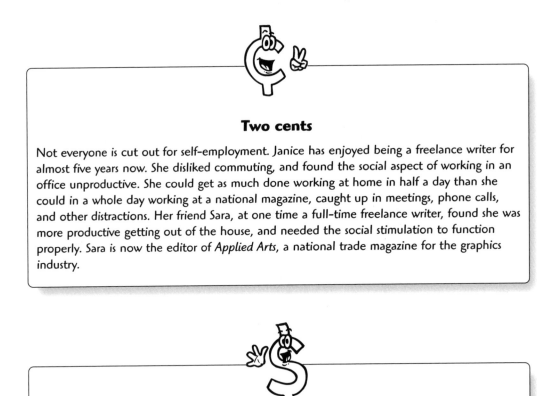

Two cents

Not everyone is cut out for self-employment. Janice has enjoyed being a freelance writer for almost five years now. She disliked commuting, and found the social aspect of working in an office unproductive. She could get as much done working at home in half a day than she could in a whole day working at a national magazine, caught up in meetings, phone calls, and other distractions. Her friend Sara, at one time a full-time freelance writer, found she was more productive getting out of the house, and needed the social stimulation to function properly. Sara is now the editor of *Applied Arts*, a national trade magazine for the graphics industry.

Money Talks

Disney began in 1923 when Walt Disney and his brother Roy set up their first animation studio in their garage. Their first contract was from Universal Studios for six short animated cartoons, and in it Walt unwittingly sold the rights to the characters. The brothers Disney were soon out of business. Walt then created another character, which he kept, named Mickey Mouse.

pleasure of doing something they love with the flexibility of working near their family. If it is respected by family members and treated like a business, a home-based business can work well.

What can you do from home? There are so many options that we can list only some of them. You can find hundreds of ideas from different books that are out there on the subject of home-based businesses. Here are a few (to get you started) that are generally easy to commence and very affordable:

➤ Start a Web page

➤ Provide child care

➤ Offer auto detailing

➤ Create a mobile auto repair or bicycle business

➤ Go into furniture repair

➤ Be a handyman

➤ Start a mail-order business

➤ Offer a pet-sitting, or dog-walking service

➤ Become a bookkeeper

➤ Offer word-processing services

➤ Go into desktop publishing

➤ Become an interior designer

➤ Open a hairdressing salon

➤ Start a house-cleaning service

Many of these businesses require minimal start-up capital and can be nice part-time or full-time moneymakers.

Money Talks

In 1999, teen entrepreneurs Albert Lai, Michael Hayman, and Michael Furdyk sold their company, mydesktop.com, to the American company Internet.com for undisclosed seven-figure deals. The young men (two of them were still in high school) set up the online publishing company, which dispensed advice and information on computer technology, in their homes. They have since moved on to their next project, BuyBuddy.com, which focuses on electronic commerce.

Two Cents

Sony Electronics was started in 1946 with $500. One of the cofounders of the company was a man who failed his entrance exam at Toshiba for that peculiarly Japanese phenomenon called "lifetime employment." Necessity is indeed the mother of invention, and in this case, literally!

Honey, Let's Have a Talk

Telling a spouse that you want to start your own business can be an emotional experience. When Dave finally had everything ready to be able to leave the protective womb of the law firm and strike out on his own, his wife was six months pregnant. (Let's just say she was not thrilled with his timing.) But the moment had come, he had written his business plan, had found an investor, and had created a little money cushion, so the time was right (well, almost right). It took a lot of discussions and prioritizing, but everything worked out quite well.

Besides a business plan, you also need to create a family plan. A lot of issues must be discussed and agreed upon if one partner is going to become self-employed. (Azriela's first book, *Honey, I Want to Start My Own Business*, goes over these issues in detail.) Among the myriad issues that must be examined are the following:

How will you finance the business?

What are the chances of success?

How long will it likely take to turn a profit? What will you do if it takes longer than you anticipate?

Can the other spouse make up the lost income for the first few months until the business gets going?

Can it be a part-time business until you see how it's doing?

What kind of time commitment will be involved?

How stressful will it be?

Where will the business be headquartered?

How will it affect the family? If you run it from your home, how will you separate work and family?

How do you feel about taking such a risk?

What role will your spouse have in the business?

How will it affect your relationship?

Who will pick up the kids from school?

Will this affect the roles you have agreed to in your relationship?

Remember, there is no such thing as "my business" when you are married. Even if your spouse will not be in the business, he or she is still your partner, one way or another.

A decision as big as starting your own business is a major life-changing event. It will affect your financial life, your emotional life, and possibly even your sex life. The business will cut into your time with your spouse (unless you start it together) and will change your perceptions of yourself and your spouse.

Do not underestimate the risk involved in going off on your own; make sure that you and your spouse both agree that the dream is worth the

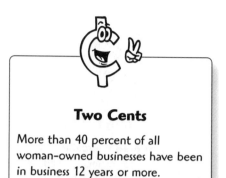

Two Cents

More than 40 percent of all woman-owned businesses have been in business 12 years or more.

risk. The first Friday without a paycheque is a bit jarring, to put it mildly. Although the rewards of making more than you did at your job are considerable, it may take a while to get to that place, so you better be prepared. The bottom line is: starting a business is exhilarating, stressful, exhausting, fun, exciting, frightening, and fulfilling, all rolled into one, so be prepared for some changes.

Financing

Finding the money to start your own business (or the money to cushion you until your new income is rolling in) is probably the biggest challenge you will initially face. For

Over Your Limit

Small businesses fail for reasons such as a poor market for the product or service, financial mismanagement, or the entrepreneur's character. More specifically, the entrepreneur may have made mistakes such as: improperly identifying the market; failing to prepare a proper business plan; going ahead with too little start-up capital; underestimating capital requirements and costs; failing to secure "back-up capital"; failing to negotiate firm terms with suppliers; or growing too rapidly. Other problems, such as lack of commitment or complacency; lack of experience; domestic pressures affecting the owner/manager; inability to recruit competent employees; dishonesty; or poor communication also contribute to business failures. For more information or support in starting your own business, contact the Canadian Federation of Independent Business at www.cfib.ca. Besides offering resources to the entrepreneur, the group also publishes books available at local bookstores or libraries.

Cheque It Out

A **business plan** is a roadmap to your business for others to read. In it, you explain what the business is, how it will be run, how much everything will cost, how much you can reasonably expect to make, and how long it will likely take to make that money.

Over Your Limit

Beware of business loan brokers who require an up-front fee to process a bank loan. Some of these outfits just send your application to banks they know can't lend to you and charge you upwards of $500 for their services. Always investigate the broker and triple-check the contract for the refund and fee policies.

most entrepreneurs, initial funding comes from savings, family, and friends.

In Praise of Self-Reliance

In Chapter 19, "What the Rich Know That You Don't," we discussed the 10 percent solution, which is saving 10 percent of your income every month in order to fund your dreams. That is the best way to start your own business. It is just so difficult to get out of debt that if you can somehow afford to finance the venture yourself, you would be wise to do so.

Lacking that, maybe your parents or a rich uncle might be interested in giving you a little gift to help you get started. Especially if they have seen you struggle with debt and climb your way out of it, they might be inclined to help you out.

Friends, Romans, Countrymen, Lend Me Your Money!

This entire book has been about getting out of debt, and we are loath to recommend getting into debt for any reason, so we cannot endorse the idea here either. However, we also understand that financing a business, depending upon its size, is no simple matter and that a loan is sometimes necessary. Not all debt is bad debt, so we won't nag.

That disclaimer begs the question: How do you convince others to invest in your dream? You must be able to show them that you have a viable idea that you are capable of executing. Usually, this is done through a business plan.

You write your business plan ostensibly for others, but you also write it for yourself. In it, you thoroughly and methodically analyze your proposed business and how it can be expected to turn a profit. By writing a business plan and going through each step of your proposed business, you force yourself to critically analyze your dream. Will it fly? Will it turn a profit?

The business plan is shown to lenders and investors alike. Even your Uncle Seymour might want to see it before he lends you $10 000 to make sure that you know what you are doing.

An institutional lender will ask for your projected financial statements, proposed legal structure, profit analysis, sales goals, and so on. You will also be asked three questions:

1. How much do you want to borrow?

2. How will you use the loan?

3. How will you repay the loan?

You had better know the answers to these questions before you ever set foot in the bank.

The Least You Need to Know

➤ You need to be sure that starting your own business is for you before you ever do it.

➤ Picking the right kind of business is usually a matter of following your passion.

➤ Working from home has many advantages.

➤ You need to discuss with your family the effect that a new business will have on everyone.

➤ Finding the money to get started may be your biggest obstacle.

Chapter 24

Life After Debt

In This Chapter

➤ Money management

➤ Rules for the proper use of credit

➤ Help beyond this book

Whew. If you have gotten this far, you have absorbed a lot of information. You may be out of debt by now, or you may be just beginning the process. Either way, we salute you. Changing habits, especially financial ones, is no easy task.

Keep in mind three things if you are to get out and stay out of debt. The first is use money intelligently. Second, as you progress, you must be concerned with the proper use of credit. Finally, utilize resources beyond this book to help you when you need it.

Be Smart with Your Money

Getting out of debt and staying out of debt demands that you respect how important each dollar is. One less dollar owed to a creditor is a dollar that you can put to more selfish goals. As Ben Franklin said, "A penny saved is a penny earned."

When it comes to using and spending money, the essential idea boils down to this:

Money Talks

A study was made of a graduating class at Yale one year. Upon graduation, students were polled to see how many had specific goals and how many had those goals written down. Only 3 percent had written down their goals. That study found that at the 20-year class reunion, the 3 percent who had written down their goals were the most accomplished personally, professionally, and financially.

You must watch what you spend and what you make. If you spend more than you make, you go back into debt; if you make more than you spend, you stay out of debt.

Keep Track of Your Spending

If you keep track of how much you are spending, the odds are greatly increased that you will get out of debt. Probably the best way to keep track is to have some sort of budget. As discussed in detail in Chapter 7, "The 'B' Word," you need not create a budget that immobilizes you. In fact, creating an impossible budget is the worst thing you can do. A budget that enables you to prioritize your expenditures is all you need.

Call it whatever you want—a plan, a budget, a priority list—it doesn't matter. What matters is what this thing can do for you:

➤ It can free up money and let you spend it in accordance with what matters to you most.

➤ It may nudge you toward being a bit more conservative with money, which may not be altogether bad.

➤ It can help you free up some money to earmark toward getting out of debt or saving up for some investments.

➤ Most importantly, it takes the blinders off.

Even just keeping closer track of what comes in and where it goes out will allow you to make better, more informed decisions about your money. You begin to turn the money tide when

Two Cents

Cosmetics pioneer Madame C. J. Walker was once asked how she got her start. "I got a start by giving myself a start," she replied.

you stop going into debt and start getting out of debt. A budget can help do that.

Staying Out of Debt

Why is it so easy to go into debt, but so difficult to get out of debt? For the same reason it's easier to gain weight than lose weight. We don't know exactly what that reason is. Someone must know, but it sure isn't us.

What we do know is that as you work your plan, following these three simple rules will ensure that you stay out of debt.

Rule Number 1: If you can't afford it, don't buy it or do it.

Going into debt with a well-thought-out plan for how you will pay it back is one thing. That is debt you can afford. Going into debt with no plan and no means of paying it back is another matter altogether. One helps; one hinders. One is good debt; the other is bad debt.

Hector and his brother Jaime are a good contrast. Hector wanted to start his own import-export business. He created a budget and a business plan and figured that he needed $10 000 to get started. His best friend was willing to lend Hector the money on two conditions. First, Hector had to agree to repay $500 a month. Second, the debt would be secured by a lien on Hector's house. Hector's business projections concluded that he would be able to afford the $500 payment, so he agreed to the deal, got the loan, and started his business.

Jaime makes about $2000 a month and saves nothing because his combined bills total what he earns. Nevertheless, Jaime, depressed over Hector's newfound success, wanted to show his brother that he was making money, too, so he charged a $1500 big-screen television. He had no means and no plan for paying it back. If you can't afford it, don't buy it (unless it is an emergency, of course).

Rule Number 2: Make more than you spend.

This rule is a corollary to rule number 1. If you do nothing but follow this rule, you need never have unnecessary debt again.

Rule Number 3: Just say no.

Staying out of debt requires self-discipline. Say no to the enormous pressure all around you to go into debt. Say no to your child who wants that new Nintendo that you can't afford. Say no to yourself. The only way to go into debt is to say yes to debt. By saying no to debt you cannot afford, you are saying yes to prosperity and abundance, which is ironic. By saying no to debt, you create prosperity and thereby are still able to get and do what you want, only without any debt.

Ten Percent Is All We Ask

The budget solution works best when you combine it with what we have called the "Ten percent solution." If you are able to save 10 percent of your net take-home pay, you are on the way to financial prosperity.

Budgeting will allow you to get out of debt, but saving and investing allows you to get ahead. You can do whatever you want with that 10 percent: leave it in the bank, start a business, or invest it in the stock market, for example. That's your choice. The important thing is that you begin to make your money grow.

Two Cents

If you were 60 years old, cut your spending by $5 a day, and began to invest that money getting a 6 percent return, then by the time you turned 65 you would have $10 500. If you began at age 50, you would have $43 000, and if you started at age 30, you would have $203 000.

The thought of saving 10 percent of your income may still seem impossible, but getting rid of, say, $20 000 in credit card debts probably seemed impossible at one time, too. Both goals are a matter of priorities. When you went into debt, whatever it was you wanted or did to create that debt was more important than the debt itself. That was your priority at that time. That's fine; you're human; we're human. Debt happens.

By buying this book, you have decided that it is now time for different priorities. Certainly, if you want to get out of debt, then not incurring more debt will have to be more important than things you want to purchase or do. For example, staying out of debt has to be more important than charging a trip to the Bahamas that you can't afford. It's a matter of priorities. What's more important: the trip or the debt? In order for you to stay out of debt, the answer has to be the debt.

One of these priorities should be to pay yourself 10 percent of your income before you pay anyone else. If that seems impossible, just pretend that you are another one of your creditors whom you are committed to repaying. Pay your bill to yourself first.

If you get out of debt, watch what you spend, and invest for the future, your financial prosperity is almost assured.

On the Proper Use of Credit

We have said all along that not all debt is bad debt. When you do, consciously, choose to go into debt again, there are ways to do so wisely:

1. Exercise caution when taking on debt. Think twice. Is there a way to do this (whatever it is) without incurring more debt?

2. If you do go into debt, borrow when it's free or practically free. Remember that most credit cards charge no interest if you pay the balance once the bill comes. That means you are borrowing money for free. By the same token, if you are going to keep a running balance, do so on the card with the lowest interest rate.

3. Use credit to create a good credit rating. The better your credit rating, the less it will cost you to borrow money when you do need it in the future. Use a credit card and pay it off consistently. Pay your car loan and mortgage on time. Pay off a loan. The better a credit risk you become, the more money you will save down the road.

4. Debt is best when it funds investments rather than consumption. You will have something to show for the invested debt.

If you value your money, you will not make the same debt mistakes twice.

Help Beyond This Book

We hope that we have given you a lot of help, tools, ideas, and ways to get out of debt. Yet that may not be enough. There are people and groups you can contact that may be of great assistance.

Counselling

Sometimes, debt is about more than money; it's about anger and stress, anxiety and depression. Indeed, money problems are among the most stressful problems a person can have. They can be injurious to your mental health, your physical health, and your relationships. Dealing with the stress of money and its attendant problems sometimes requires professional help, and we wholeheartedly recommend it in the right circumstances.

Besides helping with the stress of the matter, money counselling can also help uncover other issues that your financial problems may be masking. Sometimes, money is the symptom and not the cause. Various resources for counselling are listed in the appendixes.

Two Cents

After creditors have received three on-time payments through a credit counseling agency, they usually stop the phone calls on good faith that the debt is being repaid in a timely manner.

And Now, the End (or a New Beginning) Is Near

Thank you for allowing us to help guide you through what is likely a tough situation. We hope that we have provided solutions, made the journey easier to understand, and maybe put a smile on your face a time or two. You deserve a life of prosperity and abundance. If we made that more likely, then we have all done our jobs.

Live long and prosper!

The Least You Need to Know

➤ Cutting back, staying out of debt, and saving a little bit are the keys to long-term financial health.

➤ Using credit wisely is important if you want to stay out of debt.

➤ There is help beyond this book.

Code of Ethics for Trustees in Bankruptcy

Introduction

The Code of Ethics for Trustees in Bankruptcy is an integral part of the General Rules of the Bankruptcy and Insolvency Act.

The Code establishes a standard for services to be provided by licensed bankruptcy trustees. It addresses the information that trustees must provide to creditors, the treatment of funds entrusted to trustees, conflicts of interest, and the sale and purchase of the property of a business or individual who has filed for bankruptcy. It also contains standards for advertising by trustees and for maintaining the good reputation of the trustee community.

Note: The following text reflects Sections 34 to 53 of the Bankruptcy and Insolvency General Rules.

34. Every trustee shall maintain the high standards of ethics that are central to the maintenance of public trust and confidence in the administration of the Act.

35. For the purposes of sections 39 to 52, "professional engagement" means any bankruptcy or insolvency matter in respect of which a trustee is appointed or designated to act in that capacity pursuant to the Act.

36. Trustees shall perform their duties in a timely manner and carry out their functions with competence, honesty, integrity and due care.

37. Trustees shall cooperate fully with representatives of the Superintendent in all matters arising out of the Act, these Rules or a directive.

38. Trustees shall not assist, advise or encourage any person to engage in any conduct that the trustees know, or ought to know, is illegal or dishonest, in respect of the bankruptcy and insolvency process.

39. Trustees shall be honest and impartial and shall provide to interested parties full and accurate information as required by the Act with respect to the professional engagements of the trustees.

40. Trustees shall not disclose confidential information to the public concerning any professional engagement, unless the disclosure is

    (a) required by law; or

    (b) authorized by the person to whom the confidential information relates.

41. Trustees shall not use any confidential information that is gathered in a professional capacity for their personal benefit or for the benefit of a third party.

42. Trustees shall not purchase, directly or indirectly,

    (a) property of any debtor for whom they are acting with respect to a professional engagement; or

    (b) property of any estates in respect of which the Act applies, for which they are not acting, unless the property is purchased

        (i) at the same time as it is offered to the public,

        (ii) at the same price as it is offered to the public, and

        (iii) during the normal course of business of the bankrupt or debtor.

43. (I) Subject to subsection (2), where trustees have a responsibility to sell property in connection with a proposal or bankruptcy, they shall not sell the property, directly or indirectly,

    (a) to their employees or agents or persons not dealing at arms' length with the trustees;

    (b) to other trustees or, knowingly, to employees of other trustees; or

    (c) to related persons of the trustees or, knowingly, to related persons of the persons referred to in paragraph (a) or (b).

    (2) Where trustees have a responsibility to act in accordance with subsection (1), they may sell property in connection with a proposal or bankruptcy to the person set out in paragraph (1)(a), (b) or (c), if the property is offered for sale

    (a) at the same time as it is offered to the public;

    (b) at the same price as it is offered to the public; and

    (c) during the normal course of business of the bankrupt or debtor.

44. Trustees who are acting with respect to any professional engagement shall avoid any influence, interest or relationship that impairs, or appears in the opinion of the an informed person to impair, their professional judgment.

45. Trustees shall not sign any document, including a letter, report, statement, representation or financial statement, or associate themselves with any such document, that they know, or reasonably ought to know, is false or misleading, and any disclaimer of responsibility set out therein has no effect.

46. Trustees may transmit information that they have not verified, respecting the financial affairs of a bankrupt or debtor, if

   (a) the information is subject to a disclaimer of responsibility or an explanation of the origin of the information; and

   (b) the transmission of the information is not contrary to the Act, these Rules or any directive.

47. Trustees shall not engage in any business or occupation that would compromise their ability to perform any professional engagement or that would jeopardize their integrity, independence or competence.

48. Trustees who hold money or other property in trust shall

   (a) hold the money or property in accordance with the laws, regulations and terms applicable to the trust; and

   (b) administer the money or property with due care, subject to the laws, regulations and terms applicable to the trust.

49. Trustees shall not, directly or indirectly, pay to a third party a commission, compensation or other benefit in order to obtain a professional engagement or accept, directly or indirectly from a third party, a commission, compensation or other benefit for referring work relating to a professional engagement.

50. Trustees shall not obtain, solicit or conduct any engagement that would discredit their profession or jeopardize the integrity of the bankruptcy and insolvency process.

51. Trustees shall not, directly or indirectly, advertise in a manner that

   (a) they know, or should know, is false, misleading, materially incomplete or likely to induce error; or

   (b) unfavourably reflects on the reputation or competence of another trustee or on the integrity of the bankruptcy and insolvency process.

52. Trustees, in the course of their professional engagements, shall apply due care to ensure that the actions carried out by their agents, employees or any persons hired by the trustees on a contract basis are carried out in accordance with the same professional standards that those trustees themselves are required to follow in relation to that professional engagement.

53. Any complaint that relates to a contravention of any of sections 38 to 52 must be sent to the Division Office in writing.

Exemptions Allowed During Bankruptcy

The following exemptions are allowed during bankruptcy according to each province:

BRITISH COLUMBIA

➤ Equity in a home in Greater Vancouver and Victoria   = $ 12,000. In the rest of the province   = $ 9,000;

➤ Equity in Household items   = $ 4,000;

➤ Equity in a Vehicle   = $ 5,000; The vehicle exemption drops to $2,000 if the debtor is behind on child care payments (to facilitate the enforcement of Maintenance Orders)

➤ Equity in work tools   = $ 10,000;

➤ Equity in essential clothing and medical aids is unlimited.

ALBERTA

➤ Food required by the debtor and his/her dependants during the next 12 months;

➤ Necessary clothing of the debtor and his/her dependants up to a value of $4,000;

➤ Household furniture and appliances up to a value of $4,000;

➤ One motor vehicle not exceeding a value of $5000.00;

➤ Medical and dental aids required by the debtor and his/her dependants;

➤ Where the debtor is a bona fide farmer and whose principal source of livelihood is farming 160 acres if the debtor's principal residence is located on that 160 acres and that the 160 acres is part of the debtor's farm;

➤ The equity in the debtor's principal residence, including a mobile home, up to a value of $40,000.00;

➤ If the debtor is a co-owner of the residence, the amount of the exemption is reduced to an amount that is proportionate to the debtor's ownership interest;

➤ Personal property (i.e. tools, equipment, books) required by the debtor to earn income from the debtor's occupation up to a value of $10,000;

➤ Where the debtor's primary income is from farming operations, personal property required by the debtor for the proper and efficient conduct of the debtor's farming operations for the next 12 months.

SASKATCHEWAN

For Non-Farmers:

➤ Household furniture and personal effects to a value of $4,500 per person;

➤ Tools of the trade to a value of $4,500;

➤ A motor vehicle, if required for employment;

➤ $32,000 equity in your home ($64,000 if jointly owned);

➤ Certain life insurance policies;

➤ Certain pensions.

For Farmers:

➤ Furniture, furnishings and appliances to a value of $10,000;

➤ The cash equivalent of produce sufficient to provide food and fuel for heating until the next harvest;

➤ All livestock, farm machinery and equipment, including one car or truck, necessary for the next twelve months operations;

➤ One motor vehicle, if required for business or profession, but not in addition to the one above;

➤ Tools and equipment to a value of $4,500 used by a farmer in his trade or profession;

➤ Equity in personal residence to a value of $32,000 ($64,000 if jointly owned);

➤ Seed grain equal to two bushels per acre of land under cultivation;

➤ Cash equivalent of crop equal to:

➤ unpaid harvesting costs;

➤ living expenses to next harvest;

➤ necessary costs of farming until next harvest.

➤ The homestead;

➤ Certain life insurance policies;

➤ Certain pensions

MANITOBA

➤ Furniture, household furnishings and appliances not exceeding total value of $4,500;

➤ Necessary and ordinary clothing of the debtor and family;

➤ Food and fuel necessary to family for period of six months or cash equivalent;

➤ If debtor is a farmer:

➤ animals necessary for farming operation for 12 months;

➤ farm machinery, dairy utensils and farm equipment necessary for ensuing 12 months;

➤ one motor vehicle if required for purposes of agricultural operations.

➤ Home quarter.

➤ Tools, implements, professional books and other necessaries not exceeding a total value of $7,500 used in practice of trade, occupation or profession;

➤ One motor vehicle, if necessary for work or transportation to and from work, not exceeding $3,000 in value;

➤ Articles and furniture necessary to performance of religious services;

➤ Seed sufficient to seed all land of debtor under cultivation;

➤ Health aids, including wheelchair, air conditioner, elevator, hearing aid, eye glasses, prosthetic or orthopaedic equipment, necessary to debtor or family;

➤ Chattel property of municipalities and schools;

➤ Actual residence of the bankrupt, equity of $1,500 each if in joint tenancy, or $2,500 if not in joint tenancy.

ONTARIO

➤ Necessary and ordinary wearing apparel of the debtor and his family not exceeding $1,000 in value;

➤ The Household furniture, utensils, equipment, food and fuel that are contained in and form a part of the permanent home of the debtor not exceeding $2,000 in value;

➤ Necessary tools, equipment, vehicle and books to value of $2,000 used in the practice of the debtor's trade or profession;

➤ In the case of a person engaged solely in the tillage of the soil or farming, the live stock, fowl, bees, books, tools and implements and other chattels ordinarily used by the debtor in his business, profession or calling not exceeding $5,000 in value.

➤ In the case of a person engaged solely in the tillage of the soil or farming, sufficient seed to seed all his land under cultivation, not exceeding 100 acres, as selected by the debtor, and fourteen bushels of potatoes, and, where seizure is made between the 1st day of October and the 30th day of April, such food and bedding as are necessary to feed and bed the live stock and fowl that are exempt under this section until the 30th day of April next following.

QUEBEC

➤ The movable property which furnishes his main residence, used by and necessary for the life of the household, up to a market value of $6,000 established by the seizing officer;

➤ The food, fuel, linens and clothing necessary for the life of the household ;

➤ The instruments of work needed for the personal exercise of his professional activity;

➤ Family papers and portraits, medals and other decorations ;

➤ Property declared by a donor or a testament to be exempt from seizure except in certain cases ;

➤ Judicially awarded support and sums given or bequeathed as support;

➤ Benefits payable under a supplemental pension plan to which an employer contributes on behalf of his employees, other amounts declared unseizable by an Act governing such plans and contributions paid or to be paid into such plans;

➤ Periodic disability benefits and expense reimbursements under a contract of accident and sickness insurance;

➤ Property of a person that he requires to compensate for a handicap;

➤ A certain portion of salaries and wages based on the number of dependants.

* Nevertheless, the property referred to in first and third items above may be seized and sold by a creditor holding a hypothec thereon.

NEW BRUNSWICK

➤ Furniture, household furnishings and appliances used by the debtor or a dependent to a realizable value of $5,000 or to any greater amount that may be prescribed;

➤ Food, clothing and fuel necessary for the debtor and his family;

➤ Two horses and sets of harness, two cows, ten sheep, two hogs and twenty fowl, and food therefor for six months;

➤ Necessary tools, equipment and books to the value of $6,500 used in the practice of the debtor's trade or profession;

➤ Necessary seed grain and potatoes required for planting purposes to the following quantities: forty bushels of oats, ten bushels of barley, ten bushels of buckwheat, ten bushels of wheat and thirty-five barrels of potatoes;

➤ One motor vehicle having a realizable value of not more than six thousand five hundred dollars at the time the claim for exemption is made, or not more that any greater amount that may be prescribed, if the motor vehicle is required by the debtor in the course of or to retain employment or in the course of and necessary to the debtor's trade, profession or occupation or for transportation to a place of employment where public transportation facilities are not reasonably available;

➤ Necessary medical and health aids;

➤ Pets belonging to the debtor;

➤ Pension plans.

NOVA SCOTIA

➤ Necessary wearing apparel, household furnishings and furniture;

➤ Necessary fuel and food;

➤ Necessary grain, seeds, cattle, hogs, fowl, sheep and other livestock;

➤ Necessary medical and health aids;

➤ Farm equipment, fishing nets, tools and implements used in debtor's chief occupation, not exceeding $1,000;

➤ Motor vehicle not exceeding $3,000.

NEWFOUNDLAND

➤ Food required by debtor and dependants during the next 12 months;

➤ Medical and dental aids required by debtor and dependants;

➤ Domesticated animals which are kept as pets and not used for business purpose;

➤ Fuel or heating as a necessity for the debtor and his or her dependants;

➤ Clothing of the debtor and his or her dependants, of a value totalling $4,000;

➤ Appliances and household furnishings (which are defined as washing machine, clothes dryer, "reasonably necessary" bedroom suites and bedding, oven and stove top burners, "necessary" dishes and kitchen utensils, and "necessary" strollers, cribs and highchairs), of a value totalling $4,000;

➤ Motor vehicle of the debtor, value totalling $2,000;

➤ Items of a sentimental value to the debtor, a value totalling $500;

➤ The debtor's equity in his or her principal residence, $10,000;

➤ Personal property used by and necessary for debtor to earn income from occupation, trade, business or calling, $10,000.

From BankruptcyCanada.com

Credit Counselling Services

USEFUL ADDRESSES

BRITISH COLUMBIA

The Debtor Assistance Program provides free counselling for people in debt and helps devise repayment plans for consumers with financial difficulties. Debt counsellors can offer guidance on money management, help arrange repayment schedules affordable to the debtor and acceptable to the creditor, assist in developing personalized budgets and advise on bankruptcy procedures.

Debtor Assistance Offices:
Burnaby:
342 - 5021 Kingsway, Burnaby, B.C. V5H 4A5
Tel: (250) 660-3550

Kamloops:
6th Floor – 235 First Avenue, Kamloops, B.C. V2C 3J4,
Tel: (250) 828-4667

Nanaimo:
Direct line to Victoria, Tel: (250) 741-3615

Prince George:
Direct line to Kamloops, Tel: (250) 565-4325
Victoria: 1st Floor – 1019 Wharf Street, Victoria, B.C. V8V 1X4,
Tel: (250) 387-1747

Credit Counselling Society of British Columbia
200-435 Columbia St., Westminister, BC V3L 5N8
Tel: (604) 527-8999 or 1-888-527-8999
Non-profit credit counselling service.

ALBERTA

Credit Counselling Services of Alberta,, Suite 225, Sunrise Square,
602-11th Ave. S.W., Calgary,
Alberta, T2R 1J8
Tel: (403) 285-2201, Fax: (403) 265-2240

SASKATCHEWAN

Provincial Mediation Board, Department of Justice
5th Floor, 2103 11th Ave., Regina, SK S4P 3V7
Tel: (306) 787-5550, Toll Free: 1-888-374-4636
Fax: (306) 787-8168

MANITOBA

Community Financial Counselling Services
203-290 Vaughn St., Winnipeg, MB R3B 2N8
Tel: (204) 989-1900, Fax: (204) 989-1908

ONTARIO

Ontario Association of Credit Counselling Services
PO Box 189, Grimsby, ON, L5M 4G3
Tel: (905) 945-5644, Fax: (905) 945-4680
Referral Line: 1-800-263-0260
Ontario consumers can call the Referral Line to find out the phone number and
location of the counselling service centre nearest them.

Credit Counselling London
www.creditcounsellinglondon.on.ca
150 Kent St.
Suite 1
London, Ontario
N6A 1L3
1-519-433-0159
FAX: 1-519-433-4559

Credit Counselling Service of Southwestern Ontario
www.debtdoktor.org
Windsor-Essex Office
420 Devonshire Road
Windsor, Ontario
(519) 258-2030
Fax (519) 258-9243

Sarnia Office
568 N. Christina St.
Sarnia, Ontario
N7T 7W2
(519)337-8757
Fax (519) 337-8782

Leamington Office
South Essex Community Centre
215 Talbot St. E.
Leamington, Ontario
N8H 3X5
(519) 326-8629
Fax (519) 326-8697

Amherstburg Office
A.A.M. Community Services Building
400 Sandwich Street, Unit 31
Amherstburg, Ontario
(519) 736-5471

Forest Office
North Lambton Social Service Centre
P.O. Box 1000
59 King Street West
Forest, Ontario
NON 1JO
(book appointments through Sarnia office)

Credit Counselling Service of Metropolitan Toronto
www.creditcanada.com
Telephone: (416) 228-3328
Outside Metro Toronto: 1-800-267-2272
Fax: (416) 228-1164

Head Office, Credit Education Centre, North York Branch
45 Sheppard Avenue East, Suite 810
Toronto, Ontario
M2N 5W9

Weston
1920 Weston Road
Suite 231
Weston, Ontario
M9N 1W4

Scarborough Central
2401 Eglinton Avenue East
Suite 303
Scarborough, Ontario
M1K 2M5

Etobicoke
208 Evans Road
Suite 105
Etobicoke, Ontario
M8Z 1J7

Scarborough North
2942 Finch Avenue East
Suite 105
Scarborough, Ontario
M1W 2T4

Toronto
27 Carlton Street
Suite 301
Toronto, Ontario M5B 1L2

SCARBOROUGH EAST
2100 Ellesmere Road
Suite 211C
Scarborough, Ontario M1H 3B7

QUEBEC

Les dettes qui s'empilent, Option consommateurs
[French only]
www.option-consommateurs.org

Le Réseau de protection du consommateur
[french only]
www.consommateur.qc.ca

NEW BRUNSWICK

Credit Counselling Services of Atlantic Canada, Inc.
Harbour Building
Saint John, NB
E2L 2B6
Toll Free: 1-800-539-2227 (New Brunswick residents only)
Tel: (506) 652-1613, Fax: (506) 633-6057

NOVA SCOTIA

Consumer and Commercial Relations
Department of Business and Consumer Services
www.gov.ns.ca/bacs/ccr

Dartmouth
Access Nova Scotia
Super Store Mall
650 Portland Street
Dartmouth, N.S. B2W 6A3
Phone (902) 424-5200
Fax (902) 424-0720

Halifax
Access Nova Scotia
West End Mall
6960 Mumford Road
Halifax, N.S. B3L 4P1
Phone (902) 424-5200
Fax (902) 424-0720

Bridgewater
77 Dufferin Street
Bridgewater, N.S. B4V 3W8
Phone (902) 543-0666
Fax (902) 543-0599

New Glasgow
608 MacLellan's Brook Road
PO Box 236
New Glasgow, N.S. B3H 5C5
Phone (902) 424-5200 or
1-800-933-2101
(Toll-free within Nova Scotia)
Fax (902) 424-0720

Kentville
Access Nova Scotia
28 Aberdeen Street
Kentville, N.S. B4N 2N1
Phone (902) 424-5200
Fax (902) 424-0720

Port Hawkesbury
Provincial Building
P.O. Box 624
Port Hawkesbury, NS B0E 2V0
Phone (902) 625-2691
Fax (902) 625-4092

Sydney
Access Nova Scotia
380 Kings Road
Sydney, NS B1S 1A8
Phone (902) 424-5200
Fax (902) 424-0720

Truro
35 Commercial Street
Suite 101 Truro, NS B2N 3H9
Phone (902) 893-6280
Fax (902)893-6108

Yarmouth
328 Main Street,
Yarmouth, NS B5A 1E4
Phone (902) 424-5200
Fax (902) 424-0720

Amherst
Please call to arrange an appointment:
Phone (902) 667-3604

Antigonish
Access Nova Scotia
20 St. Andrew's Street
Antigonish, NS B2G 2L4
To arrange an appointment, call 1-800-670-4357
Fax: (902) 863-7490

PRINCE EDWARD ISLAND

Community Affairs and Attorney General
Division of Consumer Services
Box 2000, Charlottetown
PEI C1A 7N8
Tel: (902) 368-4580

NEWFOUNDLAND

Personal Credit Counselling Service
2nd Floor, Suite 101, Virginia Park Plaza,
Newfoundland Drive,
St. John's, NFLD
A1A 3E9
Tel: (709) 753-5812, Fax: (709) 753-3390

CONSUMER PROTECTION BRANCHES

If you have a problem or question regarding collection agencies or credit reporting agencies, here's a list of provincial sources of information. We've provided Web sites, phone numbers and addresses where possible.

BRITISH COLUMBIA

Consumer Assistance Directory

ALBERTA

Housing and Consumer Affairs (or direct link to offices)
www.gov.ab.ca/ma/hca/consumer
The Fair Trading Act administers Collection Practices Act and Credit and Personal Reports Act
For information call 310-0000 (toll-free within Alberta)
or call Consumer Enquiries at 427-5782

SASKATCHEWAN

Consumer Protection Branch, Saskatchewan Justice
1871 Smith Street
Regina SK S4P 3V7
Phone (306) 787-5550 (Regina), in Saskatchewan 1-888-374-4336
Fax (306) 787-9779

MANITOBA

Consumer's Bureau
www.gov.mb.ca/cca/consumb
302-258 Portage Avenue
Winnipeg, MB R3C OB6
Phone: (204) 945-3800
Toll-free: 1-800-782-0067 (in Manitoba)
Fax: (204) 945-0728
Email: consumersbureau@cca.gov.mb.ca
Collection Agencies Act and Consumer Protection Act

ONTARIO

Ontario Ministry of Consumer and Corporate Relations
Consumer Services Bureau of the Ministry of Consumer and Commercial Relations
handles complaints relating to the Consumer Protection Act and the Business Practices
Act.
www.ccr.gov.on.ca/mccr
Contact:
Toll-Free: 1-800-268-1142
Toronto: (416) 326-8555
TTY: (416) 326-8566 (for the hearing/speech impaired)
Compliance and Consumer Services
Ministry of Consumer and Commercial Relations
250 Yonge St., 32nd Floor
Toronto, ON
M5B 2N5

QUEBEC

Office de la protection du consommateur
www.opc.gouv.qc.ca

NEW BRUNSWICK

Consumer Affairs Branch, Department of Justice
PO Box 6000
Fredricton NB E3B 5H1
Phone (506) 453-2659
Fax (506) 444-4494

NOVA SCOTIA

Department of Business and Consumer Services (see above regional addresses)
Collection agencies and credit reporting agencies are governed by the Licensing and
Condominiums program. For information on filing a complaint, call (902) 424-8950 or
fax (902) 424-8652

PRINCE EDWARD ISLAND

Community Services and Attorney General, Consumer, Corporate and Insurance
Division

NEWFOUNDLAND

Commercial and Corporate Affairs Branch
Trade Practices and Licensing Division covers collection agencies and
credit reporting agencies
public.gov.nf.ca/gsl/ccbranch
P.O Box 8700
Second Floor
Confederaiton Bldg., West Block
St. John's, Nfld.
A1B 4J6
(709) 729-2660
fax (709) 3205

NORTHWEST TERRITORIES

Community Operations Division, Department of Municipal and
Community Affairs
#500, 5201 50 Avenue, Northwest Tower
Yellowknife NT X1A 3S9
Phone (876) 783-7125

YUKON TERRITORIES

Consumer Services, Department of Justice
P.O. Box 2703 (J-6)
Whitehorse, Y1A 2C6
Phone (867) 667-5111

OFFICES OF THE SUPERINTENDENT OF BANKRUPTCY

National Headquarters

365 Laurier Ave. West
Jean Edmonds Tower South
8th Floor
Ottawa, ON, K1A 0C8
Tel: (613) 941-1000
Fax: (613) 941-2862

BRITISH COLUMBIA

300 West Georgia Street
Suite 1900
Vancouver, BC, V6B 6E1
Tel.: (604) 666-5007
Fax: (604) 666-4610

ALBERTA

Standard Life Tower Building
510, 639-Fifth Avenue S.W.
5th Floor
Calgary, AB, T2P 0M9
Tel: (403) 292-5607
Fax: (403) 292-5188
Suite 725, Canada Place
9700 Jasper Avenue
Edmonton, AB, T5J 4C3
Tel: (780) 495-2476
Fax: (780) 495-2466

SASKATCHEWAN

1020-2002 Victoria Avenue
Regina, SK, S4P 0R7
Tel: (306) 780-5391
Fax: (306) 780-6947

123 – 2nd Avenue South, 7th Floor
Saskatoon, SK S7K 7E6
Tel: (306) 975-4298
Fax: (306) 975-5317

MANITOBA

400 St. Mary Avenue, 4th Floor
Winnipeg, MB, R3C 4K5
Tel: (204) 983-3229
Fax: (204) 983-8904

ONTARIO

Trebla Building
473 Albert St., 2nd Floor
Ottawa, ON, K1R 5B4
Tel: (613) 995-2994
Fax: (613) 996-0949

25 St.Clair Avenue East, 6th Floor
Toronto, ON, M4T 1M2
Tel: (416) 973-6486
Fax: (416) 973-7440

69 John St. South, 4th Floor
Hamilton, ON, L8N 2B9
Tel: (905) 572-2847
Fax: (905) 572-4066

Federal Building
451 Talbot Street, Room 303
London, ON, N6A 5C9
Tel: (519) 645-4034
Fax: (519) 645 5139

QUEBEC

Industrie Canada
Bureau du surintendant des faillites
1141, Route de l'Église, 4e étage
SAINTE-FOY (Québec) G1V 3W5
Tel: (418) 648-4280
Fax: (418) 648-4120

2665 ouest, rue King - Bureau 600
SHERBROOKE (Québec)J1L 1C1
Tel: (819) 564-5742
Fax: (819) 564-4299

Pièce 800
5, Place Ville Marie, 8e étage
MONTRÉAL (Québec) H3B 2G2
Tel: (514) 283-6192
Fax: (514) 283-9795

NOVA SCOTIA

1801 Hollis St, 5th Floor
Halifax, NS, B3J 3N4
Tel: (902) 426-2900
Fax: (902) 426-7275

Recommended Resources

Books

Balancing Act: A Canadian Woman's Financial Success Guide, Joanne Thomas Yaccato, Prentice Hall, 1999.

Building a Dream: A Canadian Guide to Starting a Business of Your Own, Walter S. Good, McGraw-Hill Ryerson, Limited, 1997.

Consuming Passions: Help for Compulsive Shoppers, Ellen Mohr Catalano and Nina Sonenberg, New Harbinger Publications, 1993.

Deloitte and Touche Canadian Guide to Personal Financial Management, Irene Jacob, Danielle Lacasse, Karen Slezak, Nicholas Seed, Prentice Hall, 1998.

Dollar Pinching. A Consumer's Guide to Smart Spending, by Shelly Branch, Warner Books, 1997.

Family Finance: The Essential Guide for Canadian Parents, Ann Douglas, Prentice Hall, 1999.

Financial Post Guide to Investing and Personal Finance, Doug Kelly, Top Business Writers of The Financial Post, Key Porter, 2000.

Get a Financial Life, Personal Finance in Your Twenties and Thirties, Beth Kobliner, Simon & Schuster, 1996.

How Chuck Taylor Got What He Wanted, William F. Staats and E.D. Sledge, Revised by

Clarence M. Stregger, Laurie Campbell, Fergus Millar, John Yee, Credit Counselling of Toronto, 1998.

How to Get What You Want From Your Bank, Douglas Goold, Macfarlane Walter & Ross, 1994.

Life After Debt: Free Yourself from the Burden of Money Worries Once and For All, Bob Hammond, Career Press, 2000.

Money, Heart & Mind, by William Bloom, Penguin Books of Canada, Limited, 1996.

Independent Means: A Canadian Women's Guide to Pensions and a Secure Financial Future, Monica Townson, Macmillan Canada, 1997.

The Cheapskate's Guide to Living Cheaper and Better, Leslie Hamilton, Carol Publishing Group, 1996.

The Complete Idiot's Guide® to Investing for Women in Canada, Jennifer Bayse Sander, Janice Biehn, Jim Brown, Anne Boutin, Prentice Hall, 2000.

The Complete Idiot's Guide® to Personal Finance for Canadians, by Bruce McDougall, Prentice Hall, 1998.

The Money Adviser: Canadian Guide to Successful Financial Planning, Bruce Cohen with Alyssa Diamond, Stoddart, 1998.

The Wealthy Barber: The Common Sense Guide to Successful Financial Planning, David Chilton, Stoddart, 1995.

Where does your Money Go? Gus Zylstra, Harry M. Belyea, MH BELYEA, 1994.

Web Sites

Note: The Internet is a terrific tool for getting information, but make sure you are getting information that pertains to Canadians. It is difficult to tell whether you're on a Canadian site, and often, you'll find you've linked to an American site from a Canadian site, without even knowing it. Information on taxes, investing, mortgages, student loans, bankruptcy and banking in Canada is significantly different from the United States.

www.imoney.com

www.investorlearning.ca (The Investor Learning Centre)

www.cba.ca (Canadian Bankers Association)

www.strategis.ic.gc.ca (Industry Canada, links to Consumer Information)

www.ccra-adrc.gc.ca (Canada Customs and Revenue Agency)

www.bankruptcycanada.com

osb-bsf.ic.gc.ca (Office of the Superintendent of Bankruptcy)

Glossary

alimony Money paid to an ex-spouse due to a court judgment.

annual fee The amount owed and paid to a credit card company for the right to use the card for one year (or any amount paid each year).

arrears Money that is overdue and unpaid. The term usually applies to support payments and mortgages.

bankruptcy A federal court action designed to give debtors relief from indebtedness and a fresh start.

budget A plan that allows you to allocate your financial resources where they can be best used.

child support Money paid from one parent to another for the benefit of the child.

collateral Property that is pledged as security for the satisfaction of a debt; property subject to a security interest.

collection agency A business that attempts to collect a debt that the original creditor has deemed uncollectable.

credit The ability of a person or business to borrow money, based upon credit payment history.

credit counselling Advice from a trained professional on reducing debt through various proven means.

credit report The report that details your credit history and bill-paying habits.

creditor A person to whom a debt is owed.

debtor A person who owes money to creditors; also, someone who files bankruptcy.

discharge The order of the bankruptcy court that releases the debtor from his legal obligation to repay dischargable debts.

entrepreneur A person who takes a risk with money to make money, usually by starting a business.

equity The value of property once all debts have been subtracted from its worth.

first meeting of creditors A meeting, that if called by the creditors, the bankrupt must attend. During this meeting, the debtor will be questioned about his assets and debts.

foreclosure An action whereby a secured creditor forces the sale of the collateral that was used to secure the loan.

garnishment A court-ordered method of debt collection whereby the debtor's wages are withheld to pay the debt.

home equity loan or line of credit A home loan that provides the debtor with a loan amount equal to the equity in his property and sometimes even more.

indebtedness The total amount of money you owe. Also, being in debt.

insolvent The state of not being able to meet your financial obligations.

introductory rate An interest rate, often a very low one, offered to entice you to choose one credit card over another.

judgment The official and final decision of a court.

late fees The fees charged when payment is received after the due date.

levy The legal process whereby property is seized and sold or where money has been attached.

lien A claim upon property used to secure payment of a debt. After the debt is paid, the lien is removed.

minimum payment The least you must pay to avoid any other fees. Paying the minimum will ensure that, over the course of the repayment period, you will pay the maximum.

official receiver The person to whom you file your bankruptcy application.

overspending Going into debt by spending more money than you have. Often, compulsive overspending is treated as an addiction.

personal property All property you own other than real estate.

principal The amount you actually borrowed. If you charged a $300 plane ticket, that is your principal.

proposal An alternative to bankruptcy, whereby a trustee and the insolvent come up with a repayment plan to the satisfaction of the creditors.

Registered Retirement Savings Plan an investment which is registered with the federal government in order to achieve compound growth through tax deferment until redeeming the plan at retirement.

repossession The action taken by the creditor to reclaim the property after a debtor defaults on a loan.

sue To commence a legal proceeding intended to recover monetary damages.

superintendent of bankruptcy The person(s) who handle bankruptcies in Canada.

teaser rate A very low, and short-term, interest rate offered to entice you to choose that credit card.

transfer balances To move your balance from one credit card to another—hopefully from one with a higher interest rate to one with a lower interest rate.

trustee in bankruptcy An individual licensed by the Office of the Superintendent of Bankruptcy to handle bankruptcies and consumer proposals. Though the insolvent person hires the trustee, the trustee is ultimately working for the creditor(s).

unsecured debt Debt not associated with any sort of collateral.

Charting Your Progress

Some people chart their workouts to make sure they're progressively getting stronger, faster, leaner or healthier. Why not do the same for your finances? Painting a clear picture of your current income and expenditures is a good way to baseline for your future.

By entering both your weekly expenses and your monthly bills into the following worksheet, you will be able to chart your spending habits and decide what, if anything, you should change to improve your fiscal fitness.

From a pamphlet written by the Credit Counselling Service of Toronto. Used with permission.

Monthly Expenses	Current Spending $	Necessary Changes $	Planned Budget $
Shelter			
Rent/House Payment			
Electricity			
Gas			
Water			
Telephone			
Property Taxes			
Food			
Groceries			
Work Lunches			
School Lunches			
Transportation			
Car Payment			
Gasoline			
Car Insurance			
Repairs and Maintenance			
Other Basic Expenses			
Child Care			
Child Support			
Clothing			
Laundry, Dry Cleaning			
Haircuts, Personal Care			
School Expenses			
Medical and Dental			
Insurance: Life, Health, Disability, Other			
Taxes: UIC, CPP, Income Tax			
Newspaper, Basic Cable			
Savings			
Emergencies			
Short-Term Goals			
Long-Term Goals			
Retirement			

Monthly Expenses	Current Spending $	Necessary Changes $	Planned Budget $
Credit Card Payments			
Installment Loan Payments			
Miscellaneous Expenses			
Vacations			
Charitable Contributions			
Cigarettes, Tobacco Products			
Alcoholic Beverages			
Movies, Plays, Concerts			
Books, Newspapers, Magazine Subscriptions			
VCR Rentals			
Club Dues or Expenses (Scouts, YMCA, Health Club)			
Internet Access Fees			
Sports (Spectator, Bowling, Softball, Fishing, Boating, etc.)			
Pets (Vet costs)			
Pet Food (If Not Purchased in Store)			
Snacks (At work, Convenience Stores, Vending Machines)			
Entertainment, Eating Out, Ordering In			
Dues (Professional, Union Dues, Social Organizations)			
Occupation License Fees			
Gifts and Cards (Average for Holidays, Birthdays)			
Records, CDs, Tapes, Music Supplies			
Children's Allowances			
Donations, School, Church, etc.			
Other			
Total Monthly Living Expenses			

Your Monthly Record

Name: _____

Year: _____

Month _____

Monthly Income	Gross Income $	Net Income $
Income 1		
Income 2		
Other Income (Child Support, Canada Pension, Rental Income, etc.)		
Total Gross/Net Income		
Total Net Monthly Income		
Minus Total Monthly Living Expenses		
SHORTAGE OR SURPLUS		

Index

About the Authors

JANICE BIEHN is a business writer, editor and co-author of *The Complete Idiot's Guide® to Investing for Women in Canada*. She has also contributed to such publications as *Investment Executive, IE: Money, The National Post, Today's Parent* and TD Asset Management's *Women in the Know: Planning Your Retirement Dreams*.

STEVEN D. STRAUSS is a lawyer, author and commentator and the author of the *Ask A Lawyer* series of legal advice books geared for the layperson. He has written for *Time Inc., The National Post* and has been interviewed on national radio.

AZRIELA JAFFE is the author of four self-help books for entrepreneurs and couples. She is an expert on the particular financial challenges faced by couples who work together in their own business, particularly on how couples can negotiate differences in preferences for financial risk, debt, and money management.